An introduction to SILK PAINTING

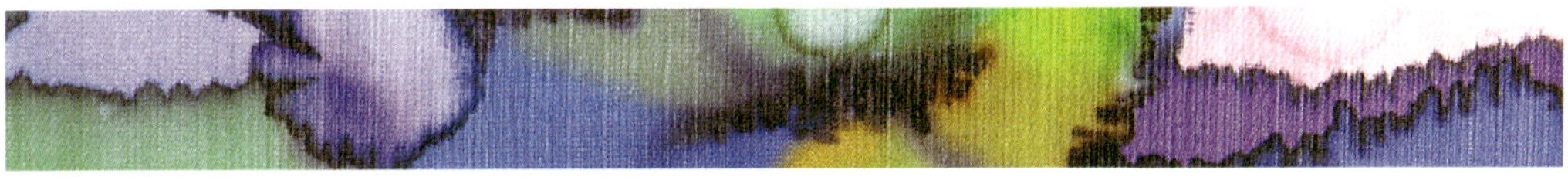

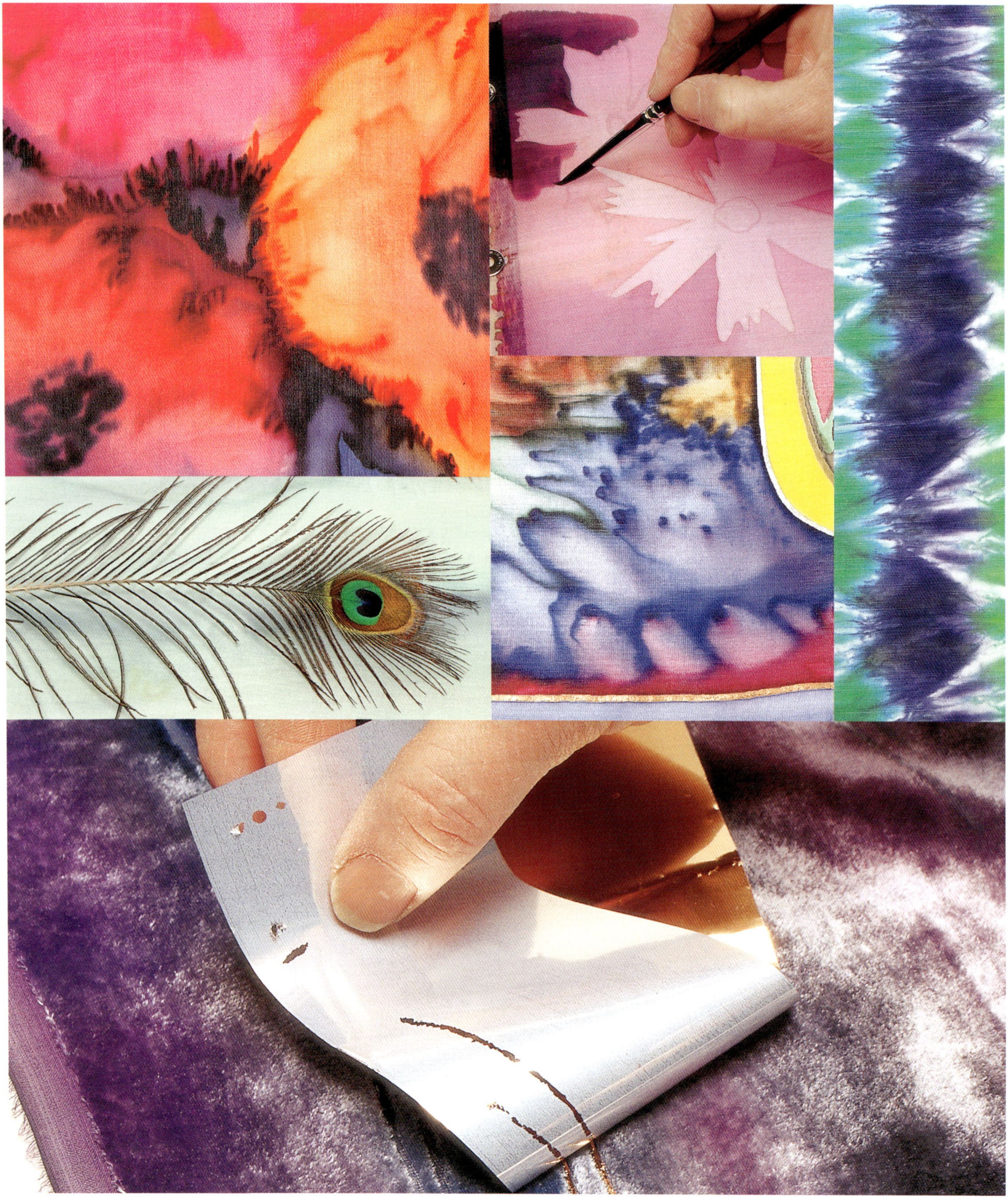

An introduction to
SILK PAINTING

Caroline Earl

Published by SILVERDALE BOOKS
An imprint of Bookmart Ltd
Registered number 2372865
Trading as Bookmart Ltd
Desford Road
Enderby
Leicester LE19 4AD

D&S Books Ltd
Kerswell,
Parkham Ash, Bideford
Devon, England
EX39 5PR

e-mail us at:-
enquiries@dsbooks.fsnet.co.uk

This edition printed 2002

ISBN 1-856056-78-3

Creative Director: Sarah King
Editor: Judith Millidge
Project editor: Sally MacEachern
Photographer: Paul Forrester
Designer: 2H Design

Set in Goudy 10/13
Printed in Singapore

1 3 5 7 9 10 8 6 4 2

Contents

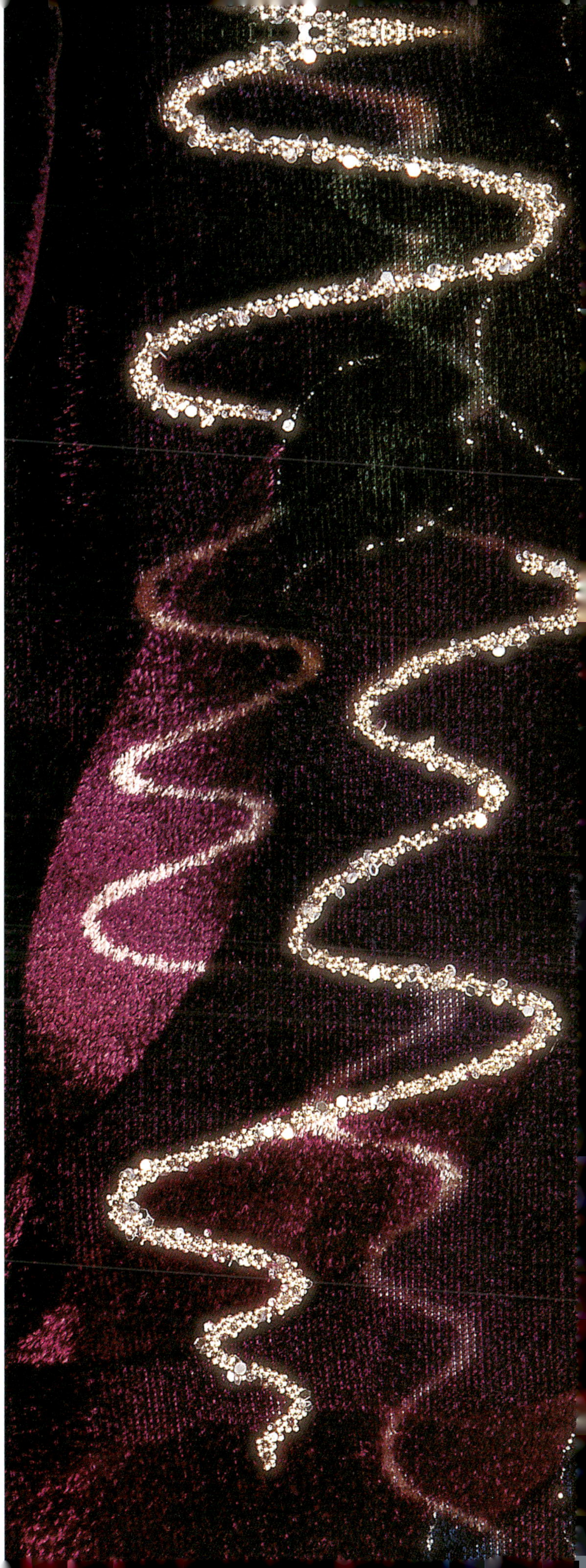

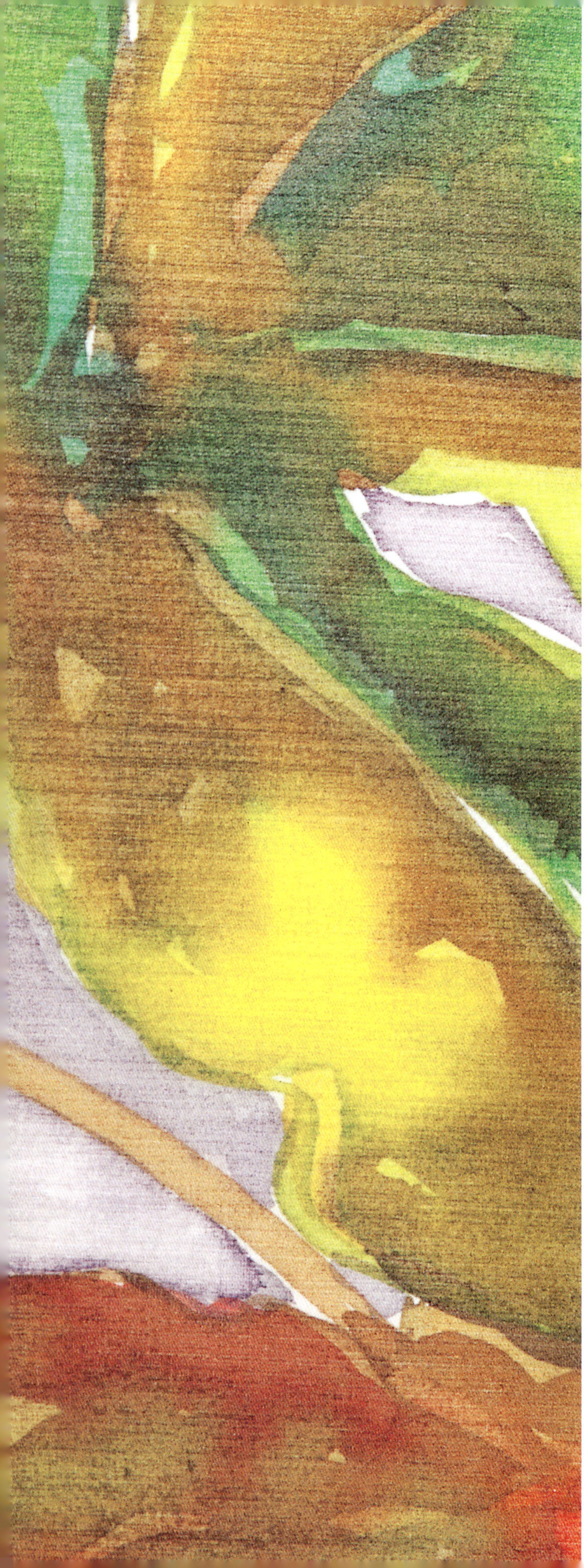

Introduction

Silk painting is a fascinating and beautiful medium. With the versatility of various silk dyes, paints and other media that form the palette of the silk painter or textile artist, it is possible to create a wide range of effects and styles. The tactile qualities of textiles and the vibrant colours of this medium are absorbing and inspiring. Silk painting provides endless possibilities for creating unique pieces of decorated silk, which can be made up into many decorative and functional items. The personal satisfaction gained from an admired scarf, or a compliment from the recipient of a painting or card gives enormous pleasure to the artist, and inspires one to do more.

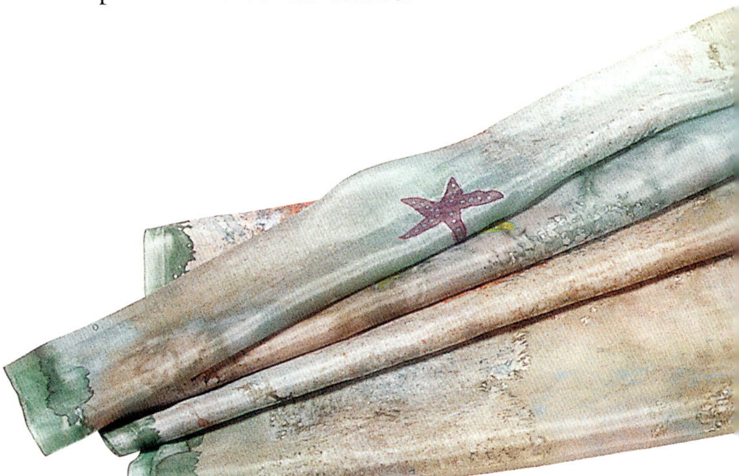

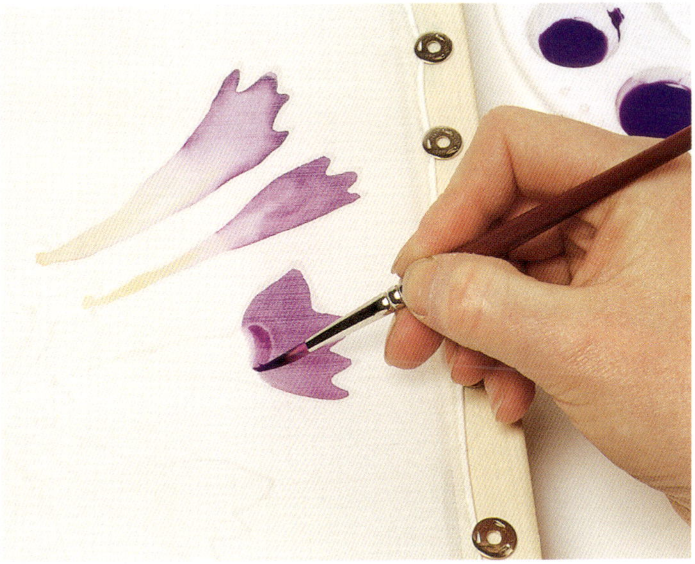

This book introduces a range of techniques that are both fun and easy. Many varied ways of applying the silk dyes, paints and mediums are clearly explained, with information on the equipment and materials you will need to start. Suggestions and information on colour, how to work up designs and a selection of patterns and projects are included to help get you started, followed by advice on how to advance and extend your silk painting skills.

I hope you find pleasure in working through this book, whether as a beginner or as a keen silk painter looking for further inspiration. For the complete beginner I add a few words of caution – be warned, silk painting is very addictive!

The historical production of silk

Sericulture, or the production of silk, has been practised for thousands of years. China, India and other Far Eastern countries produced and wove silk fabrics that were highly regarded and the prized possessions of emperors, royalty and the most wealthy members of society. Silk weaving in Britain did not become particularly important until the 16th and 17th centuries, when weavers came across from the Low Countries and France where there was already an established silk weaving industry. These immigrant silk weavers initially settled in London, particularly around Spitalfields, and gradually spread across to other areas of the country. Silk weaving quickly became an important and specialised trade, resulting in the foundation of the Guild of Silkweavers in 1629.

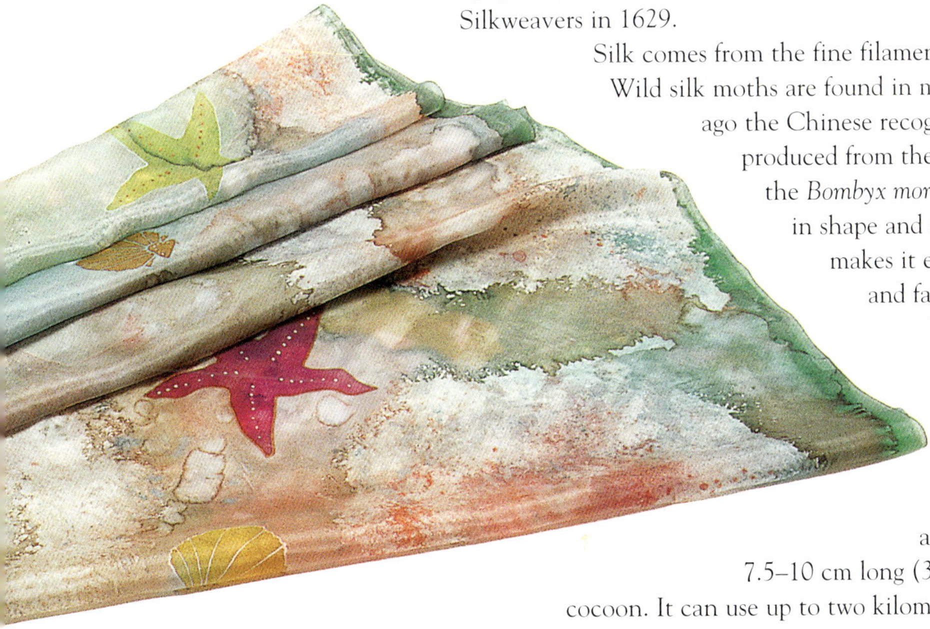

Silk comes from the fine filaments or fibres that form the cocoon of the silk moth. Wild silk moths are found in many different countries, but many hundreds of years ago the Chinese recognised the special qualities of the fine silk filament produced from the *Bombyx mori* silkworm. The cultivated silkworm of the *Bombyx mori* silk moth produces a filament which is more round in shape and smoother and finer than other silk moths, which makes it easier to unwind and work into a stronger thread and fabric.

The female silk moth lays 400–500 tiny eggs. In the late spring, the eggs start to hatch, and a new generation of silk producers emerge. These tiny silkworms feed entirely on mulberry leaves, and rapidly mature over the next four to five weeks, outgrowing and shedding their skin around four times. When the adult silkworm reaches 7.5–10 cm long (3–4 in.), it stops feeding and begins to spin its cocoon. It can use up to two kilometres (over a mile) of silk filament to produce the

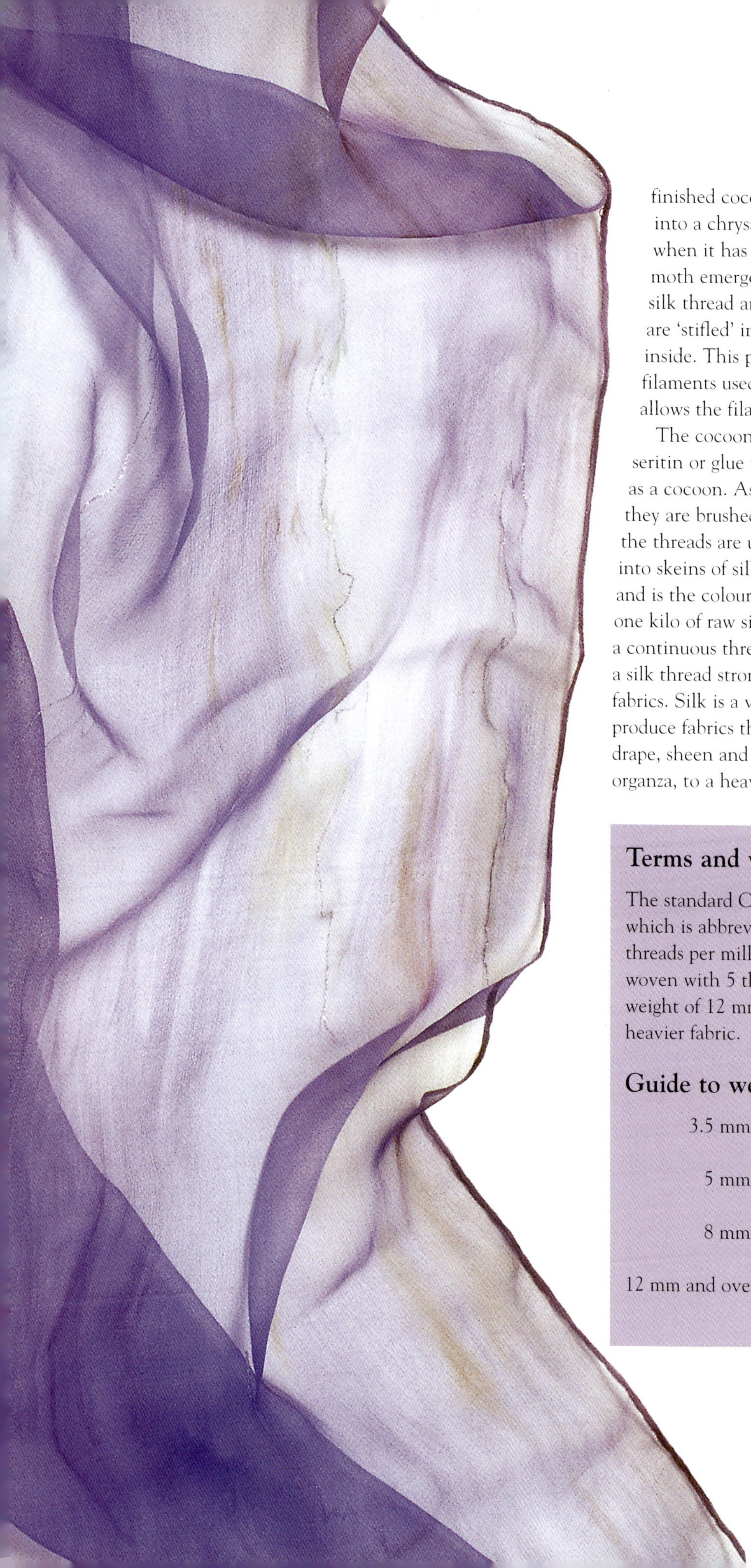

finished cocoon. The mature silkworm gradually transforms into a chrysalis inside its cocoon and after about 10 days when it has completed its metamorphasis, the new silk moth emerges from the cocoon. Silk cocoons used to make silk thread are collected before the silk moths emerge and are 'stifled' in a hot air bath, which quickly kills the chrysalis inside. This prevents the new silk moths damaging the silk filaments used to make the cocoons as they tunnel out, and allows the filament to be unwound as a continuous thread.

The cocoons are placed in boiling water to soften the seritin or glue which helps to hold the silk filaments together as a cocoon. As the cocoons float on the surface of the water, they are brushed to loosen the ends of the threads. Eventually the threads are unravelled and wound onto spools or formed into skeins of silk. At this stage the silk is known as raw silk, and is the colour of ivory. It takes about 45,000 cocoons to make one kilo of raw silk. Once the silk filaments have been spun into a continuous thread it can be plyed, or twisted together, to create a silk thread strong enough to be woven into a huge range of silk fabrics. Silk is a versatile and strong fibre which can be used to produce fabrics that vary enormously in their qualities of weight, drape, sheen and texture, ranging from a fine chiffon or silk organza, to a heavy silk dupion, taffeta or silk brocade.

Terms and weights of silk fabrics

The standard Chinese term for the weight of silk is a *mommi*, which is abbreviated to mm and refers to the number of silk threads per millimetre. A silk referred to as a 5 mm has been woven with 5 threads per millimetre, whereas a silk with a weight of 12 mm has 12 threads per millimetre and is a much heavier fabric.

Guide to weights and types of silk fabrics

3.5 mm =	a very light silk like a chiffon or mousseline silk
5 mm =	a lightweight silk like a paj or pongee silk
8 mm =	medium weight silk like a habotai, crepe de chine or georgette silk
12 mm and over =	heavyweight silk like a satin, dupion, or taffeta.

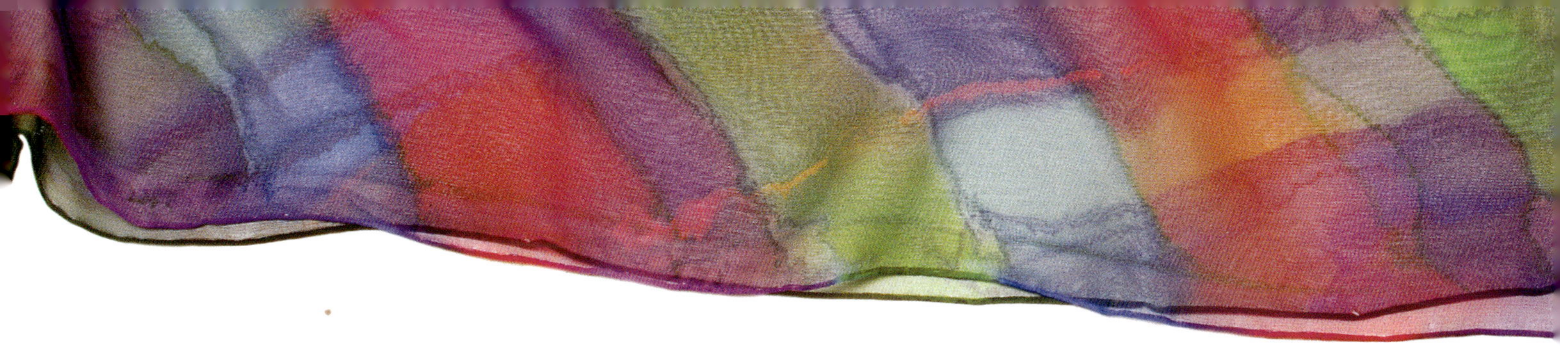

Materials and Equipment

You can start silk painting with basic equipment, although there are many items that can be gradually added to allow a more in-depth working of this versatile medium.

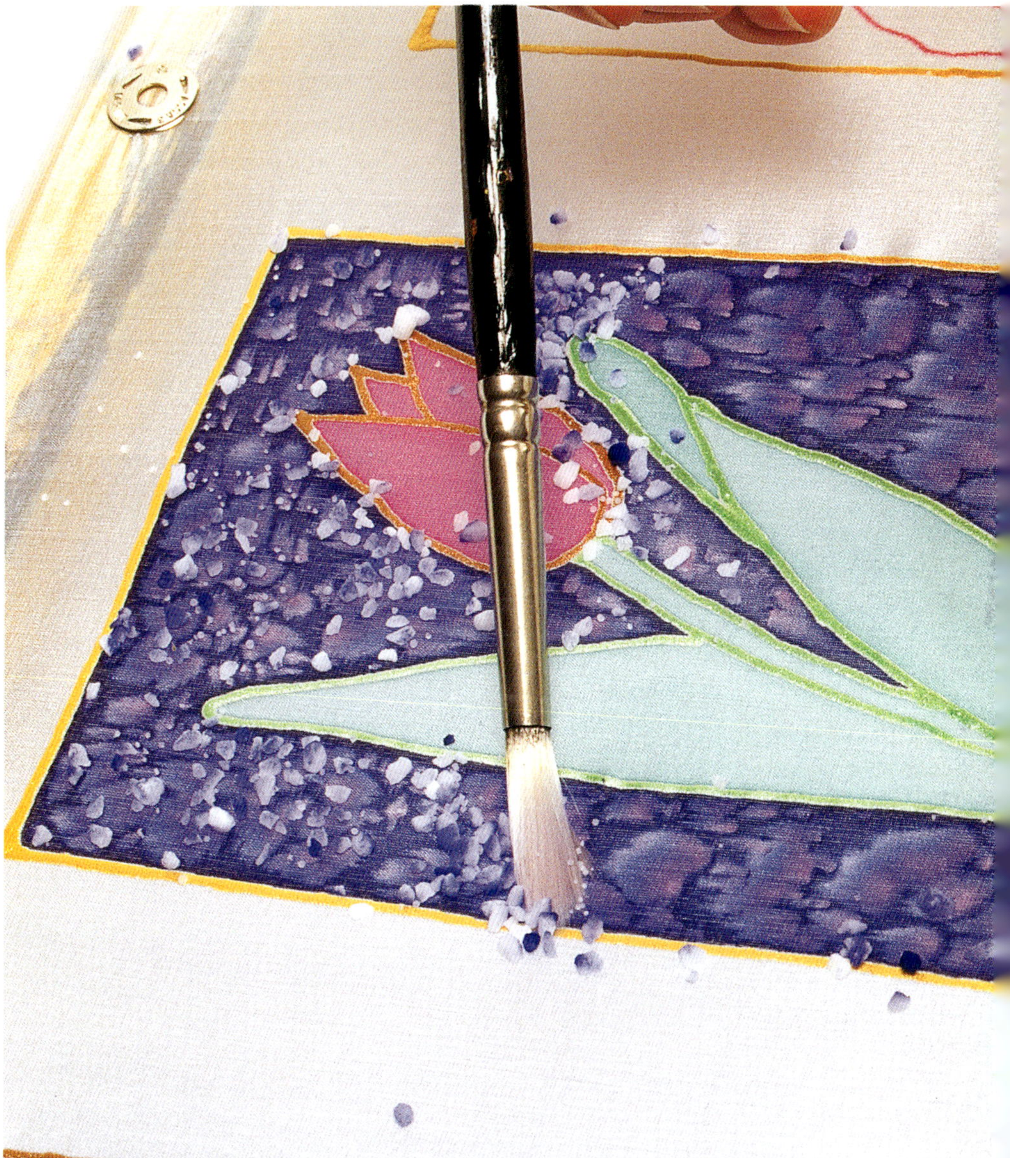

Safety

Even with something as seemingly harmless as painting, there are safety implications which should be noted. Most liquid silk dyes and paints are water-based and harmless, but procion powder dyes must be handled sensibly while they are in their powder form, so wear a mask when measuring out and mixing to avoid inhaling them. When handling any chemical, wear protective rubber gloves to avoid contact with the skin. This applies to soda ash, which is a strong alkaline solution, and fibre etch solution which could be irritating to the skin. Keep measuring spoons, utensils, bowls, jugs and any other equipment needed for silk painting and dyeing separate from the items you use in the kitchen.

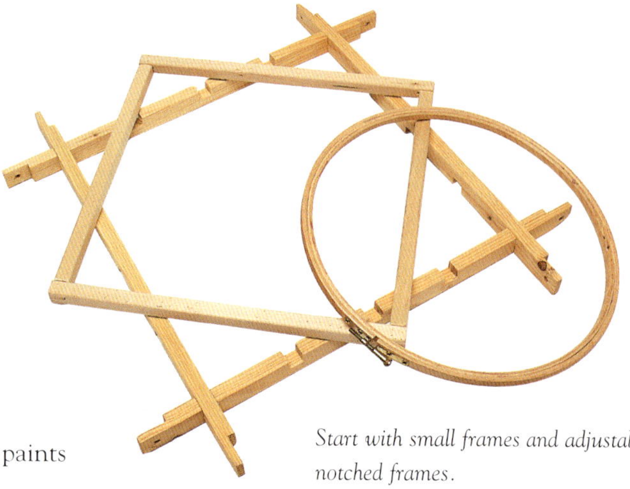

Start with small frames and adjustable notched frames.

Silk

Lightweight pongee silk is an excellent weight for the beginner to work on. It is suitable for samplers and practice pieces, as well as cards, pictures and scarves. As you become more skilled, try some of the other types and weights of silks.

Silk paints and dyes

Buy a basic selection of silk paints and dyes. Further information on silk paints and dyes is given on page 14.

Gutta and outliners

Forming barrier lines to control the flow of the silk colours is a fundamental part of silk painting. Barrier lines are formed with gutta or silk paint outliners, which come in tubes or plastic pipette bottles, and are available in a selection of colours.

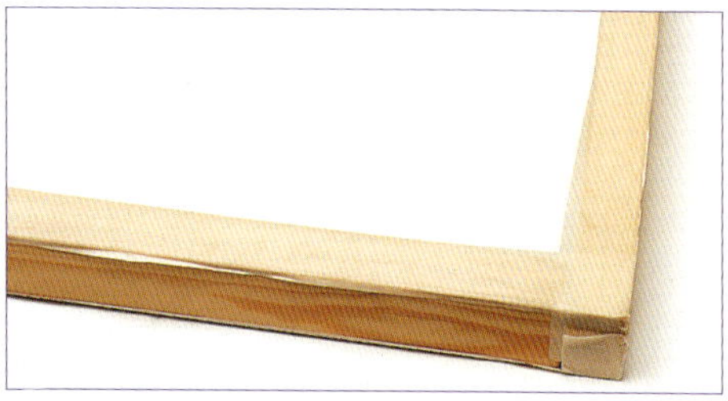

A fixed frame is easy to make yourself.

Fine metal tips

Metal tips can be fitted onto the nozzle of the plastic applicator bottles to help control the resist line. Available in a selection of nib sizes from 0.3 mm to 1.00 mm, they come with a fine cleaning wire that helps stop the hole becoming blocked when it is not being used. Stick a small piece of masking tape to the end of the cleaning wire to mark the size of the tip and help prevent loss of the fine wire if it is accidentally dropped onto the floor.

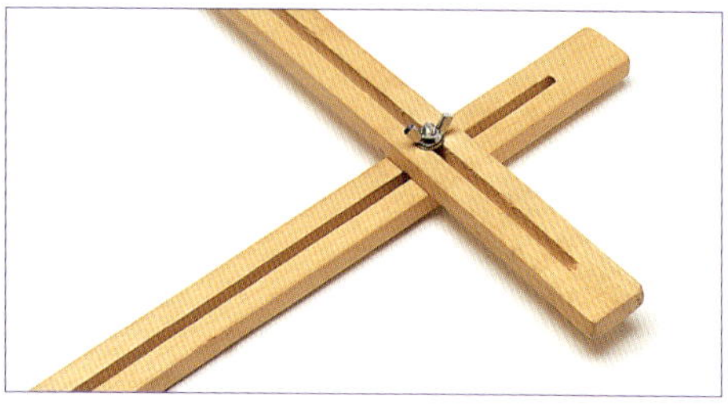

Sliding frames give good adjustability.

Silk paint thickener

Added to the silk paint or dye to change the way the colour flows.

Anti spread solution

Applied to the silk to change the colour spreading qualities of the silk.

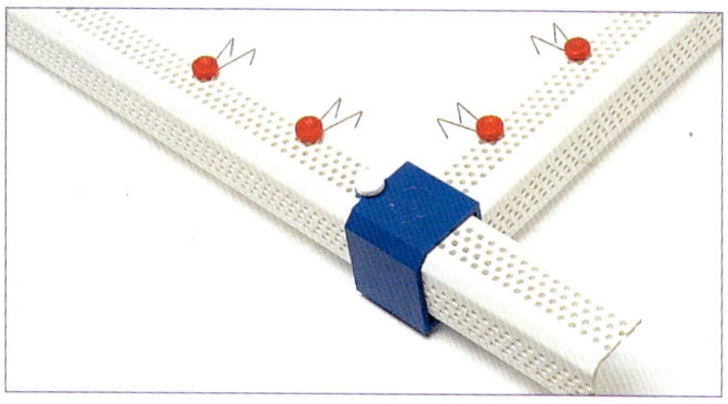

Holed frames give fine adjustability and have their own pi

Effect salts

Sprinkled on to the wet coloured silk to create texture patterns.

Frames

Most silk painting is done with the fabric supported on a frame, which stretches the silk and helps the dye to flow evenly. Frames can be as simple as an old wooden picture frame, or four pieces of wood fastened together to make up a rigid square or rectangle. If you make your own frame, choose wood that is not too hard, so that the silk pins will easily push into it. A frame that allows some sort of adjustment is more efficient both for stretching the silk and to accommodate different sizes of material. Frames can be made of wood, plastic or metal. Investigate a selection of frames and see which type seems best.

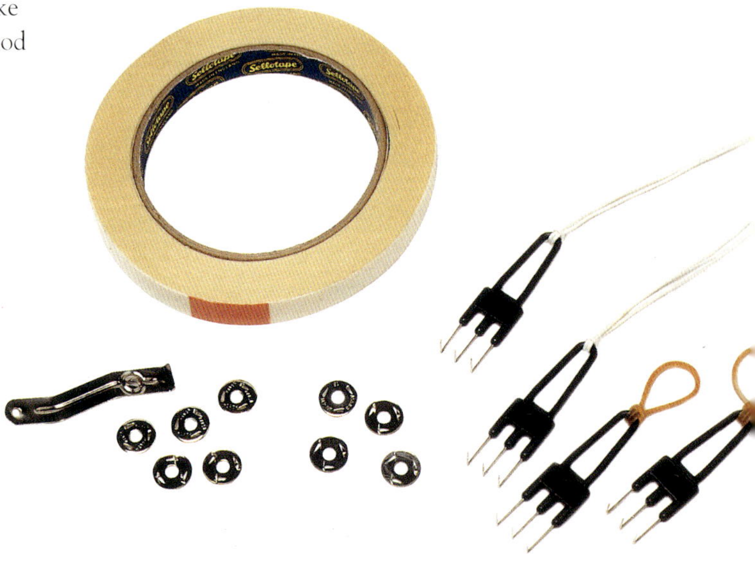

Silk pins, stenter pins & double sided tape

Silk pins, stenter pins and double-sided tape

Silk pins are usually employed to fasten silk to a frame. The simplest are three-pointed silk pins, which divide the fibres of the material rather than making holes as the silk is tensioned. These pins are made of steel, and can rust if the salt-effect crystal deposits employed made of steel, and can rust if the salt-effect crystal deposits employed in some projects are not washed off occasionally.

Stenter or claw pins are an alternative to three-pointed pins. Stenter pins are particularly useful for awkward sized pieces or when if you want to paint right up to rolled edges on the silk. It is possible to create your own stenter pins (see page 23 for instructions). Some frames come with their own pins.

Double-sided tape is another alternative, and is good for large areas of silk that do not have a ready rolled edge. See page 22 for instructions on how to use this method of tensioning the silk.

Paint brushes

A good selection of paint brushes is essential, as they are the main tool for applying and moving the silk paints and dyes. Soft round watercolour brushes that form a good point, or Chinese brushes are suitable. Brush quality varies enormously, but spend as much as you can afford, and then make sure you look after your brushes properly. Brush sizes between 2 and 12 are probably most useful to start with, plus a larger Chinese or foam brush for backgrounds and large areas. Use old brushes, decorating brushes or hog brushes when working with wax. Silk dyes should not damage or stiffen brushes, but heat-fix paints can slightly stiffen brushes after a period of time. Use your best brushes with steam-fix dyes, and save the second-best for heat-fix paints.

Mixing palettes, cups, spray bottle

A small multi-welled mixing palette is essential for silk painting. A good selection of wells will encourage colour mixing which adds far more variation and depth to your work. For larger pieces of work or backgrounds, plastic cups, jam jars or a larger palette well is necessary to avoid running out of colour before the area is fully coloured. Palettes can be made of china or plastic. Some paints and dyes can stain plastic palettes although china palettes should not be affected. Pump-action spray bottles are very useful for spraying colour or water.

A large water pot is also essential. Change the water frequently as dirt on the brush will spoil the clarity of the colours.

Pipette droppers

Plastic pipette droppers are useful for carefully lifting up colour or water with the minimum of spillage. Most pipette droppers have marked graduations on the side, which allow accurate recording and re-mixing of colours.

Paper towelling and cotton buds

Paper towelling or kitchen roll is essential for wiping the inevitable blob that forms at the beginning of the outliner tube when you first start silk painting, and for drying off the brush between rinses, to keep the colours at the correct depth. Paper towelling can quickly absorb excess quantities of dye or water on the silk, and cotton buds are useful for small spaces.

Soft pencils and disappearing pens

If you are not tracing from a pattern placed under the silk, use either a very soft 4B pencil, or a disappearing pen to draw directly onto the silk. Disappearing pens are available as auto-fade pens whose ink vanishes after a period of time, or as water-soluble pens, where the ink disappears after contact with water.

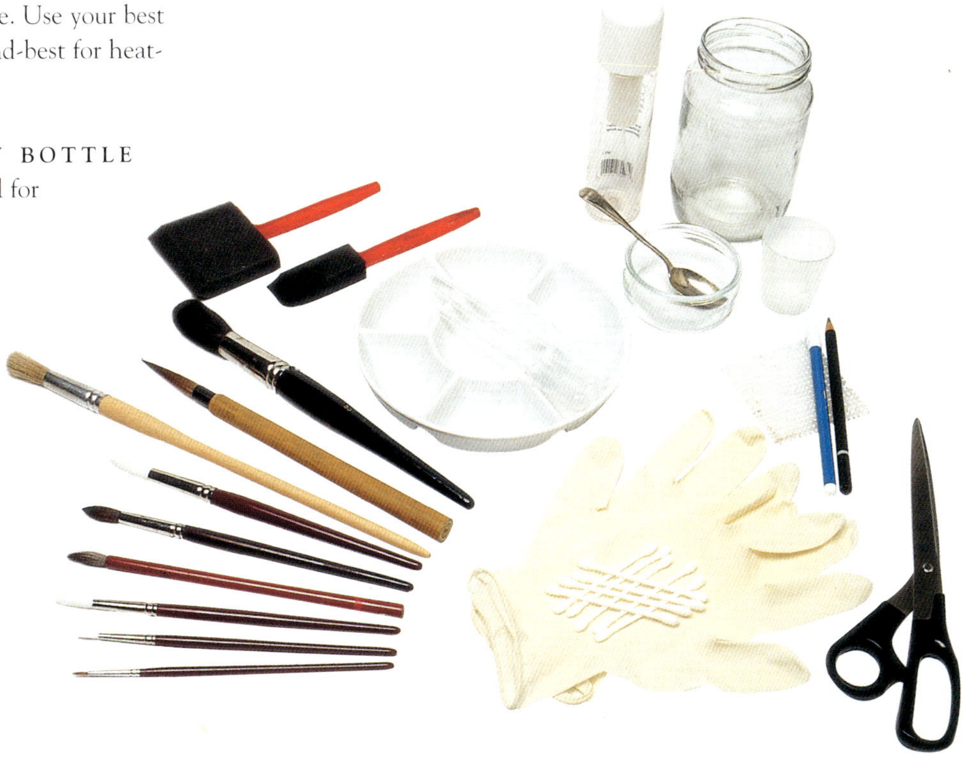

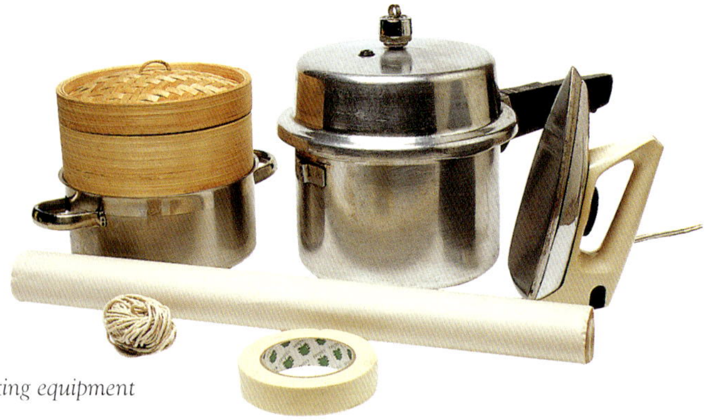

Fixing equipment

Fixing equipment

Heat-fix silk paints are normally fixed by ironing. Use a flat iron in preference to a steam iron when heat-fixing. An iron is also used to remove any wax used as a resist on the silk. It is also possible to oven-cure heat-fix paints. Please refer to page 40 for further information on this process

Other silk dyes are set by steam fixing. The work is rolled up with wallpaper lining or cotton which absorbs any excess dyes during the steaming process, and then steamed in a saucepan or pressure cooker. See the section on steam-fix dyes on page 16 for further information.

Hairdryer

A hairdryer can speed up the process of drying outliners, water and colour washes. It can also be used to selectively dry particular parts of a design or to help create watermarks.

Scissors

Use sharp scissors for cutting the silk and for careful trimming and finishing techniques.

Metre rule or yard stick

This can be used to draw neat straight gutta lines in a geometric design or to create a border. The ruler can also be used to help measure and calculate quantities required for a particular design or project.

Plastic canvas square

A 10 cm (4 in.) square of plastic canvas makes a simple measuring grid for quickly marking out even corner point marks when creating a border design and is available from sewing or craft shops. Make a series of larger holes, at intervals of your choosing, on the diagonal line of the square. It can then be placed into each corner of your silk while it is stretched out on the frame, and the corner points marked with a water-soluble pen or soft pencil in the appropriate hole to create a border of the required depth. The edges can also be used to mark out border widths. See page 46.

Synthrapol

This is a concentrated liquid detergent that can be added to the rinse water to help wash out loose dye particles from the silk. Please refer to the manufacturer's instructions for a guide on dilution rates.

Protective clothing

Wear rubber gloves to protect your skin, especially when using chemical-based mediums. It is also sensible to wear an apron as most paints and dyes have the capacity to stain clothing even before they are properly fixed.

Bowls, spoons, jugs and jam jars

Have a bowl, measuring jug, teaspoon, tablespoon and a good collection of jam jars, preferably with screw top lids, ready to use when measuring out, mixing up and storing dyes. These should labelled and kept purely for craft purposes and not used in the preparation of food.

Wax

Wax is used as a resist or barrier, and requires a few specialist pieces of equipment. Paraffin wax granules are easier to use than blocks of wax, as they can be topped up with additional granules more easily than breaking off a chunk of wax. Beeswax can also be added, which makes the wax more pliable and less likely to crackle. Wax should be melted in a thermostatically controlled wax pot. If this is not possible, use a double saucepan to melt the wax, checking that the water in the base does not dry out. Wax should never be left unattended while it is being heated, and should be left in a safe place even while it cools down.

Wax is applied to the fabric with a tjanting, or canting, a traditional Javanese pen-like tool. Available in a selection of styles and sizes, the bowl which holds the wax can be round or pointed. It is normally made from brass or copper which retains the heat and helps to keep the wax molten. The fine spouts vary in size to produce lines of various widths, and there are double and triple cantings which produce several lines at once.

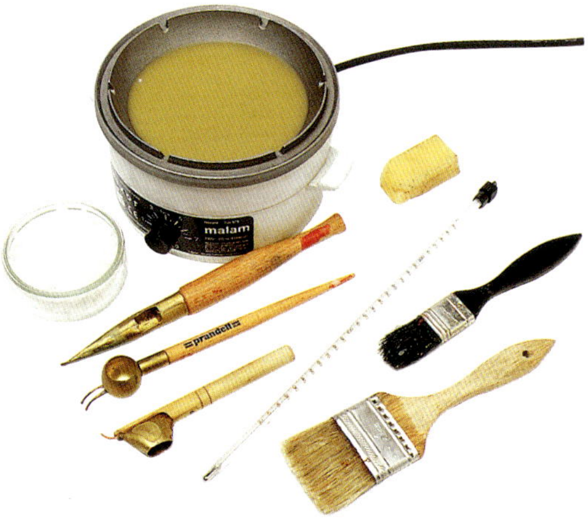

Wax pot, cantings & wax

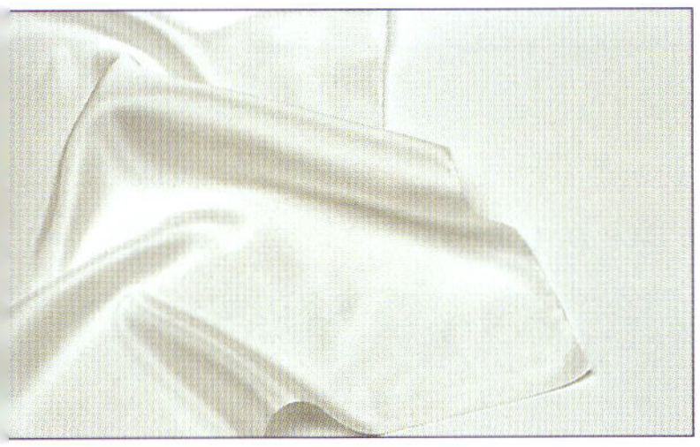

Pongee white silk

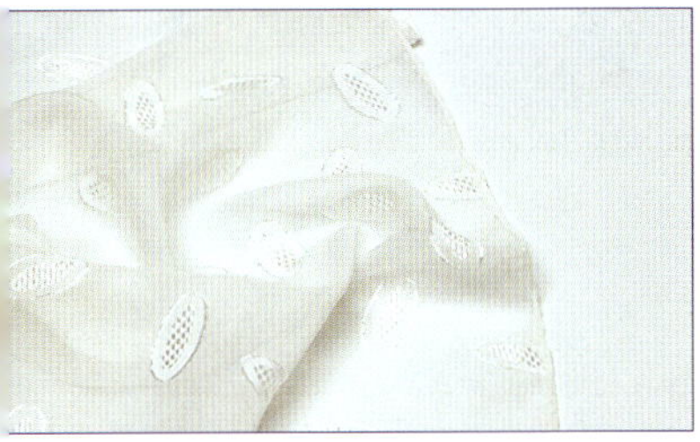

Pre-devored white silk - satin

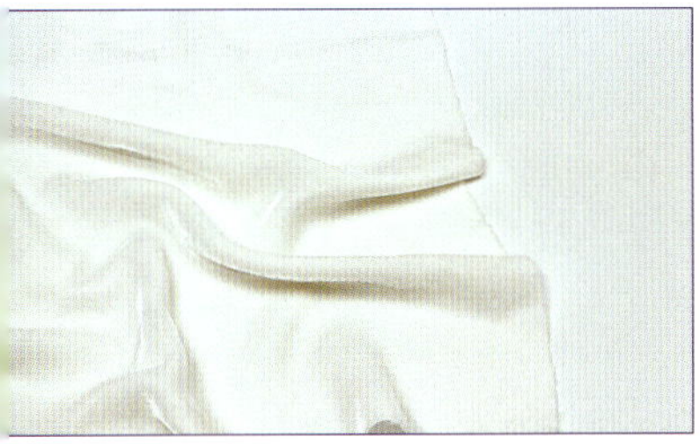

White velvet

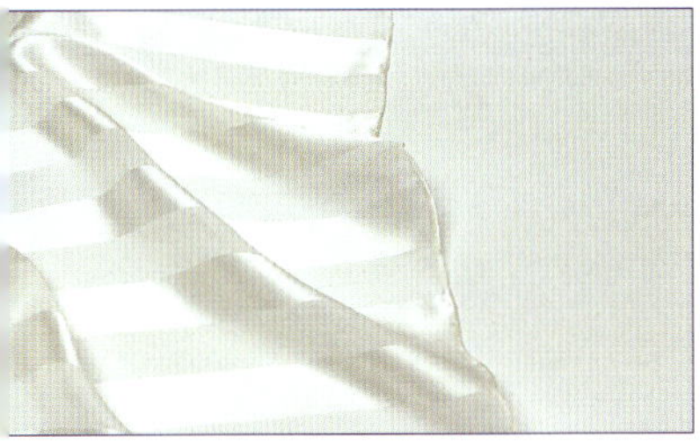

Silk/satin stripe, white

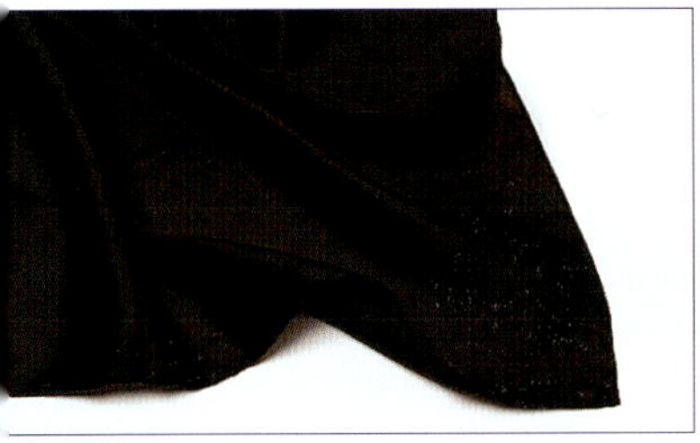

Black silk

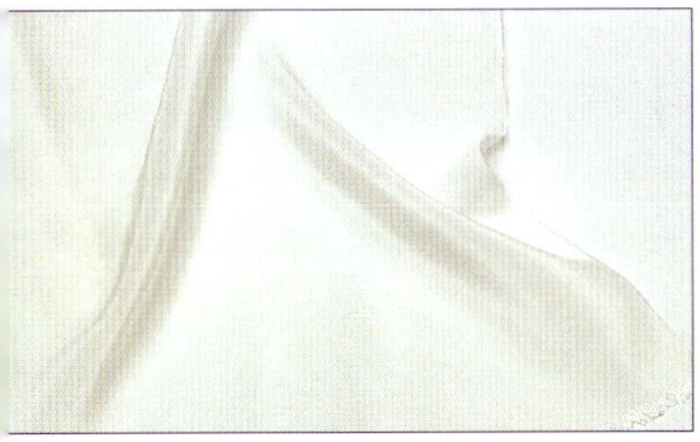

Crêpe de chine

Silk fabrics suitable for painting

Despite the huge range of silk fabrics available, not all are suitable for painting by the inexperienced painter. As a general rule, you should initially avoid fabrics with an uneven surface or slub in their weave, as it can be difficult to ensure that both the resist and dye have sufficiently penetrated the whole of the silk fabric. It is best to start working on smooth, evenly surfaced silks, like the pongee, paj, and habotai silks, which all enable the resist to seal the silk easily, and the silk dyes to move effectively across the surface.

Pongee or habotai silk comes from China and is particularly good for the inexperienced silk painter. Available in a range of weights, it has a white, smooth, even surface with a good sheen which helps to enhance the finished painting. Lightweight and inexpensive, it has a less tightly packed weave, so silk dyes spread very easily across the surface. A lightweight silk can be used for many projects: floaty scarves, hair ties, cards, pictures and test pieces.

Medium weight habotai silk has the same smooth surface, but is more dense in weave and has a slightly thicker thread giving a stronger and heavier fabric. This weight is suitable for projects such as cushion covers, scarves, pieces where creative embroidery or quilting is to be added, or clothing where a less translucent appearance of the silk is required.

The heavyweight habotai silk provides a substantial fabric for use in upholstery projects, clothing, kimonos, and for screen panels, banners and wall hangings. Any silk can be backed with another fabric or interfacing to add further strength, although bear in mind that the drape of the fabric will be affected.

The heavier the weight of silk, the slower the dye will spread across its surface. This makes some silks, such as crêpe de chine, more suitable for working designs without the use of a linear resist (a barrier to limit the spread of the dye). You may need to use more of a brushing action to evenly distribute the colour, rather than relying on the silk's natural capillary action to spread the colour across the surface of the stretched silk. Greater quantities of dye will be needed to penetrate and colour all the fibres of the silk. However, once distributed, the colour will appear slightly more intense on a heavier silk than on a lighter weight, as the fabric is more dense in construction.

Once you have done a few samplers and practice pieces on various weights of smooth surfaced silks, you may like to try working on other types of silk. Silk velvet, silk satin, crêpe de chine, jacquard, georgette and chiffon silks are all suitable for painting, each offering different qualities to the finished piece of work.

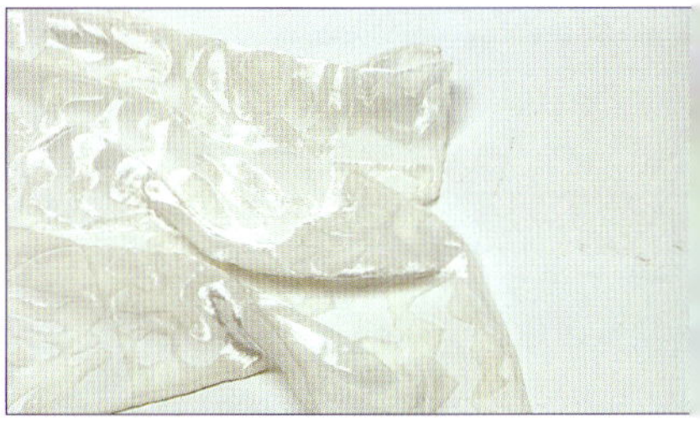

Pre-devored white silk - velvet

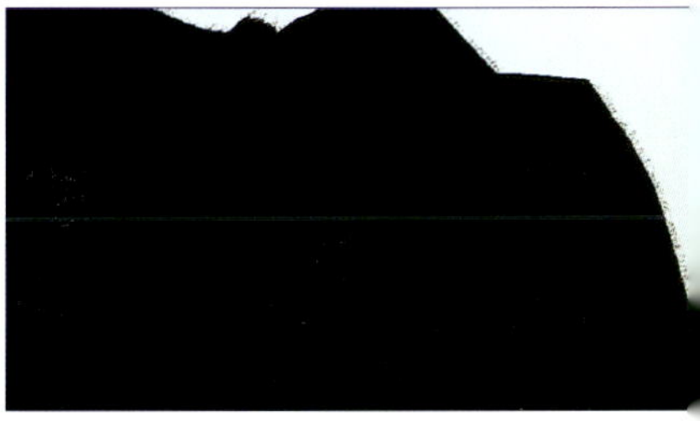

Black velvet

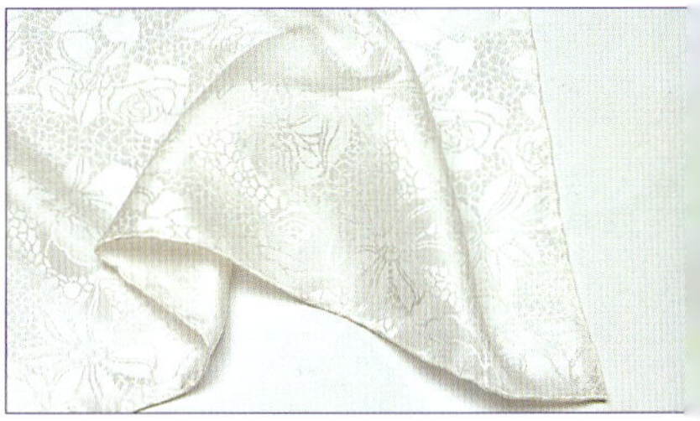

White jacquard pattern

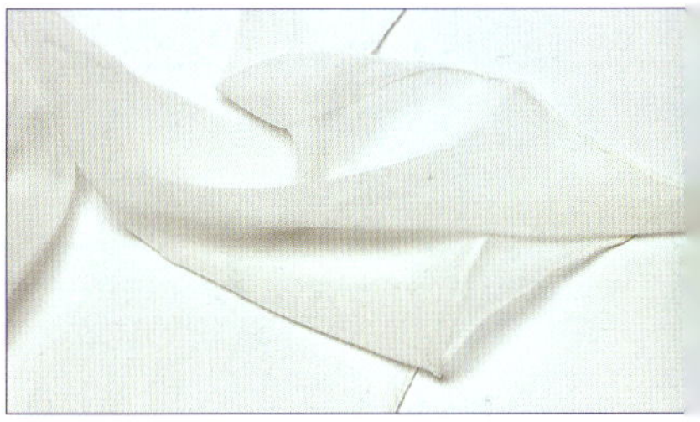

Chiffon

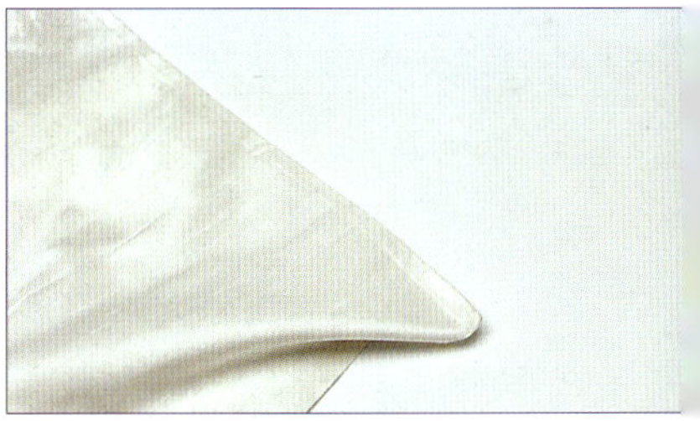

Dupion silk

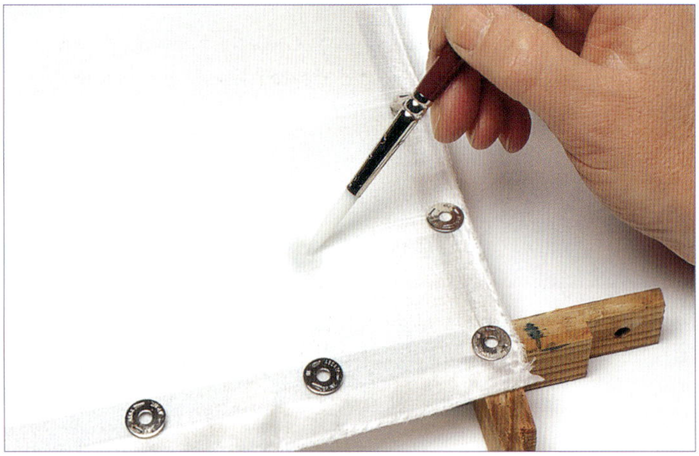

Dab a spot of water onto the silk to test its flow qualities.

Testing a piece of silk for painting
Before starting work on a piece of silk, check whether it has any 'dressing' in the surface that will impair the flow of the silk paint or dye. To test whether the silk is ready for painting, just dab a small spot of water on one corner and watch whether the water spreads out easily. If the spot of water sits on the surface like a small bead and does not sink into the silk or spread across the surface, the material contains some dressing that is preventing the absorption of the water. The silk must therefore be washed in hot soapy water before being used for painting. However, if the spot of water sinks into the silk and spreads out freely and evenly, it is ready for working, as water reacts in the same way that the paints and dyes will spread.

Silk paints and dyes

A wide range of paints and dyes is available, although for best results it is preferable to use ones that have been specifically formulated for use on silk fabrics. These allow the colours to be fixed permanently into the fabric using a variety of different methods.

With a wide selection of paints and dyes to choose from, it can be confusing choosing the most suitable. Most people start with a heat-fix silk paint because of the simplicity of the fixing process, and then progress to try steam-fix dyes, or possibly acid dyes and procion dyes. All of these types of paints colour silk effectively and permanently. It is often possible to substitute one dye type for another, so if you prefer to work with heat-fix paints just substitute your preferred paints, taking into consideration any changes necessary for their particular working and fixing requirements.

It is not simply a case that one paint or dye is better than another. Each type is different, offering various qualities that could be beneficial to a particular type of silk, to the project being worked, or that may suit one person more than another. A silk paint or dye should therefore be selected on its suitability to the project being worked, and the preferences of the individual artist.

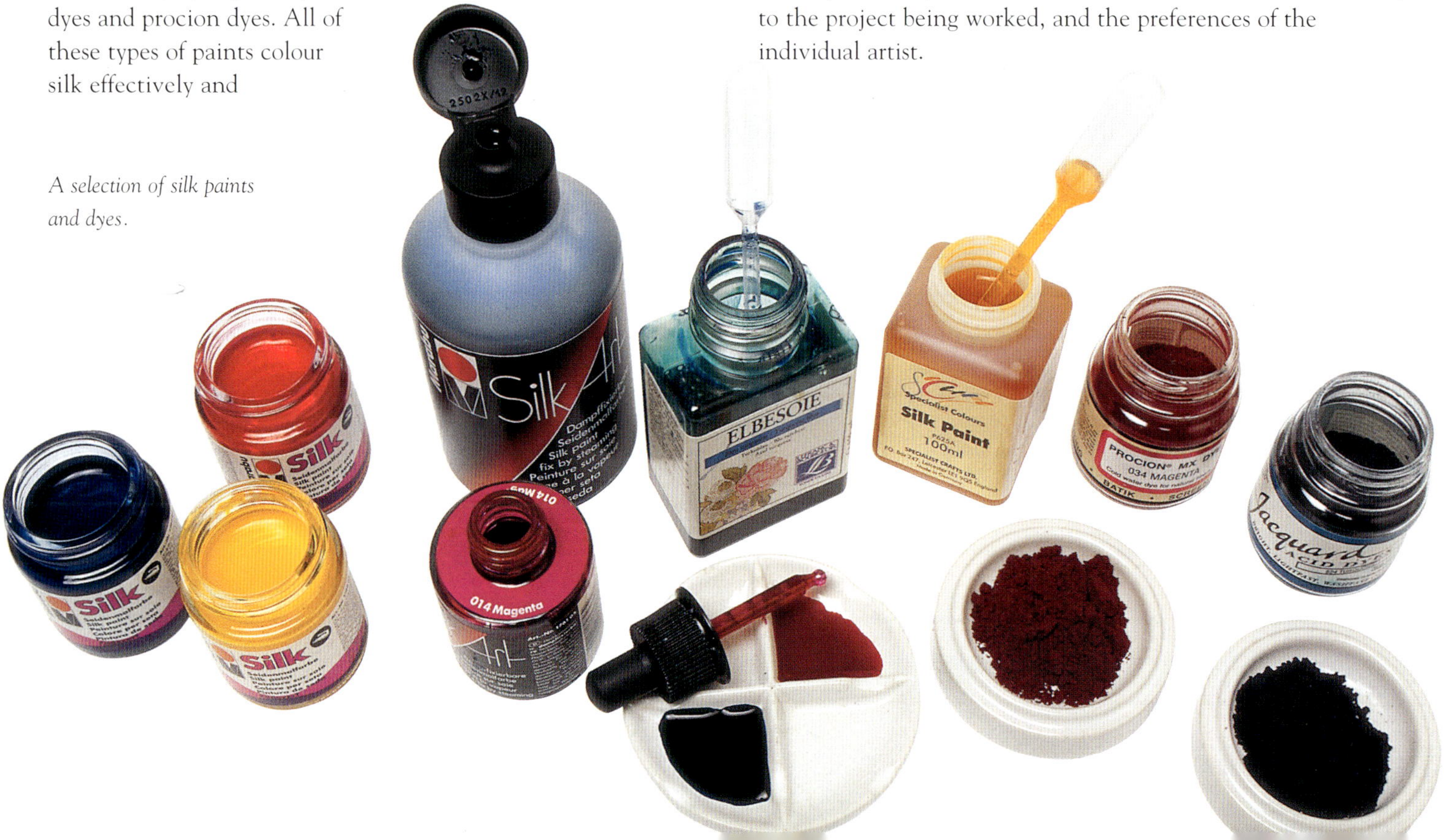

A selection of silk paints and dyes.

HEAT-FIX SILK PAINTS

The most frequently used paints are heat-fix, water-based, acrylic silk paints that can be intermixed with one another for a wide range of colours, and diluted with water for paler tints. These are popular because they are easy to use and can be simply fixed with the heat from an iron. Heat-fix silk paints work by coating the silk fibres rather than penetrating them, and you can normally feel the difference between a silk paint and a silk dye. Another quality of a heat-fix paint is that they cannot be further worked or moved into new patterns on the silk once dry, although further layers of paint can be applied on top. This means that achieving a constant, even colour across a large area, such as a background, can be quite difficult for the novice silk painter. With a heat-fix paint, if any part of the area being painted dries before being completely painted, a join mark, or watermark is almost inevitable where the wet paint meets the dry silk paint. Once dry, these paints are simply and quickly fixed by ironing which makes this silk paint the ideal choice for the beginner or for work in schools or workshops where the length of working sessions can be an important consideration.

SETTING HEAT-FIX PAINTS

Ironing

The ironing process allows the acrylic binder and pigments to bond onto the fibres giving a durable and washable finished fabric. Iron fixing can be applied directly to the reverse of the fabric, or through a piece of paper or fine cotton fabric. Ironing also sets the heat-fix outliners, which are intended to remain in the fabric, and so give a slightly textured finish to the silk. The only exception to this is the clear outliner, which is removed on the initial washing of the fixed piece.

The reverse side of the fabric should be ironed as the outliners sit slightly proud of the surface on the right side, but are quite flat on the reverse of the fabric. Use a hot or wool setting, and give the piece a thorough ironing for two minutes, keeping the iron moving the whole time to avoid scorching any area of silk. If you detect any bubbling in the outliner, the iron is too hot, or has remained in one position for too long, or possibly the outliners were not completely dry, and the heat from the iron has caused uneven drying. Heat-fix silk paints are now much improved and only give a very slight stiffening to the finished fabric, which may decrease after a series of washes.

Dry curing

It is also possible to set heat-fix paints by gently heating the silk in a domestic oven, which is especially useful for large or awkward-shaped items. Loosely fold the silk and place it on a clean baking tray. Very light or delicate silk can be covered with baking paper. The silk can then be gently fixed in an oven, at 140°C for 10 minutes or tumbled in a tumble dryer for about 15 minutes.

STEAM-FIX DYES

Steam-fix silk colours are dyes which penetrate and bond with the whole fibre of the fabric, giving colour without affecting the softness or drape of the silk. Another advantage is that the intensity of colour is increased by the steam-fixing process. It is possible to intermix colours, and pale hues can be achieved by diluting the dyes with water and or other dilutants. Unlike heat-fix acrylic silk paints, steam-fix dyes have the capacity to re-form into different patterns on subsequent applications of dye or water until they are fixed. This gives tremendous scope for added patterning when working a design in a series of layers, even if previous layers of dye have completely dried. Once the fixing process has been applied these dyes are also washable and many can also be dry cleaned (but check the manufacturer's care instructions).

ACID DYES

Acid dyes are easy to use and give brilliant colours. They are suitable for dyeing wool, silk and other protein-based fibres. They are called acid dyes because they need hot, acidic conditions to drive the dye into the fibres, which is most easily achieved by using acetic acid or vinegar in combination with a steam setting process. Steam setting is achieved in exactly the same way as for steam-fix dyes on page 16, with the addition of a couple of tablespoons of vinegar in the water reservoir in the bottom of the pan. They also work well in the microwave techniques described on page 40.

HOW TO MIX UP POWDERED ACID DYES

Wearing a protective mask, carefully measure out one teaspoon of dye powder and place it in a clean measuring jug with a small quantity of hot, but not boiling water. To achieve stronger colours increase the quantity of dye powder. Stir to dissolve the dye powder, then add a further quantity of cold water to bring the quantity up to 220ml (7 fl. oz). Pour this liquid dye into a screw top jam jar for immediate use and short term storage. Try not to make more dye than you need for a particular project. The acetic acid or vinegar will be added at the working stage if using the microwave technique, or at the steam-fixing stage for conventional steaming.

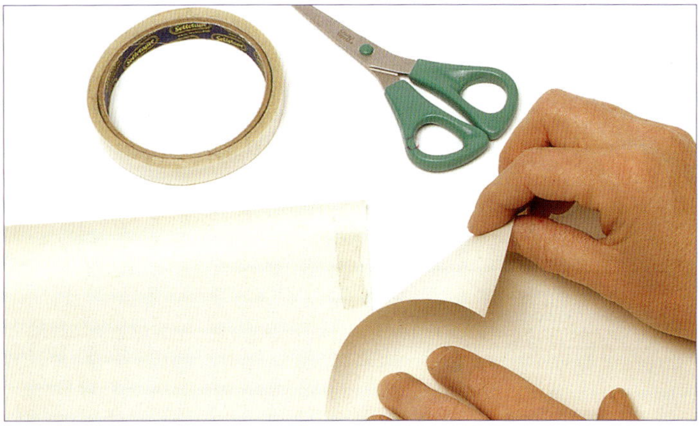

Joining and sticking fixing paper together with double-sided tape.

Fixing your work

Once the dyes are dry and the design is complete, the silk must be steamed to make the colours fast and washable. There are various way of steaming the finished work which all follow the same procedure, but the container used and the time required to set the dyes may vary.

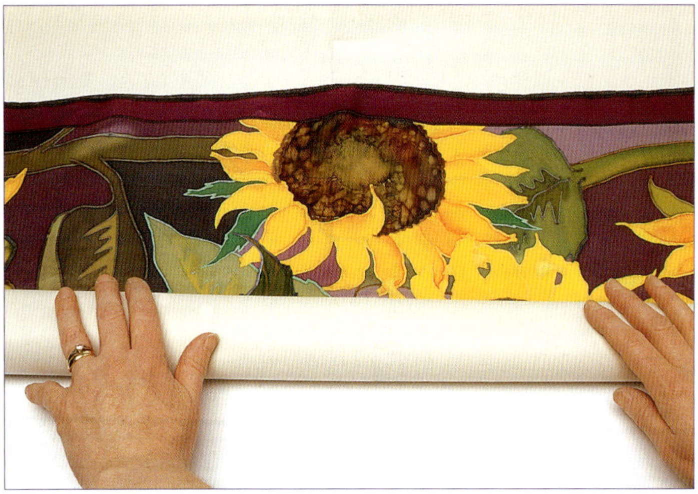

Rolling up the work in absorbant paper or cotton.

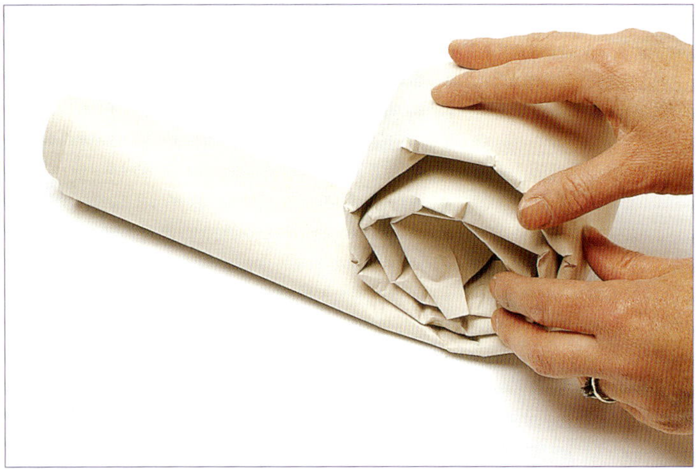

Coiling up the roll to fit into steaming pan.

Steam fixing using a pressure cooker

Place the dried, unfixed silk painted pieces onto some thin cotton material or absorbent paper such as wallpaper lining paper. Wallpaper lining may be too narrow for large pieces of silk, so simply join two strips together with a few short pieces of double-sided tape along the centre overlap. As you lay out the finished work, make sure that there is a gap of about 5 cm (2 in.) between each piece, with a similar amount at the outer edges. This will prevent the pieces touching each other as the work is rolled up.

Carefully roll up the unfixed pieces of silk, ensuring that the cotton fabric or absorbent paper is not creased. Try not to make the roll too tight; keep it loose and squashy so it is easier to coil up and fit into a pressure cooker pan. Seal up one end of the roll with tape and coil the roll, beginning with the sealed end. Secure, and seal up the other end of the completed coil with a few pieces of masking tape or sticky tape to prevent it from uncoiling. To ensure that the coil does not come undone during the fixing process, tie a piece of string around it, checking that there are no long ends of string that could trail into the water during the fixing. This coil shape is often referred to as a parcel.

Put 2 cm ($^{3}/_{4}$ in.) of water in the base of the pressure cooker pan, and then place a trivet or stand in the base of the pan for the parcel to sit on. If you do not have a trivet make one by folding a good length of kitchen foil into a stiff strip about 10 cm (4 in.) deep and coiling this up to form a stand. The parcel must not come into direct contact with the water.

Put the parcel on the trivet, and place a domed hat, made of kitchen foil shaped over a pudding basin, on top of the parcel. This prevents any droplets of condensation dropping from the lid of the pressure cooker on to the coil during steaming. It should be replaced as soon as small pin prick holes appear in the foil after a couple of steamings. Using the complete pressure cooker weights, place the lid of the pressure cooker on the base and close together.

Quickly bring the water to the boil to pressurise the pan, but once the pan is pressurised (shown by the weight rattling or the valve coming up), reduce the heat right down to a simmer setting. This should be just sufficient to maintain the pressure, and cook for 20 minutes from this point. As a rough guide, 20 minutes is sufficient for up to 2.5 metres of fabric, or an 8-foot running length of light or medium weight silk. Should the pressure drop during this time, just increase the heat slightly and add another few minutes.

After the correct cooking time, turn off the heat or remove the pressure cooker from the heat source, and allow the pressure to drop. Once the pressure has dropped you can safely open the lid of the pressure cooker, and remove and unwrap the parcel while it is still warm. If you have used water-based outliners, always open the parcel while it is still warm as it is easier to detach any silk that has stuck to the paper during the fixing. If you find that any pieces of silk are really stuck to the paper through heavy usage of outliner, particularly on chiffon or lightweight silk, do not try to force the silk away from the paper. Carefully tear the paper around the problem area, leaving the paper attached to the silk. Then place the silk with the stuck paper still attached into the rinsing water and gently agitate the silk. The water will quickly soften the water-soluble outliner and allow the pieces of paper to be removed without damaging the silk.

Allow the fixed pieces to settle and cool down before washing each piece of fixed silk in warm water with a little liquid detergent to remove any traces of water-soluble outliner, excess colour or salt deposits. As the silk fabric can only absorb a given quantity of dye, any excess dye will sit on the surface of the fabric and be washed away at the rinsing stage, so do not be overly concerned at a slight discolouration of the water. To avoid staining the silk during the rinsing process, gently move it around in the rinse water rather than just leaving it to soak, so any excess dye will not settle on the silk and stain it. Discard the first water and rinse again in clean water. Squeeze out any surplus water, then iron the fixed pieces of silk while damp to remove any creases and restore the sheen.

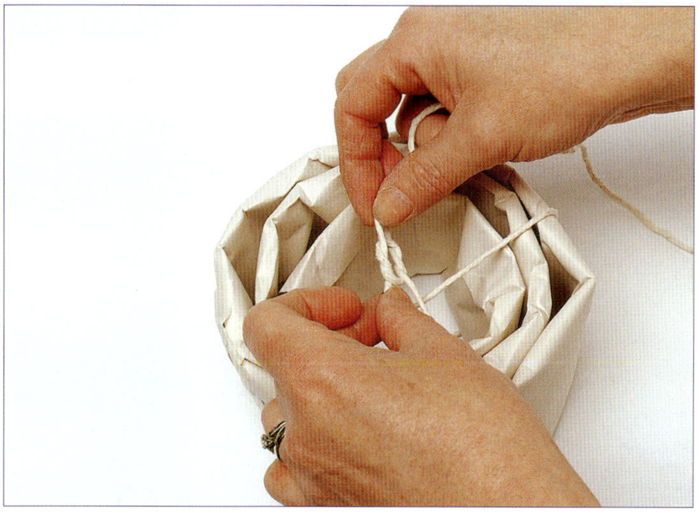

Securing the parcel with string.

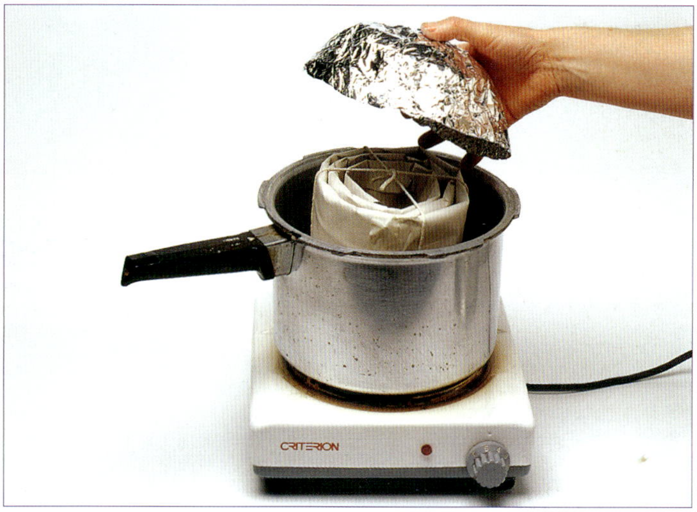

Secured parcel sitting on trivet in pressure cooker, with foil 'hat'.

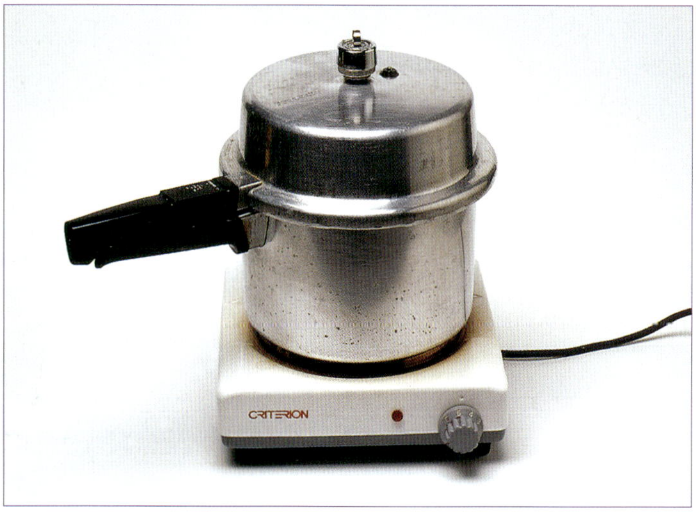

Pressure cooker on cooker ring ready for steaming.

Steam fixing in a bamboo steamer or colander and saucepan.

Follow the instructions for rolling and coiling up to form the parcel as before. Line a bamboo basket or colander with some absorbent paper, such as wallpaper lining paper, and place the parcel on it. Place a domed kitchen foil hat on top of the parcel to protect it from condensation droplets, then fit a lid on to the bamboo steamer or make a lid from kitchen foil to trap as much of the steam as possible. Place a good quantity of water in the base of a saucepan, but ensure it does not come up as far as the base of the colander or basket. Turn up the heat to bring the water up to the boil, and then reduce to a simmer, just enough to maintain a good head of steam. Steam the parcel for between one and two hours depending on the dyes used and the quantity and thickness of silk, but remember to check the level of the water from time to time, topping up if necessary to ensure there is plenty of water to create lots of steam. Once the piece has been steamed long enough to set the dyes, the silk must be washed as described earlier. As a guide, around one hour is usually sufficient for up to three metres, with larger quantities or heavier silks requiring longer.

Simple open steaming pan for Shibori work

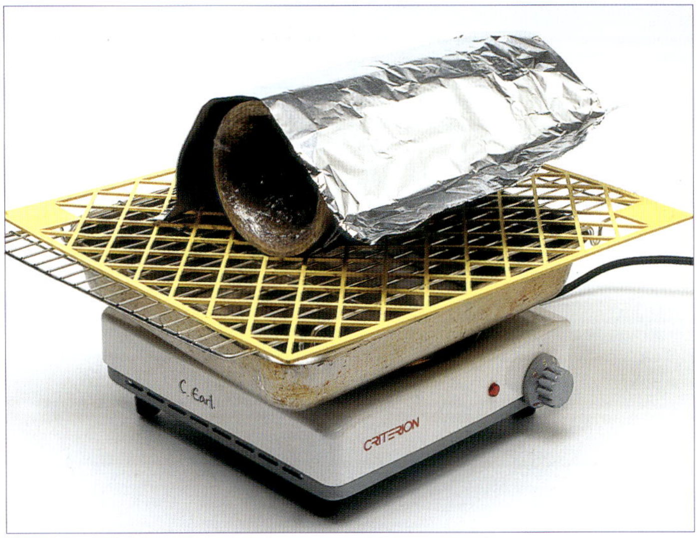

Shibori open pan steaming

Shibori is an ancient Japanese form of dyeing involving pleating, folding, twisting, wrapping, or stitching silk using bindings of fine threads or string. Shibori work can be easily fixed in a microwave, or steamed while placed on a rack over some boiling water in a roasting tin on top of the stove. An oblong roasting tin is the right shape to take a tube and can also hold a good quantity of water. The metal cooling rack will support the work above the level of the water, yet easily allow the steam to penetrate around the work. The use of a plastic sink drainer protects the silk from direct contact with the metal rack which can become quite hot over a long period of steaming, and the kitchen foil is wrapped over the work to form a lid and trap the steam. The timing for steaming work in this way will vary according to the size and thickness of the work being fixed, but will range from 40 minutes to two hours. It is important to check that there is enough water in the pan to create the steam or else the work can become scorched.

Commercial silk steamers

Designs of commercially available silk steamers vary considerably. Some are electrical, while others must be placed over a heat source. Most are cylindrical or rectangular in shape, allowing the silk to be rolled in absorbent paper, frequently on a pole, which is then suspended either vertically or horizontally, above the water source and gently steamed for several hours. Again, times vary considerably according to the model, amount and type of silk being fixed, so refer to the manufacturer's instructions for further guidance.

Which steaming method is best?

The advantage of commercially available steamers is that you do not have to coil up the paper roll containing the silk pieces, therefore reducing the potential of creasing. The disadvantage is the initial cost as they are rather expensive and, depending on the size, can take up rather a lot of floor space, so they may only be a consideration for the serious silk painter or possibly a school or college.

The results from the pressure cooker and bamboo steamer are the same as from a commercial steamer with the advantage that pressure cooking is the fastest method. As many people now use a microwave for fast cooking you will probably be able to find a second-hand pressure cooker very cheaply if you do not already have one.

The advantage of using a bamboo steamer to fix the silk dyes is that, although the process takes longer, bamboo steamers are very cheap and are available in a range of sizes, so it is a very inexpensive way of fixing your silk paintings.

Liquid fixatives

Some steam-fix silk dyes can also be set by applying a liquid fixative solution directly on to the finished, dry design as an alternative fixing method. The precise application can vary slightly so do check the manufacturer's instructions before proceeding. One way of applying the fixative solution is to completely immerse the dry, finished piece into a bath of fixative solution, agitate for the correct amount of time, and then rinse the silk in cool water to remove the excess solution together with any loose dye or salt deposits.

Other liquid fixatives require the solution to be brushed over the entire piece of work, while it is still on the frame, then left for around one hour, before washing it off along with any surplus dye, water-soluble outliner and excess salt deposits. Any fixative solution tends to slightly soften the colours, which does not necessarily make it a less effective fixing process, merely an alternative. It can be very effective to work a background, and liquid-fix it to achieve a softer look, then rework the silk with an overlaid pattern, this time using a steam fixing process to give a much more vibrant and contrasting colour strength. Since the initial colours are already fixed, they will stay in the original formation, and will not be affected when the second design is layered on top. Liquid fixing can also be used if the finished colours appear too bright once worked, and a softer appearance would be preferable for that particular piece. Not all dyes can be liquid fixed, so check the manufacturer's instructions on their suitability.

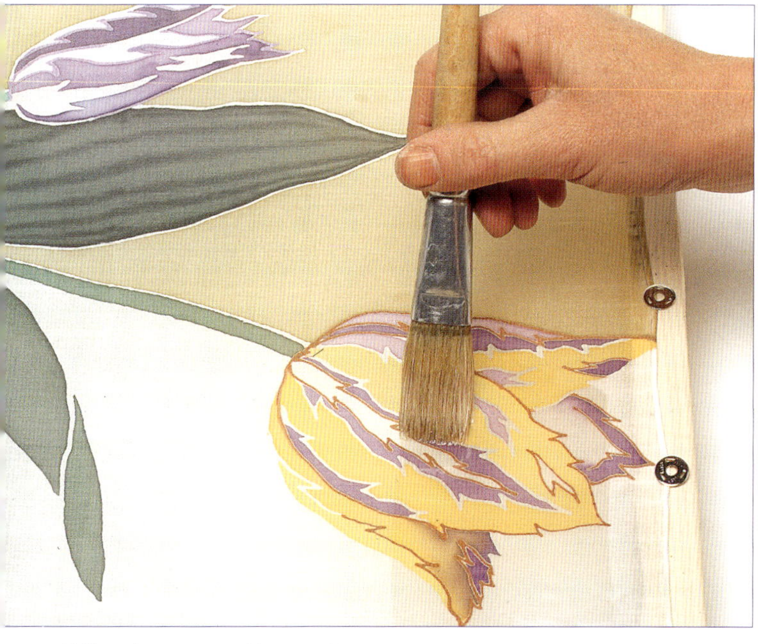

Follow the pattern with an outliner.

Outliners and resists

One of the main ways of controlling the spread of silk paints or dyes is to use a resist line as a barrier to contain the colour within a particular area. These barrier lines can be worked in a variety of resist mediums: an acrylic heat-fix outliner; a water-soluble outliner; gutta, a latex medium the consistency of honey; or a wax resist. The resist line defines the pattern and is usually drawn direct from a tube or fine nozzle on a soft plastic pipette bottle. Although it is not essential, a fine metal tip can be fitted onto the bottle nozzle to give finer control to the formation of a resist line.

The resist medium must penetrate through the stretched silk to seal the fibres on the top and lower surfaces of the silk in order to form an effective barrier line. There is no set line thickness to aim for, but the resist line should be in proportion to the design, pleasing to the artist, and functional in strength as a barrier line. As a hand-drawn line it is inevitable that the line thickness will vary, although it should not appear clumsy. The choice of colour can significantly affect the finished appearance of the silk painting, so choose outliner colours with as much care as for the selection of the dyes and paints. Resist lines are normally traced on to the silk following a paper pattern placed under the fabric, or drawn free-hand directly on to the silk. With practice it will be possible to control the thickness of the barrier line, so do not despair if your lines are not as you would wish to start with. Practise improving your outlining skills by following the exercises on pages 46–47, and by working with a clear outliner as described in the project on page 52.

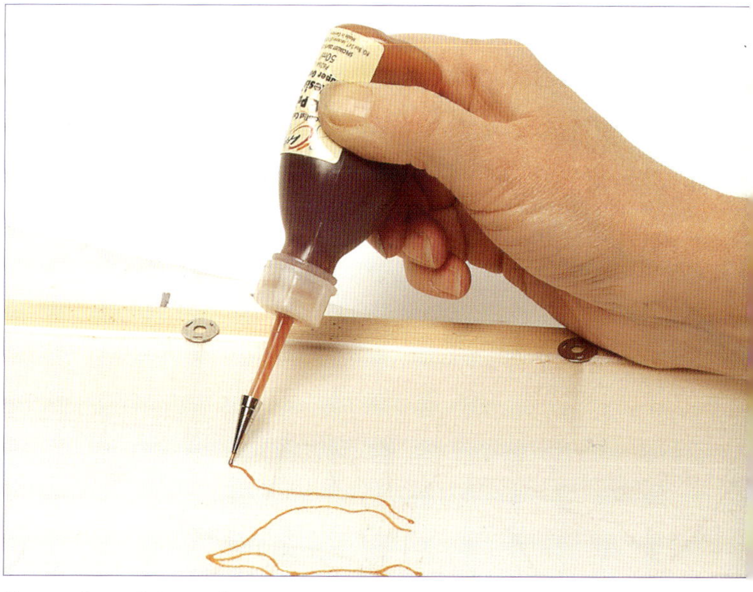

Stenter claw - fitting on frame

Water-soluble and acrylic outliners

Water-soluble and acrylic outliners are available in a selection of different colours. They can be clear, matt or pearlised. The actual outliner medium in both the water-soluble clear and coloured matt outliner is designed to wash out after the appropriate fixing method. Pearlised acrylic outliners are intended to remain in the fabric in order to give a pearlised effect and therefore give a very slightly raised or textured feel to the silk. A clear or colourless outliner has no pigment, so will give a white line if applied to a white silk and will always wash completely out of the silk leaving no trace of stiffness. However, a clear outliner can also be used to give coloured or multi-coloured lines, as it will take on the base colour of the fabric it is drawn onto: if applied to blue silk, it will give a blue resist line. You can buy ready-coloured matt, water-soluble outliners, or make your own by adding a small quantity of dye to clear outliner.

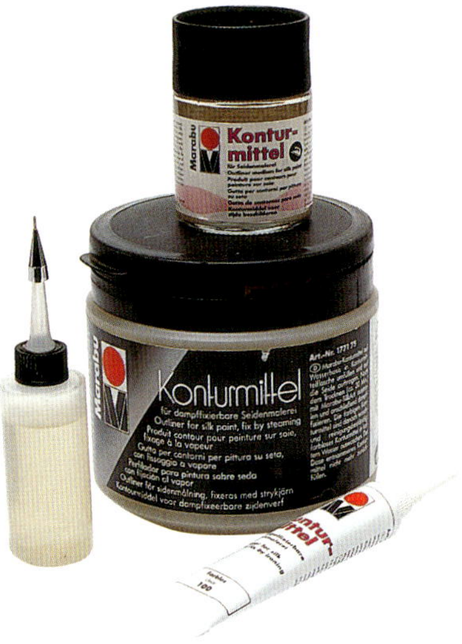

Clear water-based outliners.

A water-soluble outliner will be coloured by any paint or dye that is deliberately or accidentally brushed over it, and can lose some of its effectiveness as a barrier line if it is subjected to prolonged wetness from either colour or water. As it is receptive to colour, you can deliberately paint over a water-soluble outliner to disguise a rather chunky line or colour it to reduce the impact of the line. Water-soluble outliners are available in both heat-fix and steam-fix types, and are at their strongest as a resist line when dry, which can take around 20–30 minutes, depending on the outline thickness. Speed up the drying time by using a hairdryer, not a heat tool which can easily scorch the silk. Keep the hairdryer moving to avoid over-heating, which may result in fine bubbling in acrylic, pearlised heat-fix outliners. Paint or dye should always be applied a little distance away from the dry line, and allowed to run up to the resist line. This will prevent accidental painting over the line.

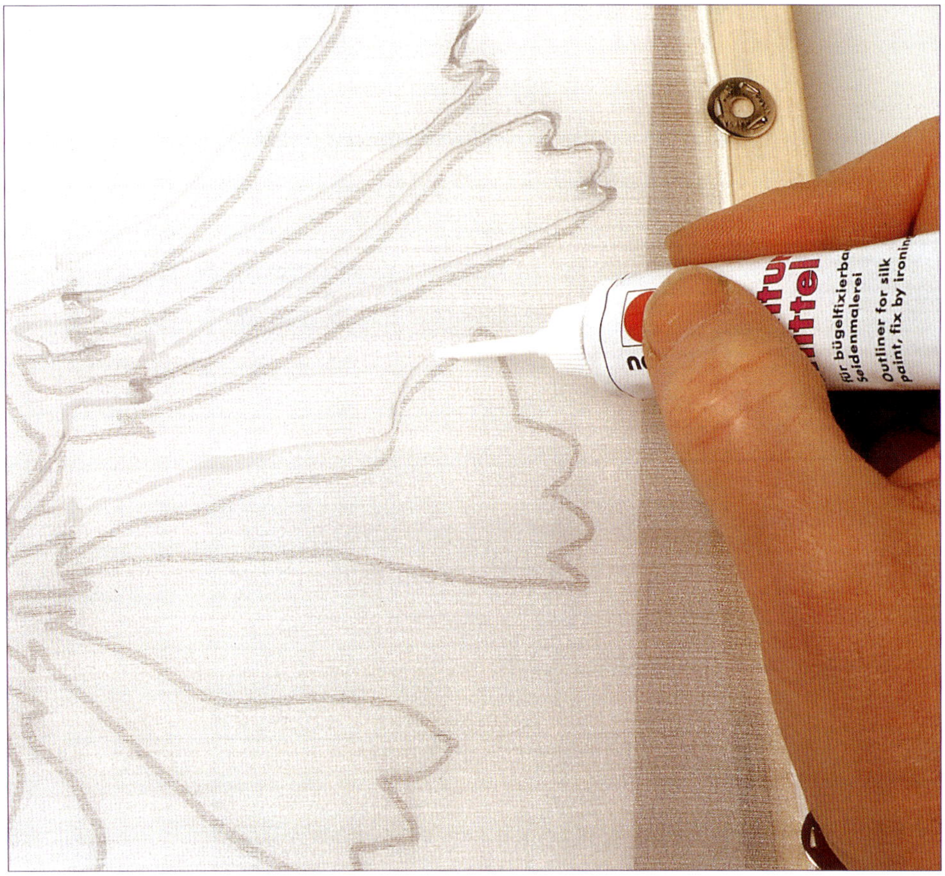

GUTTA PERCHA AND SOLVENT-BASED RESISTS

Gutta percha, usually referred to as gutta, comes from a milky latex substance collected from a tropical tree. It is processed and refined to form a resist medium that is rubbery, pliable and water resistant. There are also solvent-based resists with the same qualities.

Gutta gives a resist line that can be painted over without the dye colouring the line, as it repels colour in a the same way as a wax resist. This is useful when working-in a series of washes, or for very intricate designs where it is difficult to accurately apply the colour without accidentally brushing over the resist line.

Gutta is quite sensitive to temperature and should not be subjected to extremes of temperature. It should flow like runny honey, but may require thinning with special thinners or a few drops of white spirit to achieve a working consistency as it can thicken during storage. To prevent thickening, keep the pipette bottles in a screw-top jar that contains a little white spirit for a day or two. Any unused gutta should be poured back into the original container, as if left to air-dry in the pipette bottles it will harden and become unusable. Solvent-based gutta is most frequently available in clear and black, but you can colour your own by adding a little steam-fix dye to clear gutta. Once applied to the silk it takes about 15–20 minutes to air dry, although solvent-based gutta forms an effective barrier to the flow of silk dye even before it is completely dry. Solvent-based gutta lines will not wash out in water after the fixing process, and must be removed from the finished piece by immersing the silk in white spirit or by dry cleaning. Care must always be taken when using solvent-based products. The solvents used in gutta are flammable and should not be inhaled. Always use and store solvent-based gutta away from any heat source and work in a well ventilated area. If you do not like working with solvent-based gutta because of the smell and safety factors, substitute a wax resist for a similar working style.

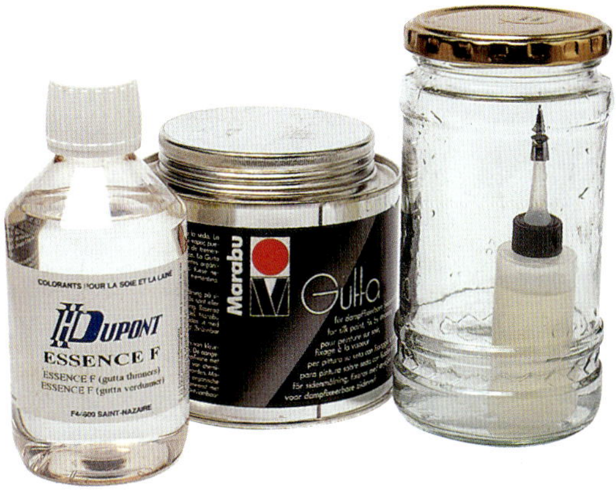

Solvent gutta & storage in jar.

WAX RESIST

Wax gives an excellent water-resistant line that preserves the colour of the silk under the waxed area even if dye colour is brushed over the top. Wax can be applied by brush, sponge, a canting or tjanting tool, wood cut blocks or other blocking or printing tools. When applied to silk, wax should look almost transparent. If it looks white or milky, it is too cool and has not penetrated the silk and the dyes may be able to creep under the wax. Wax can be removed from silk on completion of a painting by ironing the work between sheets of absorbent paper, such as old newsprint or wallpaper lining paper. Ironing will also set the silk paint colours at the same time if heat-fix colours have been used. If steam-fix dyes have been used to colour the work, the work should first be ironed to remove most of the wax, then steamed as normal to set the dyes. The steaming will also help to remove any last traces of wax.

SAFETY POINTS WHEN USING WAX

- Wax should be heated in a thermostatically controlled wax pot, or a double saucepan with a thermometer to prevent overheating, to a working temperature of 130°C.
- If the wax smokes, it is too hot; lower the heat source and avoid inhaling the smoke.
- Should the wax ignite, smother the flames with a heat-proof lid or fire blanket. Turn off the heat source, and leave the wax pot to cool down. Do not pick it up and try to move it. Never use water to extinguish the flames.
- Never leave a wax pot unattended while it is in use.

Basic techniques of Silk Painting

Tensioning silk

Most silk painting is worked with the silk fabric stretched on to a frame and held with silk pins. The simplest are small three-pointed silk pins which push into the soft wooden frame sides.

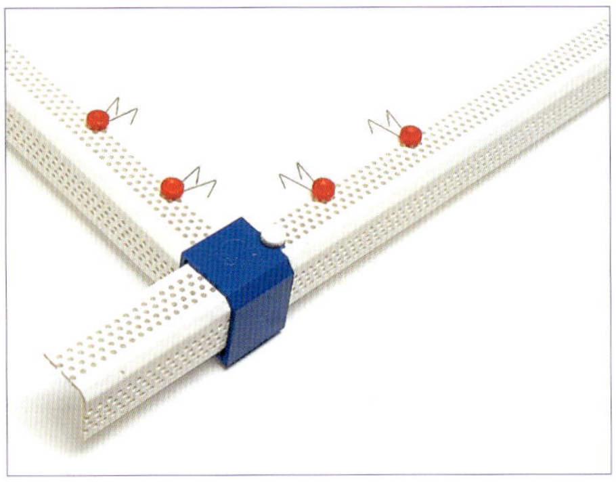

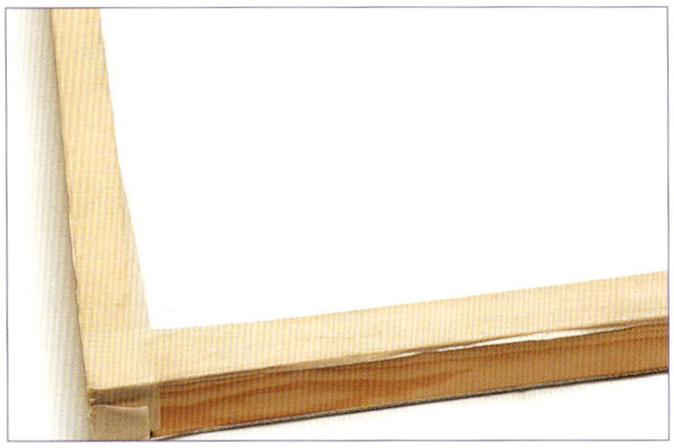

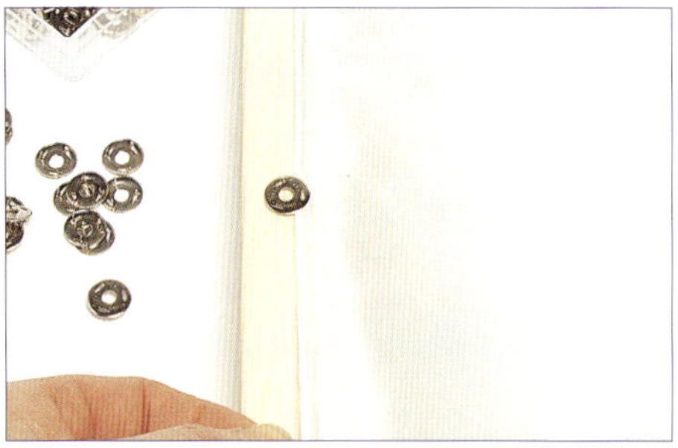

1. Select or set the frame to the correct working size, slightly larger than the piece of silk or to fit a ready-edged scarf. If you are working from a length of fabric, the silk that lies actually on the frame will not form part of the finished piece. You can cover the wooden frame with tape to help prevent the dyes marking the frame or new pieces of work.

2. Secure one corner with a silk pin. Hold the silk firmly and pull it taut along one length, then place further pins along this tensioned edge at approximately 5 cm (2 in.) intervals.

3. Repeat this procedure, working along the adjacent edge of the secured corner. Always work away from a fixed point as you will achieve a much better tension.

4. On the third edge you will need to tension both across and down the fabric, (weft and warp directions) to remove any looseness on the diagonal. Place pins opposite to those already in position, as this helps to keep the fabric square.

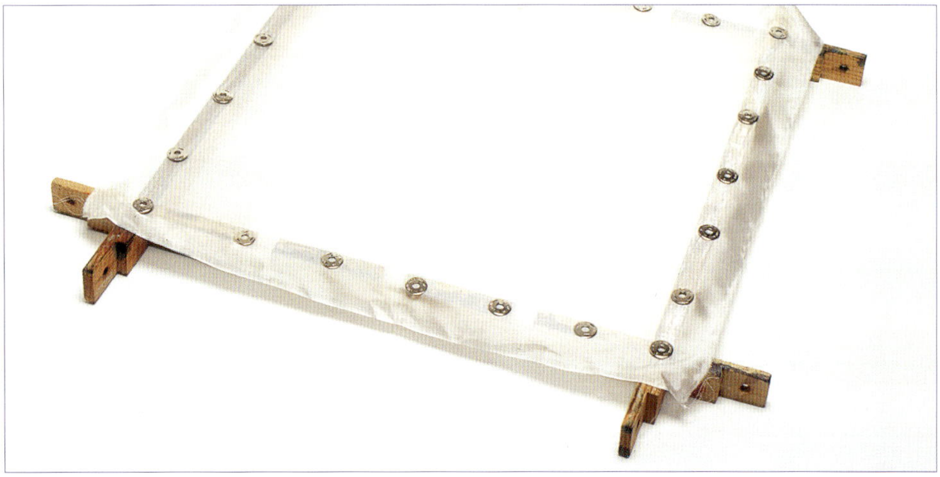

5. Tensioning the fourth side should achieve a tight and even working tension. If you run your finger across the surface you will be able to feel ridges where the pins are holding the silk. Try to avoid any floppy areas where the silk is too loose, or hard shiny ridges where the silk is too tight. Adjust and re-position pins as necessary to achieve the correct working tension.

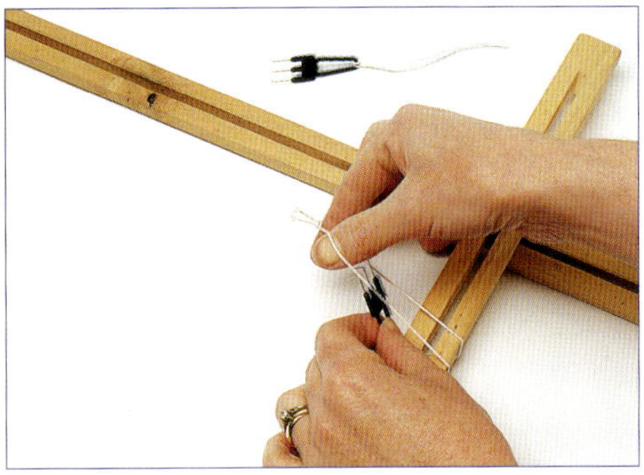
Fitting stenter claw pins on to a frame.

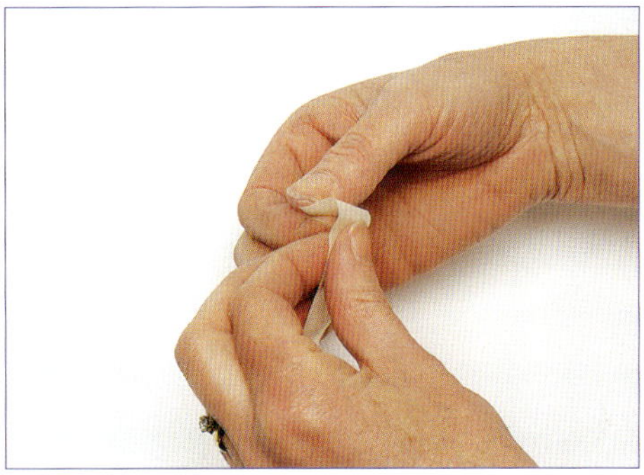
Folding tape to make your own claw pins.

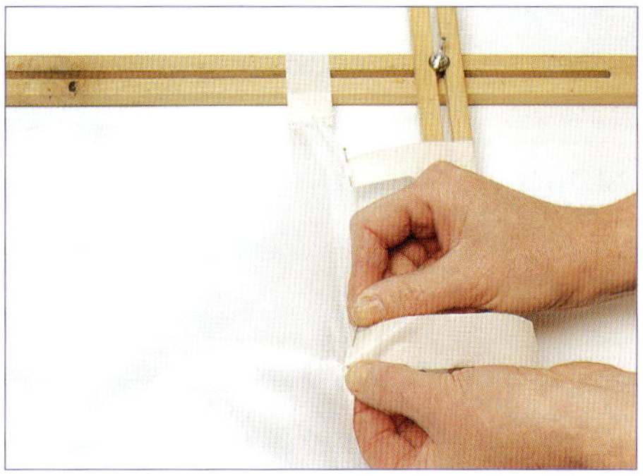
Attaching tape with pin at edge of silk.

Stenter claw pins

Stenter or claw pins are an alternative to the three-pointed pins and are very useful when working with ready-edged pieces or awkward sized pieces that will not fit your frame. If you are working with stenter pins the frame will need to be set out larger than the silk to accommodate the length of the pin and the stretch of the elastic that holds the pin on to the frame. I find that it is better to replace the elastic bands that are supplied with these pins with thin elastic, as it does not snap or perish with use.

You can make your own stenter type pins with a length of masking tape and a sewing pin. Take a length of masking tape approximately 15 cm (6 in.) long, and fold back one end on to itself. Secure this end on to the edge of the silk with a sewing pin. Stretch the length of masking tape out towards the frame, and stick the tape onto the frame to tension the silk. Repeat this pinning out at approximately 8 cm (3 in.) intervals around the piece of silk, or along any edges as necessary to achieve a working tension.

If you are working with a frame that comes with its own pins refer to the manufacturer's instructions.

Double-sided tape

Another way of fastening the silk on to the frame is with double-sided tape. Although this achieves a good tension and makes it easy to reposition the fabric, it should only be used when working with pieces of silk cut from a length, as the strength of the tape can slightly misalign the warp and weft threads as the silk is removed from the frame.

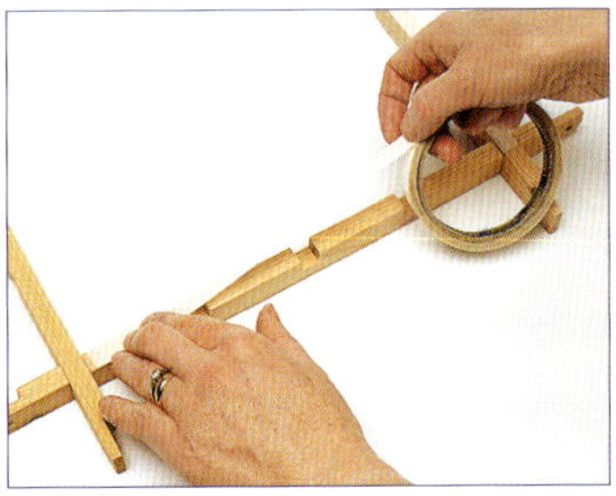

1. Set the frame out to the correct working size for the project. Take a reel of double-sided tape and secure the end at one corner of the frame.

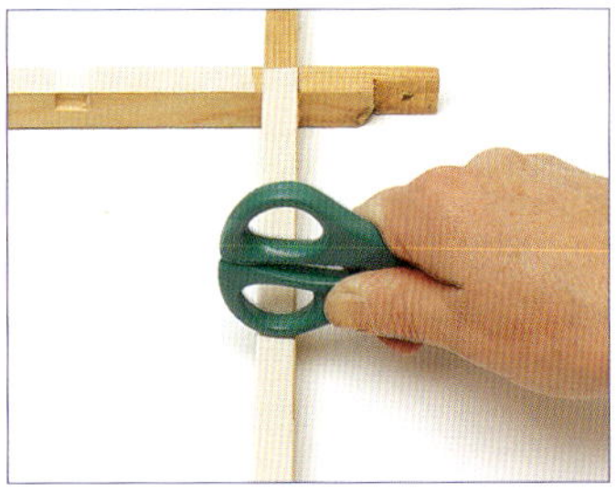

2. Run the reel of tape along the whole length of the first side, pressing it firmly into position. Cut the tape and repeat along the other three sides.

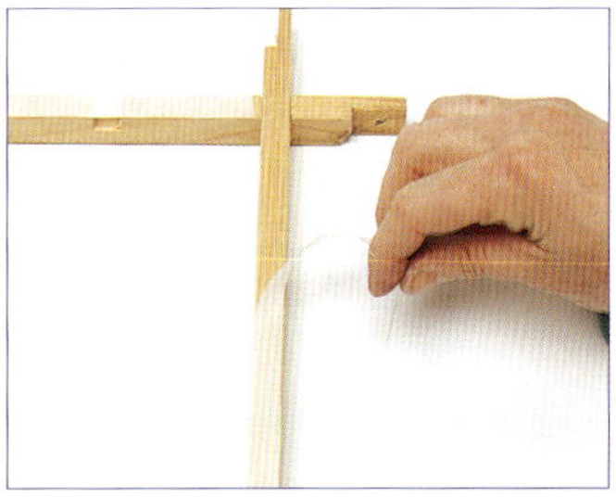

3. To position the silk, peel back one length of backing strip, and fasten down the silk, initially in one corner only. Hold the silk taut and line up the edge with the edge of the frame, then gently run a finger along the silk to secure it on to the sticky tape.

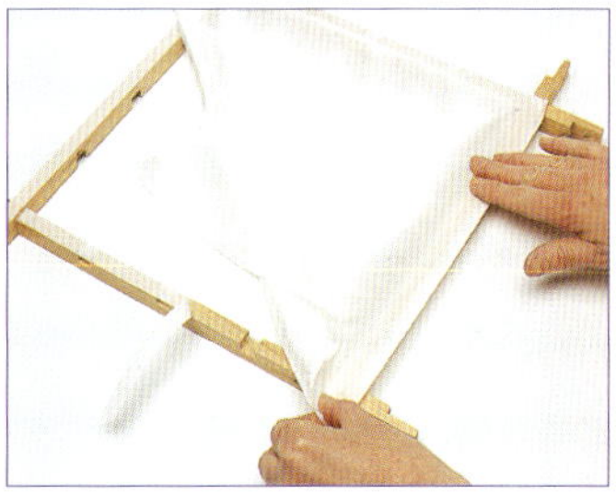

4. Peel back another backing strip and repeat this process, tensioning the silk before it is stuck on to the sticky tape. If the silk is only lightly pressed on to the tape, it can be lifted off and re-tensioned if necessary without removing the tape from the frame. This will allow the sticky tape to be re-used for tensioning further pieces.

Drawing outlines

Forming an outline or 'resist' to define the pattern and create a barrier from a resist medium is fundamental to the art of silk painting. The 'resist' forms a wall that limits the flow of paint or dye to one particular area of the pattern. Achieving neat resist lines is probably one of the hardest skills to perfect. This section suggests several different ways of applying resist mediums to help you to achieve both effective and aesthetically pleasing outlines.

How to apply gutta, water-soluble and acrylic resist lines

If you are drawing out your own design, use a dark coloured medium tip, permanent marker pen to draw the pattern on to the paper. A permanent marker pen will not smudge or mark the silk if the pattern becomes wet with contact from any of the dyes or water, and a dark pen colour is easier to see through the heavier weights of silk. Ideally, use tracing paper so you can turn the pattern over to work a reversed image, although photocopied patterns also work very well.

Place the tracing paper pattern under the frame, resting the pattern on some folded newspapers to bring it closer to the underside of the silk. Try to ensure that the taut silk does not make contact with the pattern. Only apply resist to dry silk. Select an outliner colour and hold the tube or pipette applicator bottle at approximately 45°, in the way you would hold a pen. Have a piece of kitchen paper handy to quickly wipe the nozzle free of blobs before starting. Place the applicator nozzle down to contact with the silk, look through the silk to the pattern line and gently squeeze the tube or bottle to draw out a resist line. Watch the resist line as it is drawn out so that you can immediately adjust and correct it as it is formed.

It is much easier to adjust the resist line as you draw, than have to re-draw a line, as it is difficult to match the lines and not get a blob at the joining points. A resist line that is too fine and has not penetrated the top and underside of the silk to form an effective barrier line may allow colour to seep through. A line that has been drawn out too quickly allows the tip of the nozzle to skip across the surface of the silk, resulting in a broken or dotted line which will allow colour to flow between the gaps.

Continue to trace out all the pattern lines, remembering to use more than one colour of resist if this benefits the piece, until the design is complete. Allow the lines to dry, or use a hairdryer to speed up the drying time. Make sure you remember to remove the tracing pattern before you start painting so that you do not see a double image which may be confusing. If possible, start working at the top of the design to help avoid smudging, or if there is a border, do this first to help define the outer edges of the piece and prevent colour running on to the frame itself.

If you find it difficult to work without any support for your hand, try forming a fist, and rest your drawing arm on this to steady your hand. It is also possible to apply some of the resist lines, allow them to dry and then work more of the design to avoid smudging on larger pieces. Before you start painting always thoroughly check the outlines for gaps – holding the frame up to the light often exposes any holes in the resist lines.

This is probably the most common way of working when starting out and even an accomplished silk painter can find it helpful to work out a design on paper before committing outliner to silk. Many of the projects in this book can be worked in this way by photocopying and enlarging the patterns from the back of the book.

Tracing out a design with the aid of a pencil or a water-soluble pen

If you are working on a thicker weight of silk and cannot see the pattern through it, or just prefer not to use a pattern, draw the design out directly on to the silk with a soft pencil or a water-soluble pen (also known as a disappearing pen). If lightly drawn, a soft 4B pencil should wash out, and any remaining traces of a water-soluble pen will disappear when the silk is first washed. Some disappearing pens vanish after a period of time, varying from a few hours to a couple of days.

If you are using a water-soluble pen, once the resist is applied on top and is dry, lightly mist over the silk with some water to make any remaining pen lines disappear before you start painting. One disadvantage of a water-soluble pen is that the pen line may act as a partial resist line, and stop the paint flowing right up to the real resist line. This results in small white, unpainted areas of silk showing in the finished piece.

If you are working on a heavy silk, place the pattern on the table, then turn the frame over so that the silk contacts with the pattern. Use the water-soluble pen to trace out the whole design, then turn the frame back to the correct side and re-draw all the lines in your chosen barrier medium. Remember that working in this way will reverse any image, so be careful with words and numbers.

Working a line of resist free-hand

Sometimes it is easier just to draw straight on to the silk without using a pattern. This allows for great spontaneity and freedom, allowing the design to develop as each resist line is drawn. Always keep the tip of the nozzle of the outliner tube or pipette bottle in contact with the silk, and try using your whole body to help you draw long unbroken lines, by shifting your body weight from one leg to the other as you draw.

Remember that the thickness of the line formed comes from a combination of the speed you draw the line and the amount of pressure applied to the tube or bottle. Too much pressure will result in thick clumsy lines, while too little pressure will produce lines that cannot hold the flow of dye colour. Blobs form very easily at the end of the applicator nozzle, and at the start and finish point or the sharp turn of a resist line. With practice you will be able to control this blobbing more effectively, but there are no short cuts to good resist lines. Just as with any other skill the answer is practice, practice and more practice. Bear in mind that your resist lines are hand drawn, and that the appearance of a hand drawn image has an appeal and special quality of its own. Very little in life is completely perfect, so take comfort from this as you work.

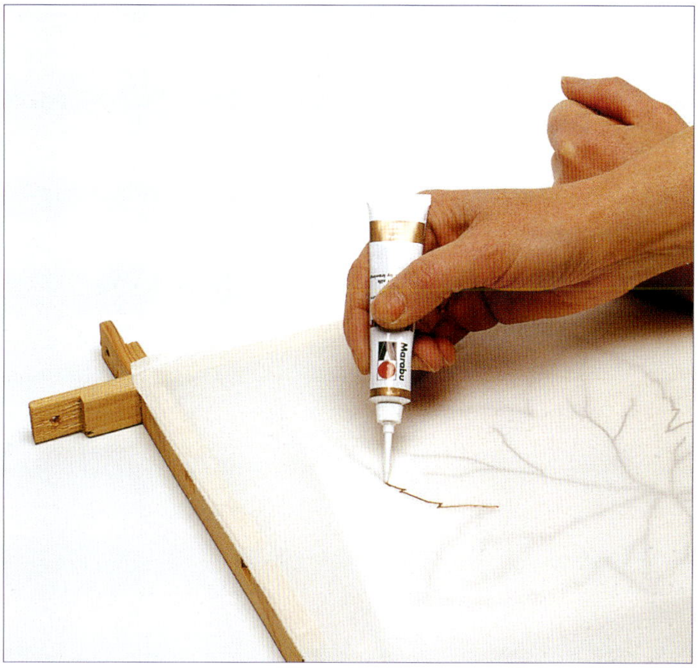

Form a fist to support your hand as you outline.

Sequential outlining with a clear resist

You can create some very interesting designs using a resist line to both define the pattern and control the spread of the dyes, but in such a way that the line is less obvious, which results in a softer, less stencilled appearance.

Lay down an initial background of dye colour, allow this to dry and draw the clear resist line on to this coloured ground. Then add further dye to re-work some areas of the design, and allow this second layer of colour to dry. Continue to work in this way, drawing out resist lines, allowing them to dry and applying further colour. This gives the finished work a layered effect where the resist lines have less impact on the design, yet the use of resist has allowed full control over the spread of colour at the working stage. When applying a series of resist lines, followed by re-working in this way, it is possible to apply the subsequent dye to any part of the design to enhance and strengthen the colour or shapes formed. It is easier to use steam-fix dyes when working in this way as heat-fix paints do not flow so readily after the second layer of colour.

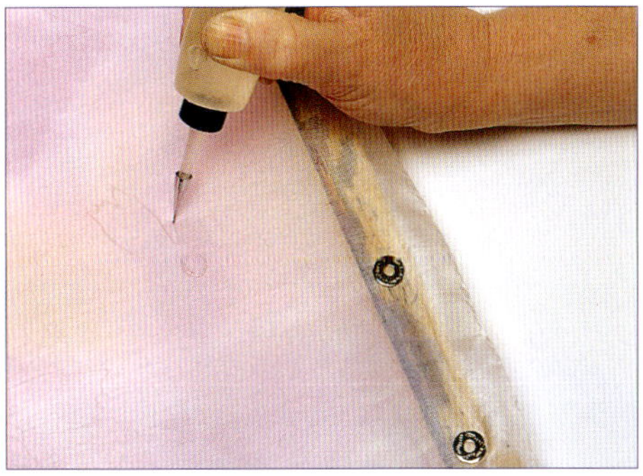

Sequential outlining - first draw out clear outlines.

Re-painting background in on sequential outlining piece.

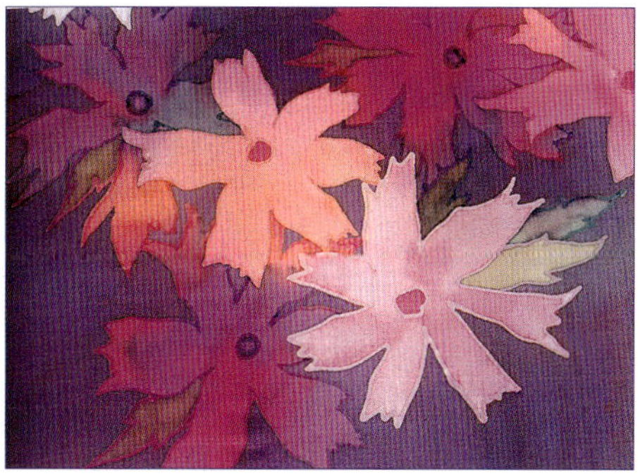

Finished shot of sequential outlining effect.

Using clear resist as an invisible barrier line

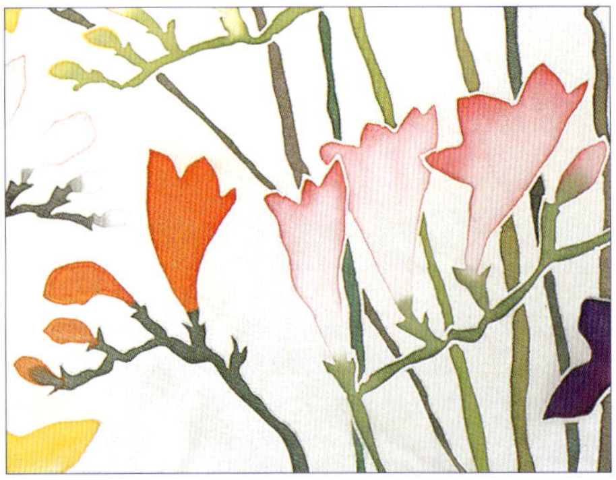

Using clear resist as an invisible barrier.

As well as working in a series of layers to minimise the impact of a resist line, it is possible to work in such a way that the resist line does not show at all. Since all colourless resist mediums, whether gutta, water-soluble outliner or wax, can be completely removed from the silk, you can use the advantages of working in a controlled way but remove the evidence of their presence in the finished piece.

The resist line used for this technique must be colourless, but can be applied to plain white or coloured silk. Once the resist lines have been drawn on to the silk, the silk paint or dye must only be applied up to *either* the inner or outer edge of the resist lines throughout the whole piece. Once the work has been fixed in the appropriate way and the resist lines removed there will be no evidence of a barrier line around the shape. A resist or barrier line will only show on the finished work if colour is applied up to both edges of the resist line.

If a design is drawn in clear resist on white silk, and painted leaving the background white, the lines will disappear completely after the work is fixed and the resist lines removed. The design motifs will appear on a white background without the apparent evidence of use of resist. This way of working can also be applied to coloured silk, as long as the silk dye or paint is only applied to one edge of the resist lines. Please refer to the projects on pages 52 and 79 for working in this way.

Ruling straight lines for borders and geometric designs

Although it is possible to work a reasonably straight line freehand with a little practice, a straight line for borders or geometric designs can easily be achieved. Find a couple of pieces of wood that are slightly higher than the height of the silk painting frame, place them on each side and rest a long ruler like a metre or yard stick on them to form a bridge. Hold the rule in position, ensuring that your fingers will not be in the way as you draw out the line by running the applicator nozzle along the edge of the rule. The spacing of the lines can be done by eye, or by marking set points along the edges of the frame or silk using a plastic canvas grid with a water-soluble marker pen.

Use a plastic canvas square grid to mark out border widths and corner points. (See the materials and equipment section on page 12 for instructions on how to make a grid from plastic canvas.) Place the plastic canvas square grid into each corner in turn, marking out the corner points with a water-soluble pen or soft pencil in the appropriate hole on the grid. Then use the supports to make a bridge and line up the rule to join up the corner marks and form an even border without lots of measuring out.

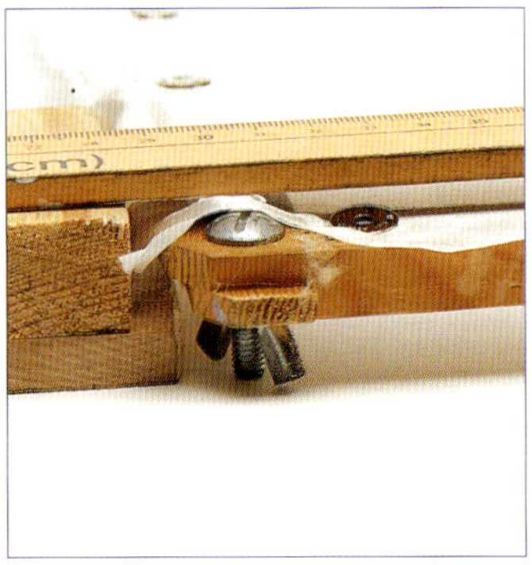

Making a bridge.

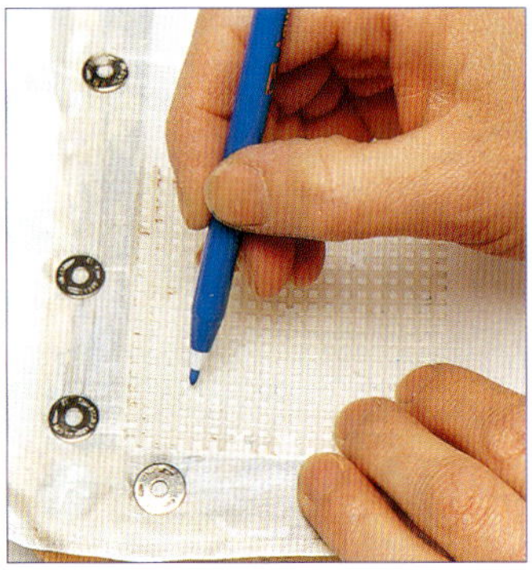

Marking out corner points with a plastic canvas square grid.

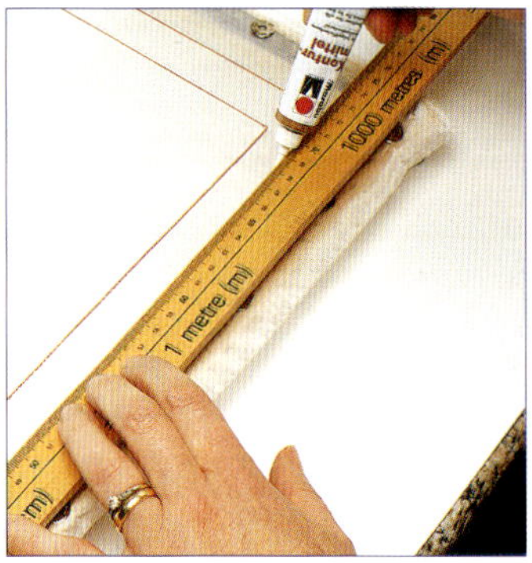

Joining up corner points using a ruler to draw out resist line.

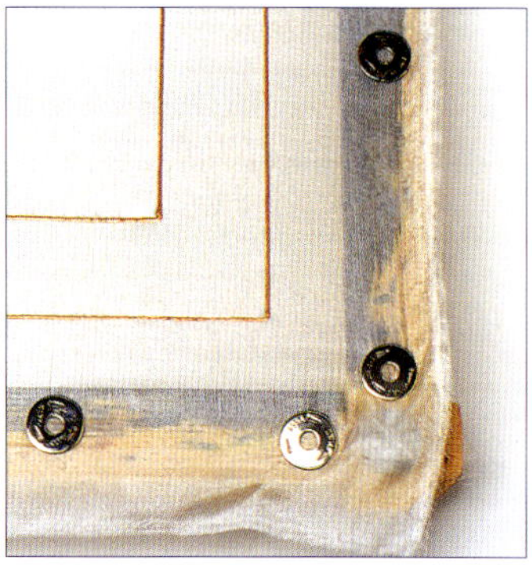

The finished marked out corner.

Using silk paint thickeners

Silk paints and dyes can be mixed with a thickener medium which takes away the normal free flowing properties of a liquid colour, and creates a medium that can be used as an alternative resist or paint medium. Silk paint thickeners are clear or honey coloured gelatinous substances. They should be added in roughly equal quantities, proportionate to the dye, and thoroughly mixed to combine the two elements into a coloured medium. For a colourless resist, apply the thickener directly on to the silk without the addition of any colour.

Before applying any colour to the silk, allow the thickener to dry or use a hairdryer. Apply the colours in the normal way, placing the brush a little distance away from the thickener lines or motifs, and allow the colours to flow across the silk up to the thickener. The paints and dyes will stop at the areas where thickener has been applied in the same way that colour stops at a resist line. Once the painting is completed and fixed in the appropriate way, the silk should be washed to remove the dried thickener medium which slightly stiffens the fabric at the working stage. Once washed, it should retain the usual degree of softness and drape expected from the silk paints or dyes used to colour the piece.

Paint thickeners can be applied by brush, sponge or print blocks to create either a pattern with a linear design, or pattern shapes of resistance. Since the application of thickener in these ways does not require the same fine hand control it can be particularly useful for people with stiffness of the hand, arthritis or anyone without good hand co-ordination skills. If using a water-soluble thickener, remember that any colour sprayed or brushed over the dry thickener will penetrate through the medium and slightly colour the silk.

The use of thickened silk paint gives a softer, less stencilled appearance to the finished piece, and allows the transition of one colour into another without a fine resist line separating the two. The strength of the barrier quality of the thickener medium can be adjusted by varying the amount of thickener applied to the silk, or by slightly adjusting the proportionate mix. To form a definite edge to the pattern, apply a generous amount of thickener medium, or create a much softer barrier by applying less thickener medium to the silk. A slightly higher proportion of dye to thickener will create a looser, weaker resist, which will also deliberately allow some spreading of the colour across the thickener.

It is possible to combine the use of resist lines and thickener within the same piece to add further interest to the work. If you do use both, do not apply gutta or outliner over the top of the thickener, as it will not be able to bond with the silk and will become detached at the washing stage when the thickener is rinsed away. (See projects on pages 64 and 87)

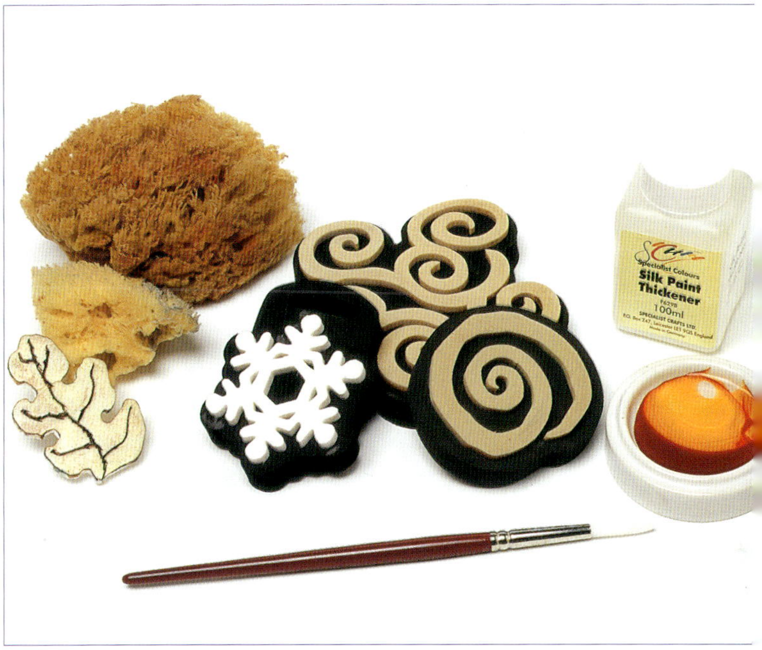

Thickener sponges/stamps & colour/thickener.

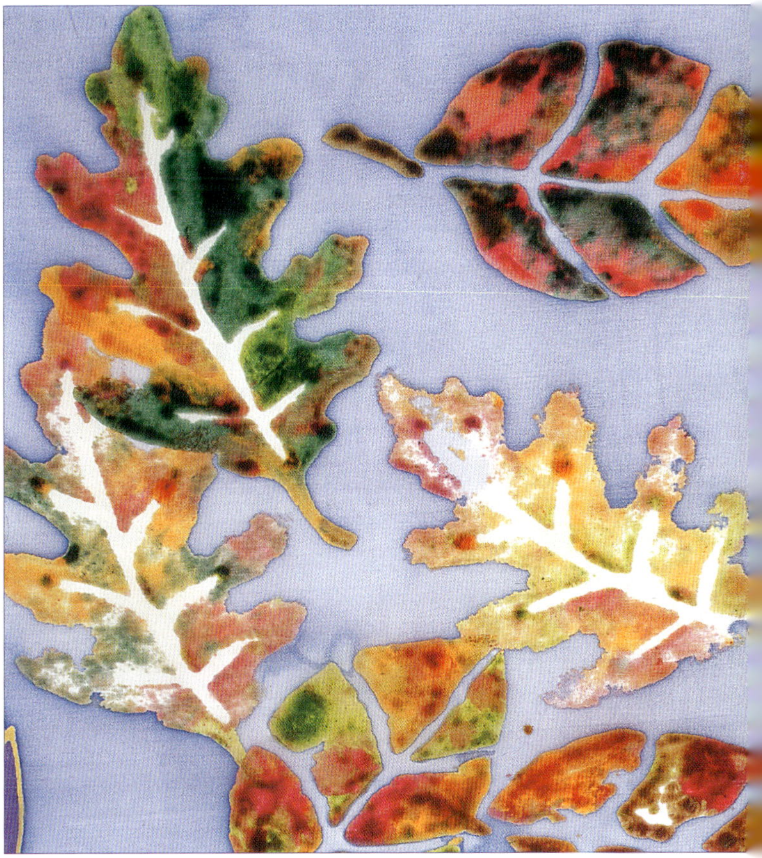

Block printed leaf design using silk paint thickener.

Applying colour

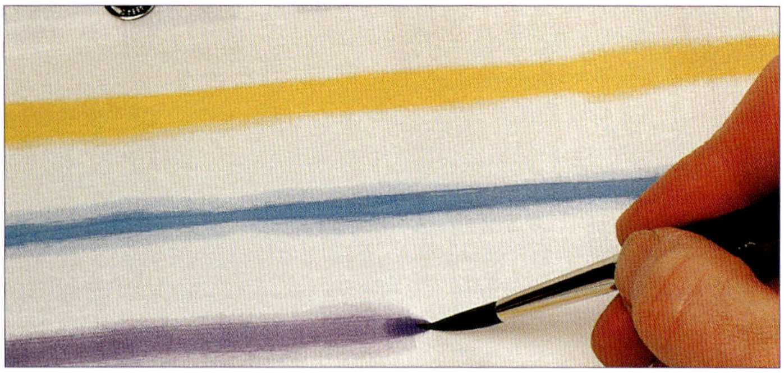

Striping colour down.

Silk paints and dyes offer a fascinating way of working because of their wonderful free-flow qualities. Brushes are an excellent tool for lifting and applying colour, and can also release colour in a controlled way. Try working a striped pattern, forming stripes of equal thickness. It is possible to achieve this just by using the tip of the brush initially, and then as the stripe is brushed out, pressing the brush down to give greater contact with the silk. Further stripes can be added to form overlapping or tartan patterns with blended or watermarked edges, depending on whether the additional stripes are added on to wet or dry silk and by varying the spreading gap.

Rinse your brushes in a large water pot, and always use a piece of kitchen towel to dry them after rinsing. This ensures that the colours remain at the correct strength, untainted or diluted.

Always allow the colour to flow towards an outline, rather than putting it down next to an outline. This spreading distance ensures the outlines are not swamped with colour and prevents the tide of colour from flowing across or under a weak resist line. It also gives you time to repair any gaps before too much colour has escaped.

The best position for placing colour on an outlined shape will vary depending on the size, complexity and colouring effect of the shape to be filled. As a general rule, place the colour in the centre of simple, medium-sized shapes, so that the colour flows evenly to the outer edges. For complex, long thin or very large shapes, it may be better to place the colour at one end and allow it to move along the shape like a tide flowing up a river estuary, gradually filling all the nooks and crannies as it progresses.

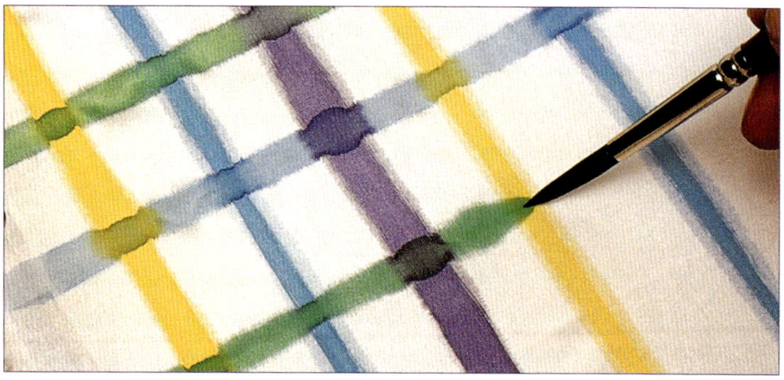

Gridding on tartan stripes.

Colouring a daisy

Take the shape of a daisy as an example to illustrate various colour placement positions.

One area of one colour: if the daisy is small to medium size and formed from one outlined shape which is to be one colour, the colour should be applied from the brush as a central reservoir in the centre of the daisy. The dry silk will absorb the colour and allow it to flow up into each of the petals. By estimating the amount of paint or dye required to colour the whole shape, it can be coloured by one application of paint or dye. However, if more is required, use the brush to re-apply a small further quantity of colour to complete the shape. Observe how the silk absorbs the colour and wait until all the dye is absorbed before adding any more if you think it necessary. If puddles of colour remain on the surface of the silk once the shape has been completely painted in, you are applying too much. Remove excess colour with a dry brush or cotton bud, to prevent it seeping across any weak barrier lines.

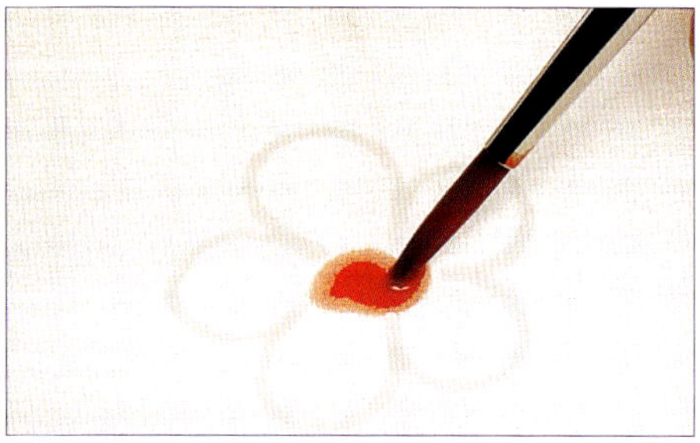

Apply colour to the centre of a shape.

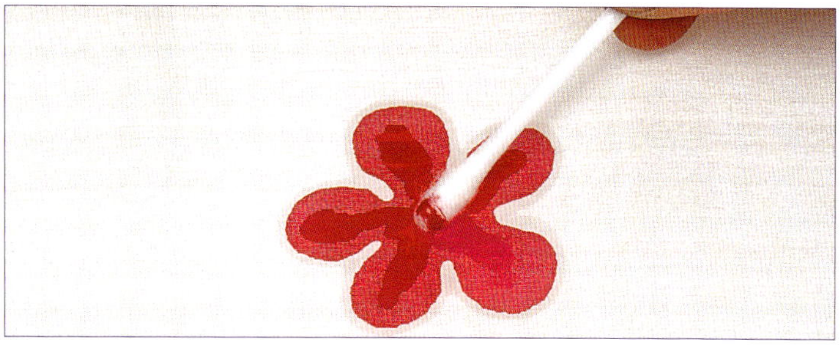

Removing excess colour with a cotton bud.

Several shapes of one colour: If the daisy shape is formed from a round centre with separate petals, which are to be the same colour, each petal should be painted individually by placing the colour in the centre of each petal, and completing it before moving on to the next one. By following this rule you will be able to concentrate properly on just one segment of the whole shape, rather than trying to paint several petal shapes at once. This method of working is of particular benefit with large or complex shapes. Once all the petals have been painted, the centre shape can also be coloured.

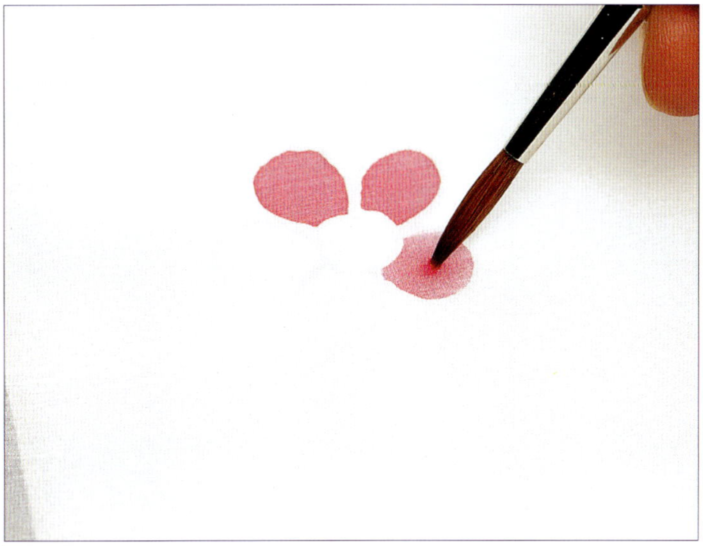

Complete each petal shape before moving on to the next one.

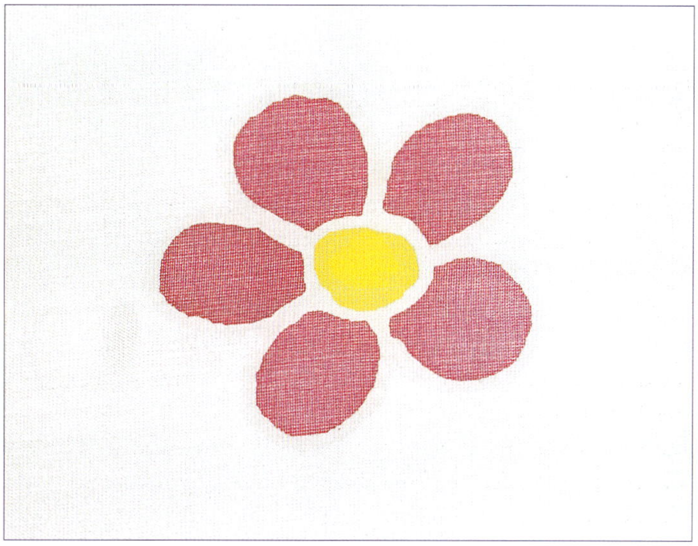

The completed daisy with the centre area painted in last.

Shapes with one colour blended at different strengths: blending colour from full strength to a lighter, more diluted colour adds depth and reality to a design. First apply a little water to the area of the petal that you wish to remain pale, near the centre, for example. This acts as a stop, and prevents the darker colour from swamping the whole shape. Then, use a small brush to work one petal at a time and apply a tiny quantity of the deeper strength colour at the tip of the petal. Quickly rinse and dry the brush with kitchen paper, then lift up a little mid-strength colour and apply this with an overlapping brush stroke. Repeat this process with a lighter tint, until you can blend into the water. Use a clean brush to blend each tint of colour into the next to achieve a gradual shading effect. Repeat this process with each petal in turn until the flower is complete, then go back and paint the centre of the daisy. This technique for shading can be applied to any shape or size of shapes by adjusting the brush sizes and varying the number of tints to fit the area of the shape being worked.

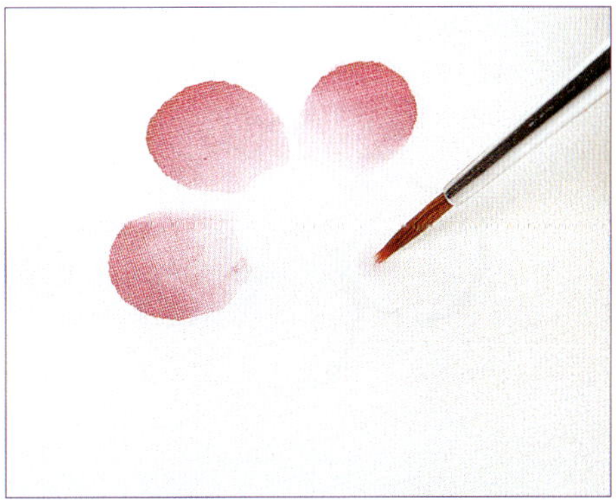

Applying the lightest colour.

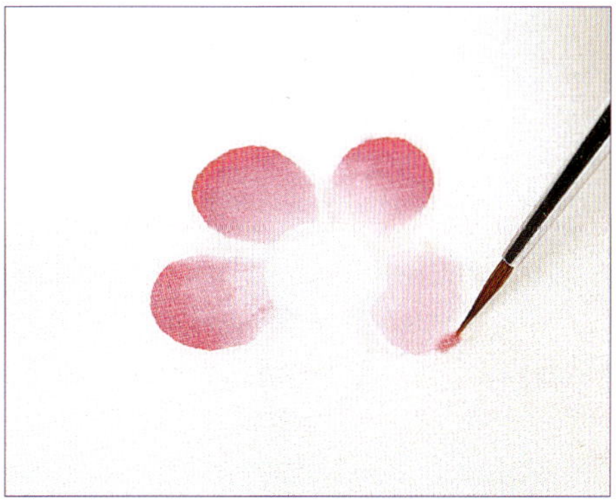

Brushing in the mid strength colour.

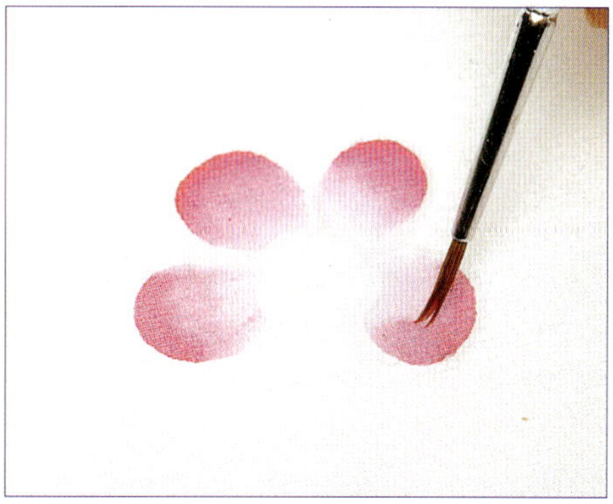

Blending in the darkest colour.

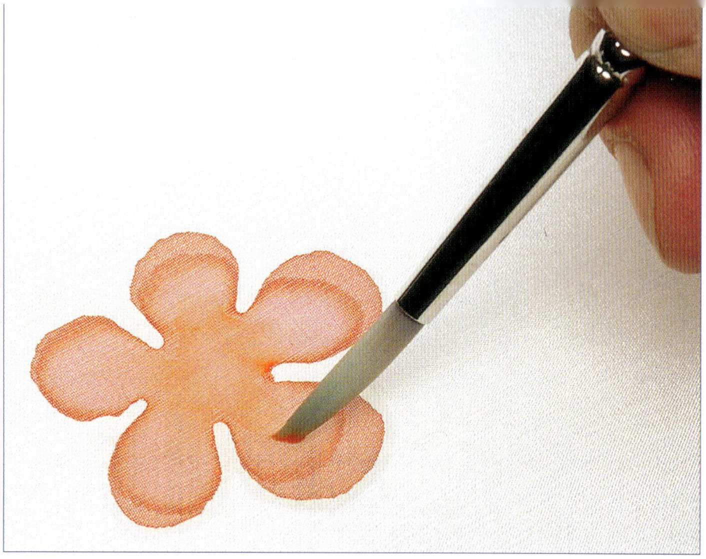

Creating a halo shading with water.

One shape halo shaded with colour at different tonal strengths: water will flow across silk in the same way as colours, so water can be used to create shading. First, place some colour in the centre of the daisy shape and allow it to flow out to the outline edge, then, before the first colour has completely dried on the silk, add a small quantity of water to the centre of the shape. The water will push some of the first colour outwards, concentrating the colour at the outline edge and giving a shaded halo effect. This effect can also be worked using another colour to displace the initial colour.

One large outlined shape: if the shape to be coloured is too large to apply colour from the centre, allowing it to spread outward, it is more effective to apply the colour at the tip of one petal and work the colour towards the centre. At the centre introduce colour into the two adjoining petals, keeping the centre spreading edge wet, and gradually move on to the next petals until the whole flower is painted in. It is possible to have both fast track and slow track leading or spreading edges. As long as you keep a leading edge wet with small top-ups of colour, you can concentrate on other areas without a hard watermark forming. Try to completely paint in one part of the shape before moving on to the next part. This avoids having to go back to an almost dry or dry area with further colour, which will cause a watermark where the wet colour displaces the damp colour.

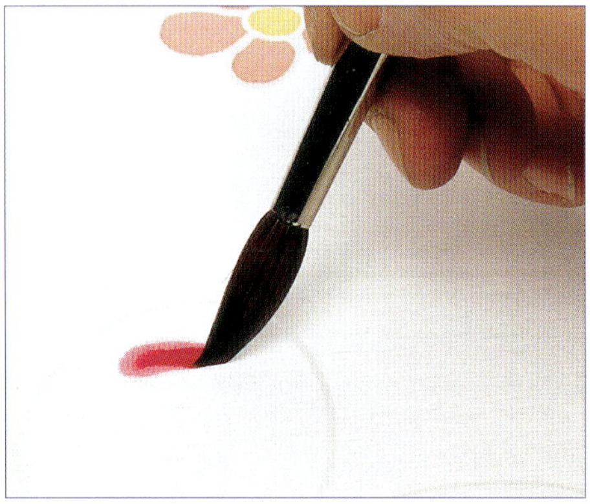

1. *Start applying the colour at the edge of the shape.*

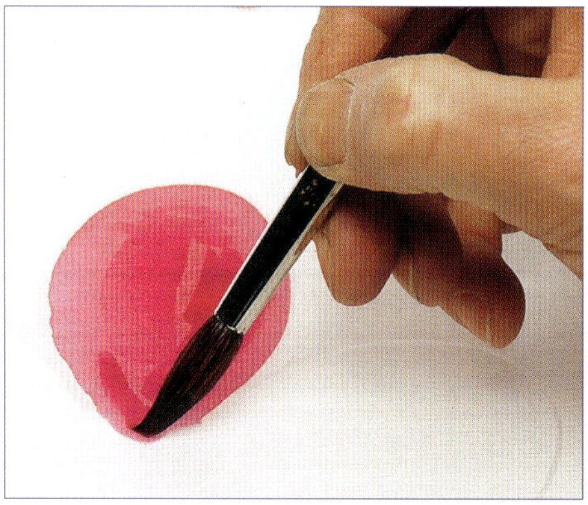

2. *Completely paint this area.*

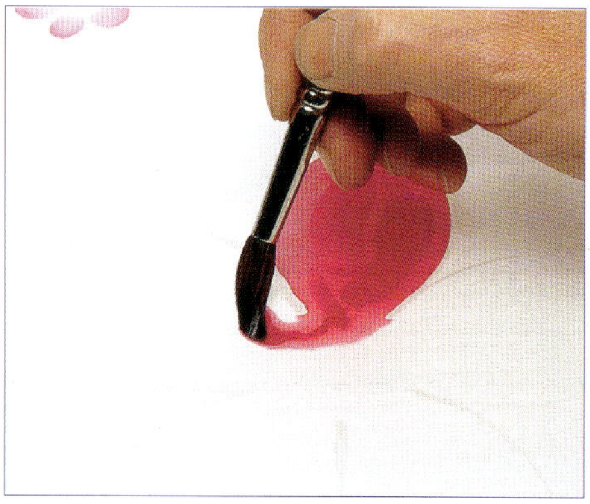

3. *Start to introduce colour into the adjoining area.*

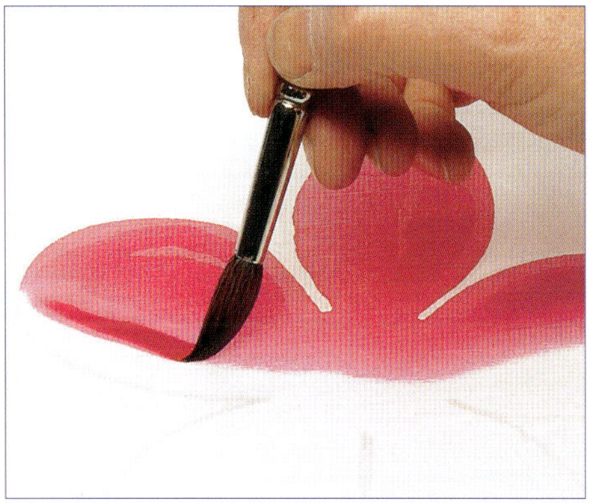

4. *Use bold strokes to keep the spreading edge wet.*

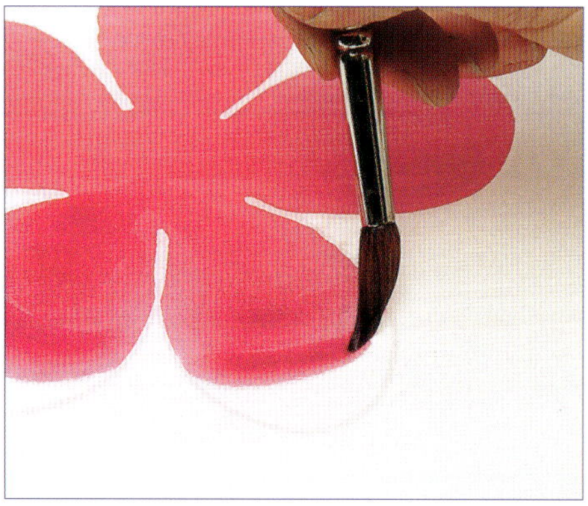

5. *If necessary, have several spreading edges and keep both moving by working them alternatively.*

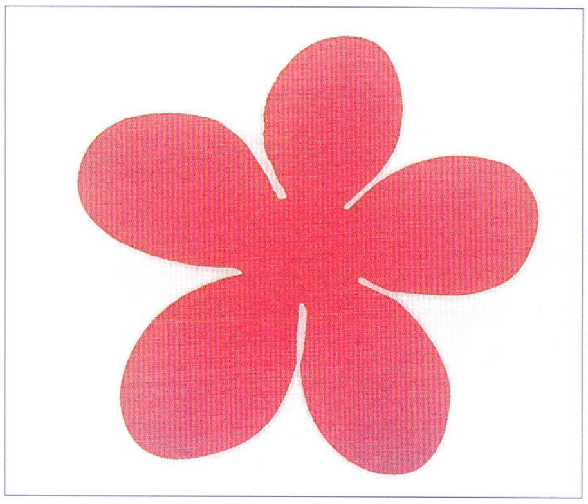

6. *The completed shape, with even colouring and no watermarks.*

Repairing leaks of colour through a resist line

Sometimes colour can seep through a resist line even though there is no obvious gap. If this happens you can reduce the impact of the escaped colour to a minimum, sometimes to a point where it will not be noticeable at all. There may be a slight change in the flow of colour across the silk in areas where you have lifted up escaped colour. Slight marks or a reluctance of flow can usually be overcome by rubbing the fabric with a brush to encourage the colour to penetrate the silk.

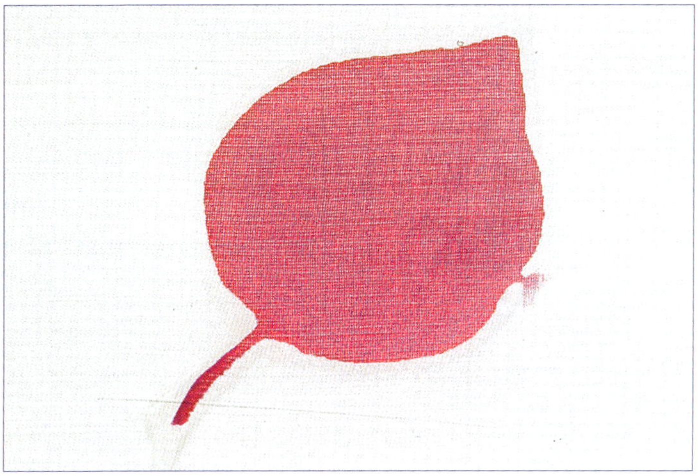

Colour seeping through a resist line

Colour can break through a resist line for the following reasons:

- The resist line was too fine or not dense or strong enough to form a barrier.
- The resist did not properly penetrate the silk, allowing the colour to seep under the line.
- Too much colour was applied, too close to the resist line and swamped it.
- The brush accidentally brushed across the resist line taking the colour with it.

Should any of these be the cause of colour seepage, the following corrective measures can be worked to improve unwanted colouring on the wrong side of the resist line.

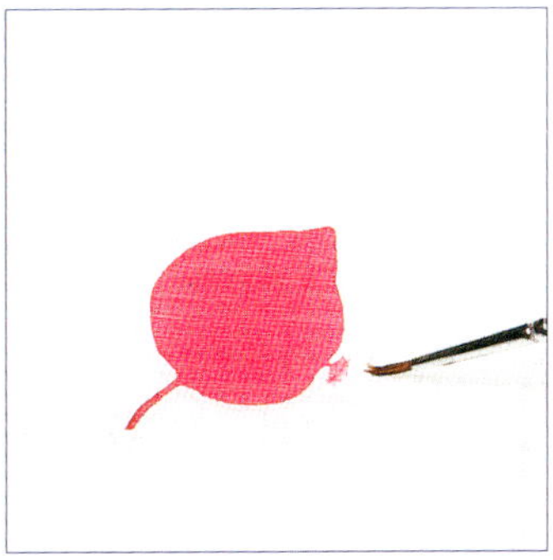

Apply water in an arc around the escaped colour.

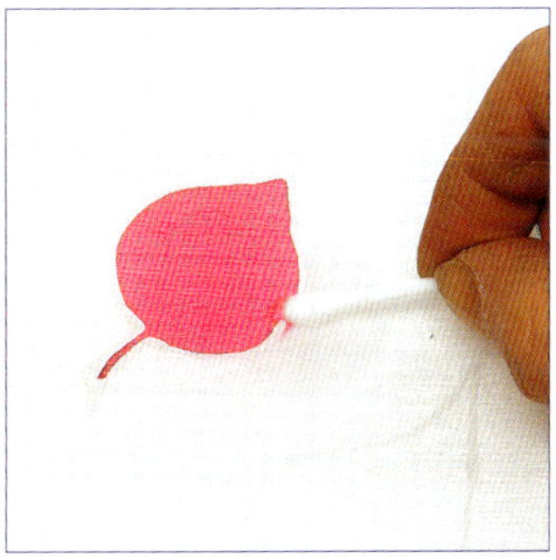

Lift up the escaped colour with a cotton bud.

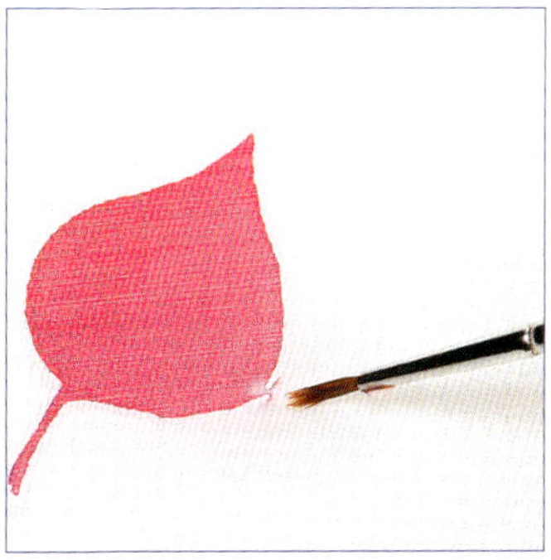

Repeat the application of water if necessary.

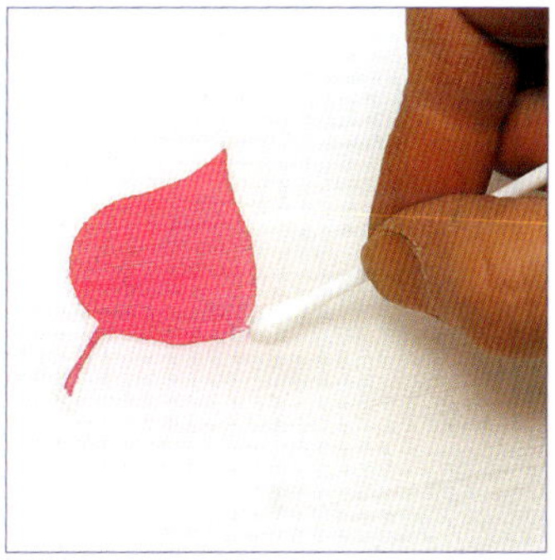

Use a clean cotton bud to dry off the area.

Following the unwanted seepage, quickly rinse your brush in clean water and apply a little water in an arc *around* the escaped colour. Do not apply water directly on the colour as this will cause the colour to spread out even further. Instead, allow the water to run up to the edge of the seepage and push all the escaped colour back towards the resist line, preventing a hard watermark edge forming. While the colour is moving back towards the resist line, use a cotton bud to wipe the surface of the silk to lift up the escaped colour. Repeat this process carefully, as many times as necessary to pick up as much colour as you can. Be careful not to swamp the area with water as this may cause further problems if the water breaks through an already weak resist line to the inside of the shape. Should this happen, blot the inside area with another cotton bud before repairing the resist line to prevent further seepage.

Colour escaping through gaps in the resist line

As soon as you see colour escaping through a gap, blot the area with a cotton bud and then close the gap by re-applying a little resist to seal the break. Then apply a little water in an arc around the escaped colour as described before. Any escaped colour from heat-set paints must be cleared up before they dry; steam-fix colours can be treated even after they have dried. If steam-fix dyes are being used, it may be easier to lift up the escaped dye if the re-applied outliner is first dried. This allows the cotton bud to be taken right up to the repaired gap without the risk of smearing the wet outliner.

Lifting up spots of unwanted colour

It can be very annoying if a spot of colour drops from your paint brush on to the silk. Should this happen the damage can be minimised by quickly rinsing and drying the brush, before lifting up clean water which is circled around the unwanted spot. The water will spread and concentrate the colour spill into a smaller spot, which should then be gently rubbed with a cotton bud to lift up the colour. Repeat this circling process with further applications of clean water until the damage is minimised. Slight colouration can normally be covered by the background colour or hidden by the addition of a little more outlining. This corrective measure will work effectively on white unpainted silk, or a dry completed area if heat-fix paints are being used.

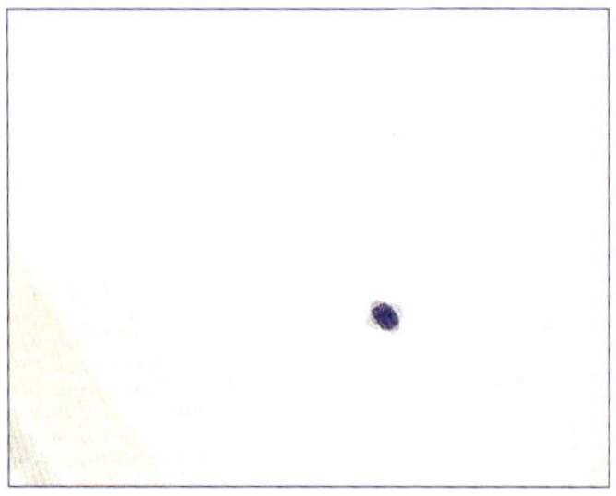

Unwanted spot of colour.

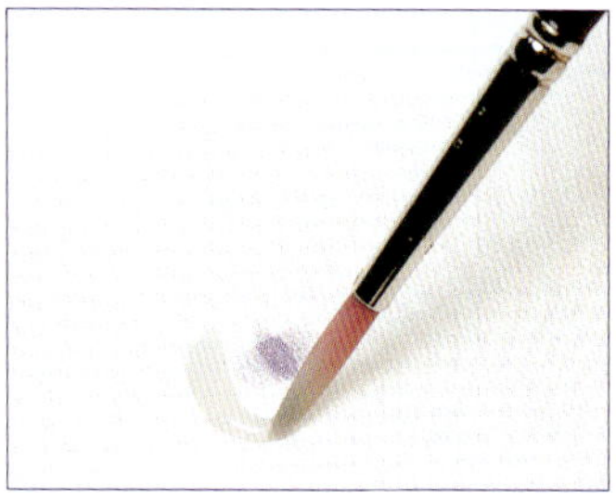

Circle clean water around the spot of colour.

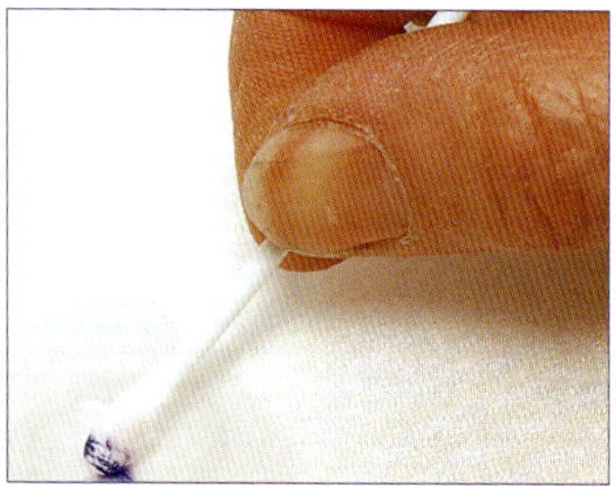

Use a cotton bud to lift up the unwanted colour spill.

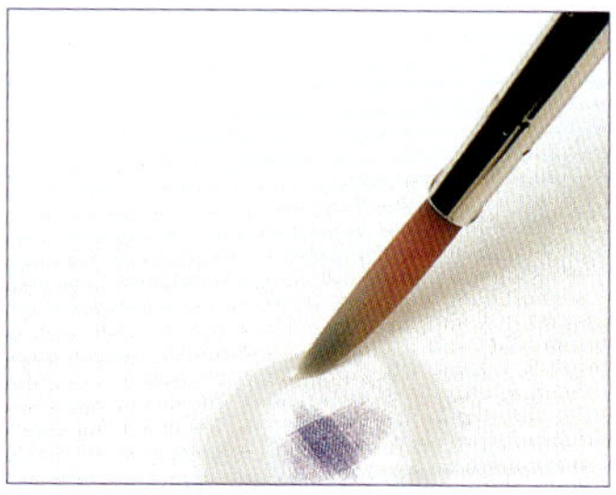

Apply more clean water if needed. Re-blot with a cotton bud.

Painting-in backgrounds

Successfully painting-in large complex backgrounds, especially if they have lots of shapes to paint around, is one of the hardest things to achieve. Minimise the size and complexity of a background at the design stage by allowing shapes to link together, or incorporate a border to reduce the overall size of the background. Always ensure you have sufficient colour before starting to paint; notice how much is in your palette before starting and then check how much remains once you have completed the background. This allows you to build up an awareness of approximately how much colour is required for a particular area.

Painting a background area of one colour

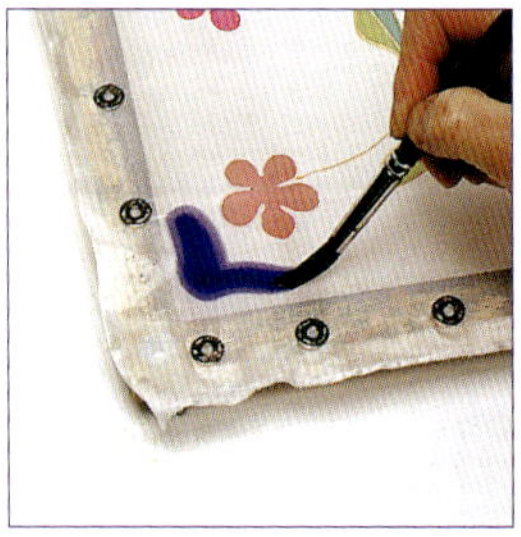

Start in a corner.

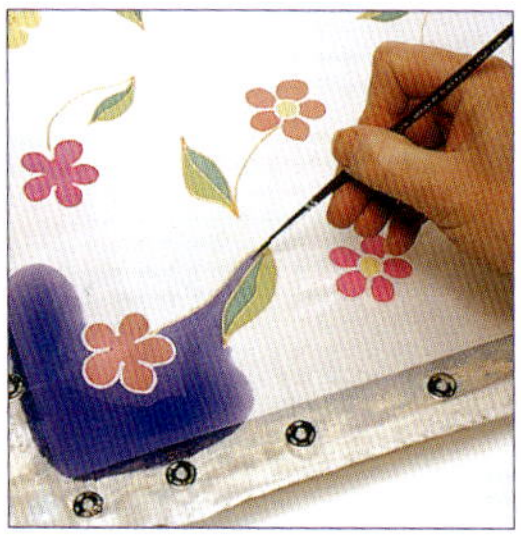

Work the colour around the shapes.

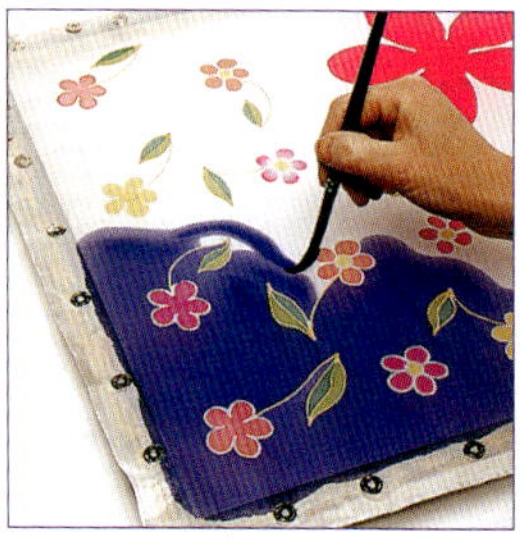

Keep edge wet with colour to prevent watermarks.

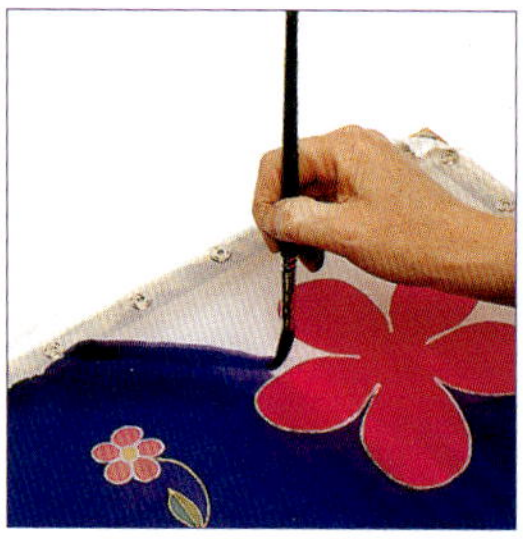

Avoid going back by totally painting-in the area.

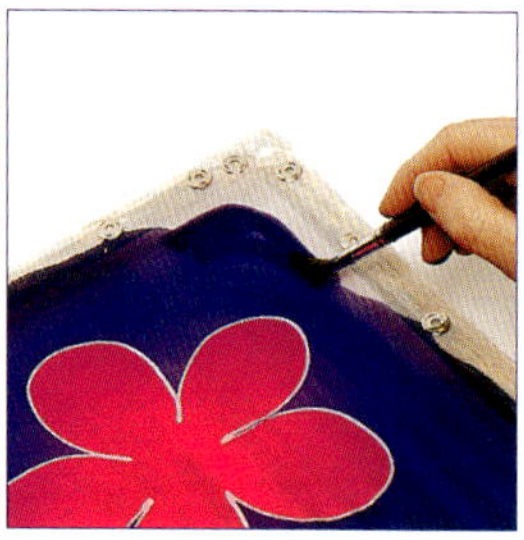

Finish in an opposite corner.

Before you start, check to see where is the best starting point. Remember the rule of the incoming tide moving up a river estuary, together with the fast and slow track methods of applying colour. Once you have decided where to start, work the colour onwards across the work in a controlled way. Top up colour along some spreading or leading edges to keep the silk wet, and fast track work on other spreading edges until they are completely painted in. When you have completed one area, go back to the slow track spreading edges, and concentrate on the next appropriate one. A corner is often a good place to start, then move down and across, while fanning out and around shapes keeping all spreading edges wet, until the whole background has been painted. Bring your palette closer to the area you are painting to prevent accidental drips landing on your work.

Ensure that you have completely painted in behind the spread of the leading edge, especially in all the small nooks and crannies, before progressing onwards, to prevent having to go back to an area that was accidentally missed, which usually results in a watermark. It is always better to allow a background to dry naturally, as using a hairdryer can cause rings to form through uneven drying.

Background areas with more than one colour

When painting in a large area or background with several colours blended together, it is better to start with the lightest colour first, gradually working towards the deeper colour. It is possible to paint backgrounds with the silk dry or pre-dampened, depending on your personal preferences and experience. Large areas of silk can be pre-dampened with either water or dilutant, or a mixture of alcohol and water in a 2:1 ratio, to help colour blending and to prevent watermarks forming.

As the dampness of the silk slows down the flow of the colour, unwanted halo marks can form along the edges of the pattern lines where the water prevents the colour from spreading right up to the resist line. To reduce this, carefully take the brush right up to the resist line, and check that the dampness is not preventing the colouring of small finely detailed shapes.

Wet-into-wet for a watercolour effect

Free-flow colour

Paints and dyes flow freely across the silk without interruption and stop at resist lines. As colour reaches the limit of its flow, a decorative edge is formed which is referred to as a watermark. Watermarks can be incorporated into a design by encouraging them to form in a particular place. They work particularly well in landscape pictures depicting hills, trees or implied features, or in floral designs where their decorative edge can be a very effective way of creating the veins of leaves and petals on flowers.

Working in this way can be more difficult than working within a set framework provided by resist lines, as the design relies much more on your control of the movement of the dyes. Steam-fix dyes are most suitable as the colours can be applied in a series of layers and moved into new positions, forming new watermarks each time. A steam-fix colour is capable of movement across the silk, and vulnerable to contact with water until it has been fixed. Layering the colours and forming watermarks is still possible with heat-fix colours, but the patterning must be done while the colours are still damp to achieve any movement of the paints, as a heat-fix colour will not move into new patterns once it has dried. Practise a few times on a sampler or try working the project on page 100 that uses this technique with minimal resist usage.

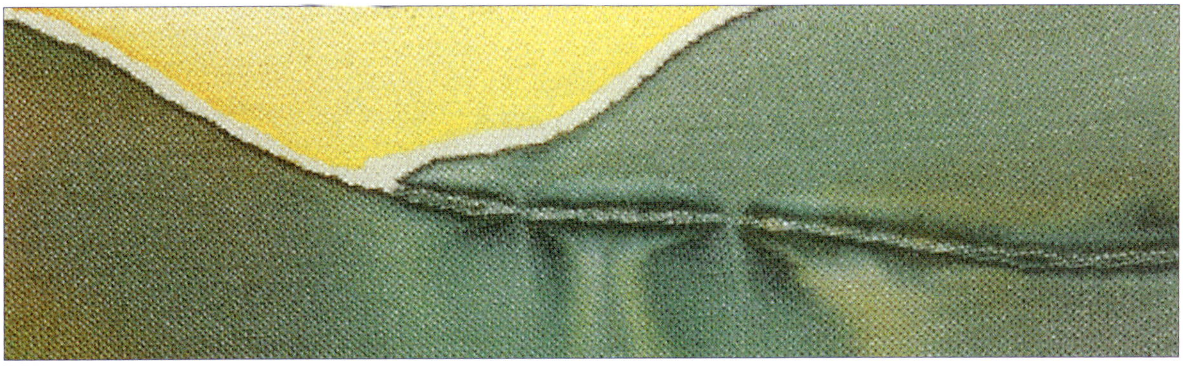

Freeflow colour on landscape card

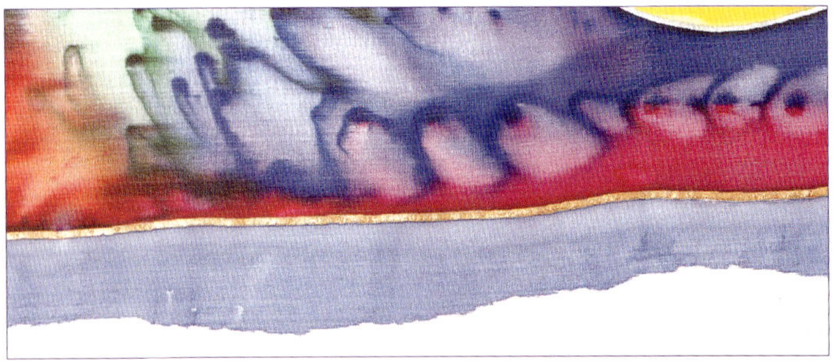

Texture patterns created with salt.

Working with effect salts

You can create some beautiful textural patterns using salt granules. Dry salt soaks up the wet silk paint or dye and forms wonderful frost-like patterns. By using various sizes of salt grains and crystals it is possible to vary the size of the pattern marks. Table salt produces very fine pattern marks, while coarse sea salt, dishwasher salt and commercial effect salt produce larger marks.

How to successfully achieve salt effect patterns

To work this technique you must place or scatter the salt on to the silk while the paints or dyes are still wet. If the work is too dry the salt cannot absorb the colour to form the patterns. You may achieve small starry patterns but not the impressive frosty flowing patterns that are associated with salt. If the work is too wet, the salt may become saturated too quickly and will not pull further patterns until the work has dried a little and the correct balance and optimum conditions are achieved. Impressive patterns develop when all the salt crystals have a little working space of their own. If the salt is too heavily applied, it produces large bleached-out areas, with little patterning.

It is best to leave the salt on the silk until it is dry, although you can reposition it while the patterns are still being formed. Never be tempted to use a hairdryer to dry a work with salt still on the silk, as it results in a shower of coloured salt landing over the whole piece. It is best to use table, sea and dishwasher salt only once and then throw it away, although it is possible to re-cycle commercial special effect salts.

Always make sure that any resist lines are completely dry before using salt, as it can become stuck in the resist line, possibly damaging it on removal. To prevent salt-effect patterns appearing where you don't want them, make sure you remove any stray crystals that have jumped on to the wrong patch of silk. If it is possible, save any salt patterning till last, making sure that all other sections are dry.

Once you have finished, it is vital to remove all the salt from the work before fixing, especially if you are steam-fixing it. Salt crystals left on the silk can cause spot marks to appear during the steam fixing process. You may notice that some of the very dark freckling marks made when working with salt disappear when the work is washed for the first time. This is just the base of the salt crystal being removed from the silk, rather than the paint or dye washing out. After the appropriate fixing method is complete, the silk should always be washed to remove any traces of salt.

Salt effect on edge of drawstring bag.

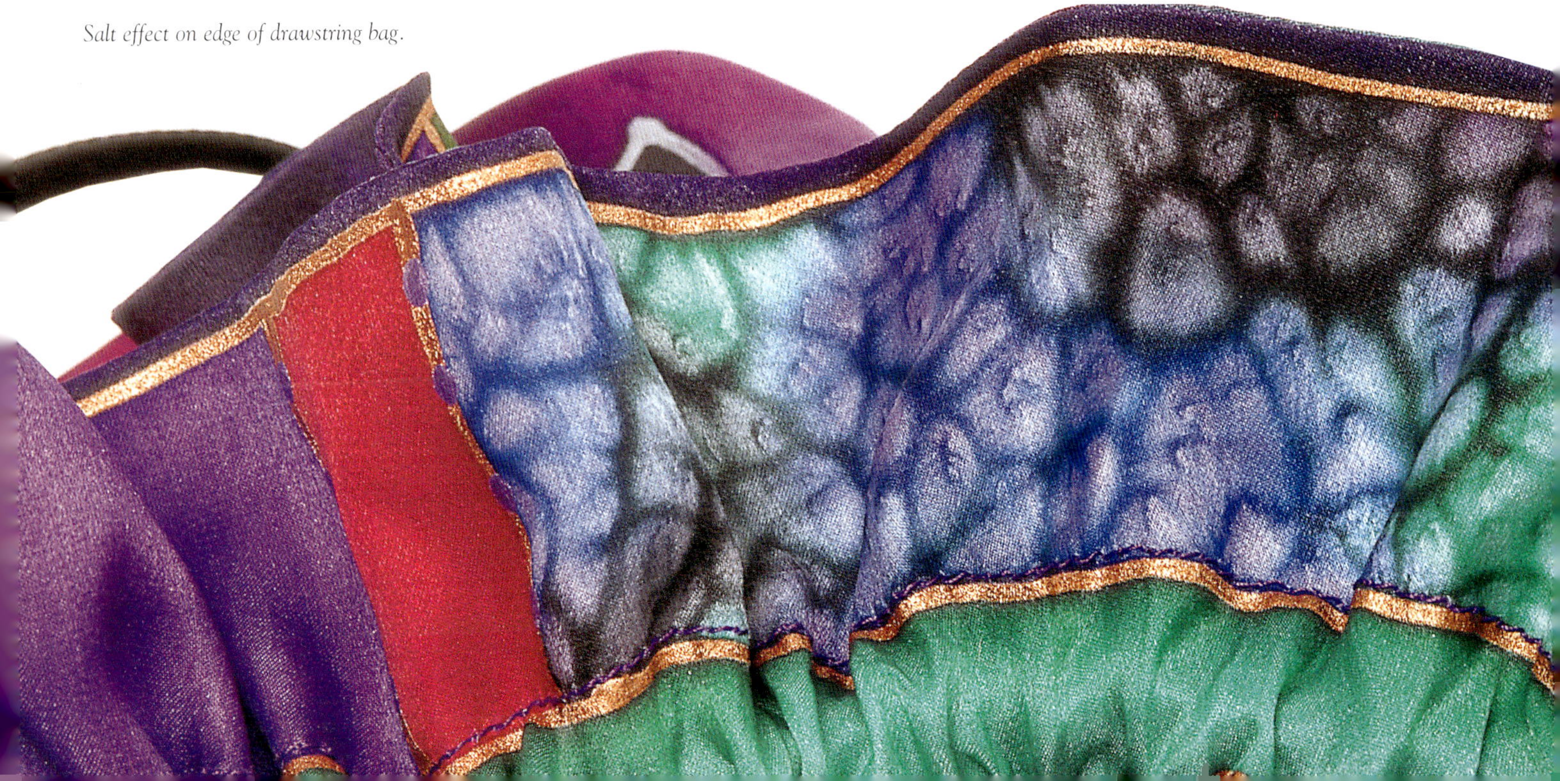

Working with anti-fusants, no-flow or anti-spreads

We have already looked at a thickener medium which changes the flow properties of the colour, but it is also possible to change the flow properties of the silk. By treating the silk with a liquid anti-spread, the colours can be applied to it in a controlled way, without the need for a resist.

Anti-spread solution, which is clear or white in colour, is available for both heat- and steam-fix colours, and can be applied to the whole or just part of the silk. Once dry, the silk will behave more like a dry cartridge paper, holding the colour where it is placed for fine work, or if the colours are applied as a wet-on-wet technique, they will mix and blend. You can work effectively in layers, or from a pattern placed under the silk in the normal way, following the shape of the pattern without applying a resist line, and giving the finished work a watercolour appearance.

On completion of the painting, the work should be fixed in the appropriate way and then washed. Anti-spread solutions can leave a slight trace of stiffness to the silk, so are more suitable for projects where the drape and flow of the silk are of less importance, for example, cards, pictures, banners and cushion panels. Please refer to the project on page 92 for practice in this technique.

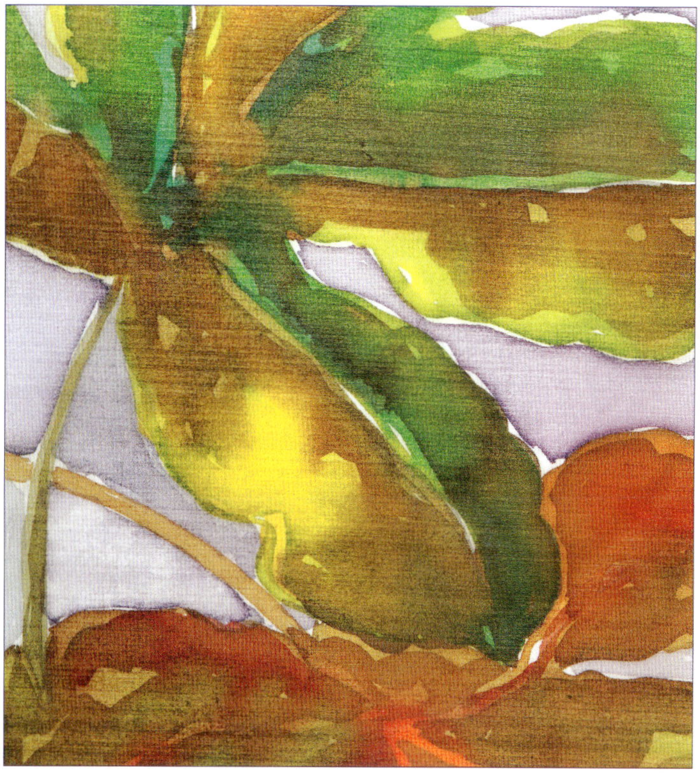

Leaves painted on silk treated with anti-spread.

Watermark patterning

As mentioned earlier, it is possible to create watermarks as texture patterning within a design. The most dramatic watermarks are formed when applying further steam-fix dyes, water, alcohol or diffusing medium on to dry areas of painted silk. The second application of dye or liquid pushes aside the first layer of colour to create a beautiful crinkly edge. The effect is softened if the work is still damp when the second or subsequent application of colour or liquid is applied, creating lovely soft rings or pattern lines of a lighter shade. This patterning can overwork and lose the dramatic effect if it is always left to dry naturally, so keep watching the developing pattern and dry with a hairdryer at the appropriate time. Cotton buds can be used to lift up excess liquid once the desired effect has formed, and control the final result. With some steam-fix dyes it is more effective to use alcohol or diffusing medium in place of water to create these watermarks.

As water, alcohol and diffusing medium all spread across the silk by capillary action, they can also be used to reserve areas as white, unpainted silk. Any of these will act as a stop to the spread of the colours if they are applied to areas of silk that you wish to remain white or very pale, before any colour is introduced. The joining line where colour and medium meet will form a soft, paler line which can be blended together by working over the area with a clean dry brush.

Watercolour effect.

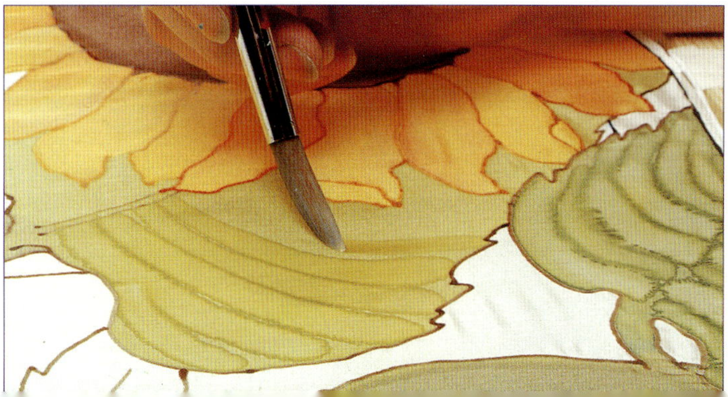

Watercolour effect on a sampler.

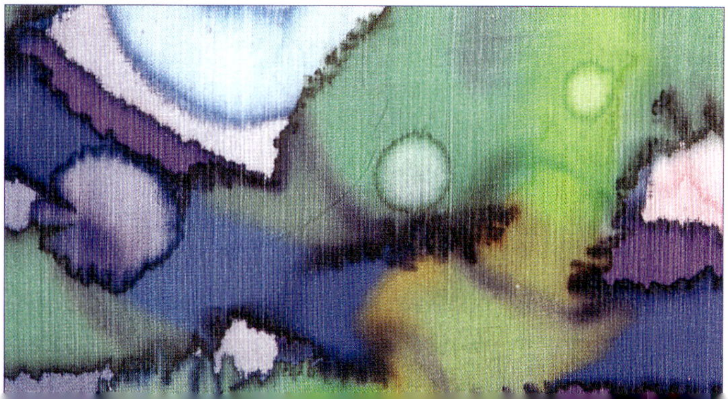

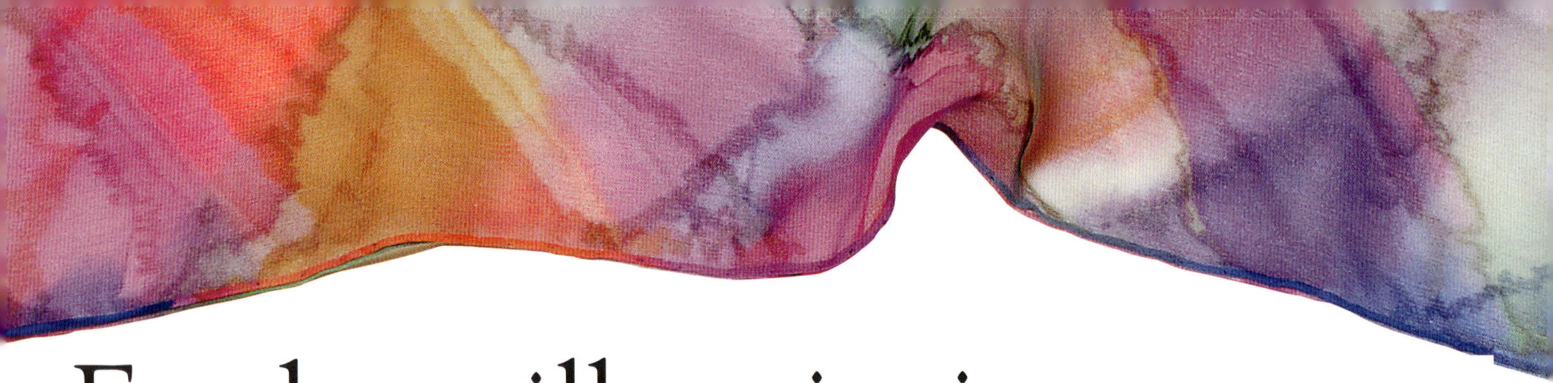

Further silk painting techniques

Working on velvet

Working on silk velvet is another strand in the silk painter's skills. The velvet most frequently used is a mix of fibres and is made up of silk, a protein fibre for the backing, and viscose, a cellulose fibre for the pile. This combination of fibres allows the use of a fibre etch gel to work a devorée pattern into the velvet, for an additional textural effect. Devorée means 'to burn out', and involves the removal of the pile by etching out or carbonising the cellulose-based fibre. The most suitable dyes to colour silk viscose velvet are either steam-fix or procion dyes. Both work well and give excellent depth of colour. If steam-ixed dyes are used, follow the steaming instructions given earlier. The advantage of working with a procion dye on velvet is that you do not have to steam the finished design to set the colours.

The fixing process is achieved by a chemical reaction from the use of a soda ash solution applied either directly into the dyes, or as a fixing bath solution. There are many different recipes for fixing procion dyes, and they often include salt, urea and soda ash in varying quantities.

Salt helps to dissolve the dye and drive it into the fibre.

Urea is available in granular form, and also helps to dissolve the dye and drive it into the fibre.

Soda ash is available as a powder, but when dissolved in water creates an alkaline solution which helps the dye bond to the fibres of the fabric.

Safety notes

- Care should be taken with procion dyes while they are in the powder state. Avoid inhalation of the dye powder and wear a protective mask when measuring out and mixing up these dyes. Rubber gloves should be worn when handling chemicals.
- The dye powder should be added to the water, not the other way around, but once the dyes have been mixed there is no danger of inhalation and therefore it is not necessary to continue to wear the mask.
- Wear a protective mask when tearing silk-viscose fabric as the fine fibres could also be an irritant if inhaled.
- Always clearly label any containers of dyes or chemicals.

Materials and equipment for painting on velvet.

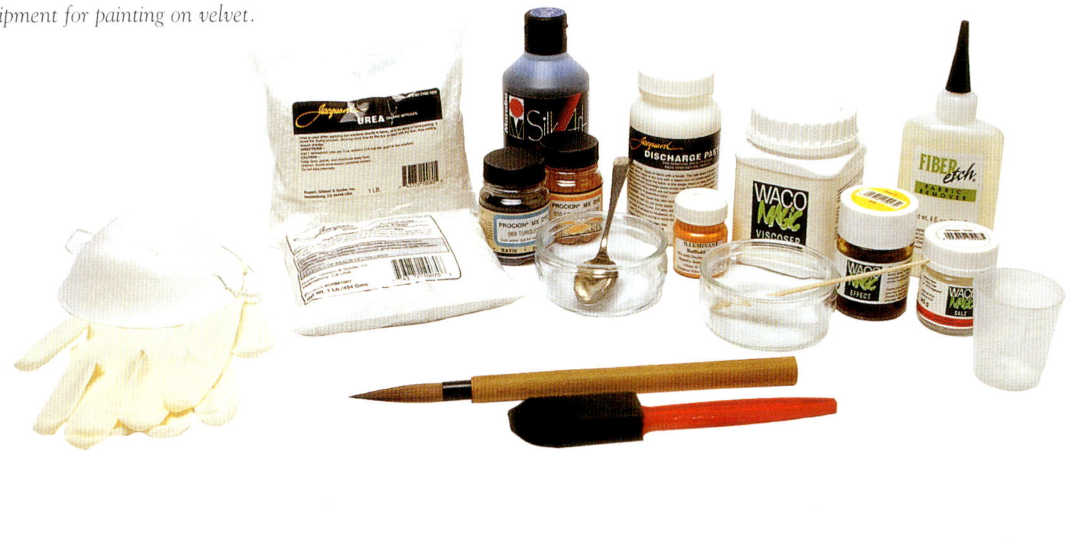

Procion dyes

Procion dyes are cold-water reactive dyes that are set with a soda ash solution. They work on many natural fibres including silk, wool, cotton, linen, paper and rayon, but are particularly good with plant fibres, making them ideal for silk and viscose mix velvets. Procion dyes are normally available in powder form and need to be mixed with water to form a liquid dye. Both procion dyes and steam-fix dyes can be applied with Chinese style paint brushes or foam brushes, without the need for resists when working on velvet.

The soda ash solution needed to set procion dyes can be added either while mixing up the dye, and be applied as the dyes are painted on to the fabric, or else applied as a fixative bath after the dyes have been poured on to the silk velvet. However, once the soda ash solution has been added to the dyes it starts the chemical reaction which bonds the dyes with the fibres, with an effective working time of approximately three hours.

These dyes can be applied with a brush to work a defined and controlled design, or by dipping the silk velvet into a large container, or adding several colours to a dyeing bucket or tray for random and blended colours. Use the following steps to work the dyeing process in a dye bath or tray.

Dyeing silk viscose velvet in a bucket or tray

Add 250 ml ($^1/_2$ pint) of boiling water to two tablespoons of ordinary table salt in a heat-proof measuring jug. Stir well until the salt has dissolved and then add cold water to make up to 500 ml (1 pint). Wearing a protective mask, measure out $^1/_2$ teaspoon of procion dye powder, (more if you want a stronger colour) and add this to a jam jar with 125 ml ($^1/_4$ pint) of the salt water solution. Stir well to dissolve the procion powder, and then top up this coloured dye solution with a further 125 ml ($^1/_4$ pint) of cold water. Increase these quantities proportionately for greater quantities of dye. Have a standard teaspoon measure, whether flat or heaped, to allow for a greater degree of consistency when re-mixing to achieve a similar strength of colour when working with powdered dyes.

Wet the velvet with water, then gently squeeze out the excess, and arrange the fabric randomly or into a semi structured pattern in the base of the bucket or tray. Pre-wetting the silk helps to achieve a more even colouring. Carefully pour the liquid dye on to the fabric and gently agitate the tray, or wear rubber gloves and mix the colours with your hands. The more you handle the fabric the more blended and muted the colours become. If the velvet is sitting in large quantities of dye, pour this away, and then leave the velvet to rest for at least 20 minutes, preferably longer. The velvet can be left for several hours to maximise the uptake and blending of colours.

Mixing up the fixative solution for dyeing in a bath or tray

A fixative solution of soda ash must be added to the dye bath to fix the dyes. Dissolve one tablespoon of soda ash in 250 ml ($^1/_2$ pint) of boiling water and stir to dissolve, then add a further 250 ml ($^1/_2$ pint) of cold water. Remove any dye liquid left in the dye bath, then pour the soda ash fixing solution all over the dyed velvet. Slightly agitate the tray to ensure that the fixing solution has penetrated all areas, and leave to cure for at least one hour.

Tip away the fixing solution and rinse out the silk velvet in cold water. Keep rinsing until the water runs clear. It may take several rinses before all the loose dye is removed; try using a little Synthrapol, a liquid detergent that helps to remove excess dye.

Lay the dyed silk velvet out on some old newspaper to dry off a little, and then iron on the reverse side while it is still just damp for a smooth, plush finish.

You can continue working and developing the fabric by adding devorée patterning or surface decoration for further textural enhancement to the dyed silk velvet. The devorée process is explained on page 39.

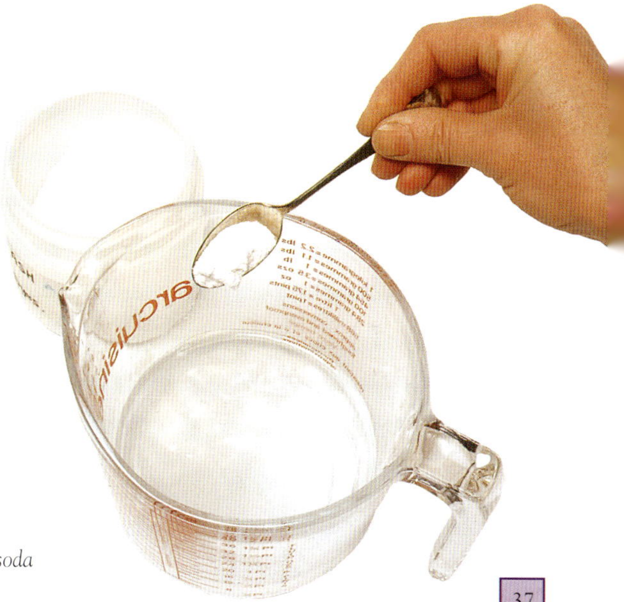

Measuring out soda ash fixative.

Painting a design on to silk viscose velvet with procion dyes

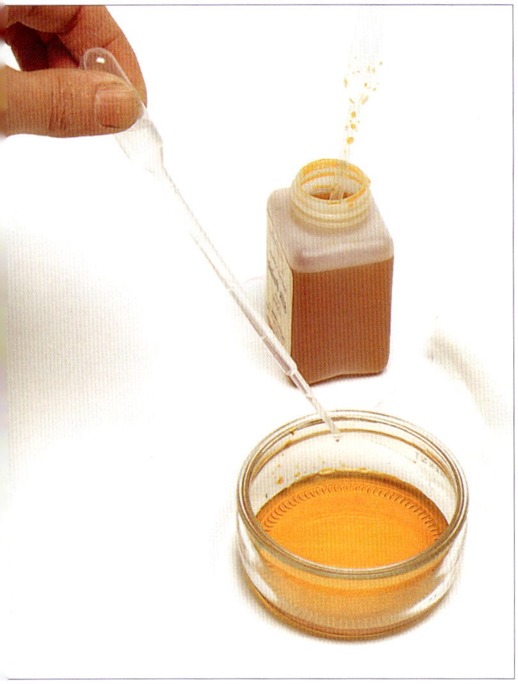

Measuring out dye and fixative in a jar.

Beautiful designs can be painted on velvet without the need for a barrier, as the thickness and absorbency of the fabric allows for only minimal flow of the dyes and fine control over the pattern cn be achieved. Adding the soda ash fixative solution to the dyes in the mixing palette starts the chemical reaction and means the dyes must be used well within three hours to allow sufficient time for the fixing to work.

Before you begin mixing up the procion dyes for painting on to silk velvet, put on a face mask. Measure out one teaspoon of dye powder and add it to a little hot, but not boiling water in a measuring jug. Stir to dissolve the dye. Then add cold water to make it up to 200 ml ($^{1}/_{3}$ pint). Pour the dissolved dye into a labelled screw-top jar, where it will keep for several weeks; however, it is better to mix up only the quantity that you need for each project.

Wear rubber gloves to make the fixative solution, and measure out and dissolve eight teaspoons of urea granules into 400 ml ($^{3}/_{4}$ pint) of hot, but not boiling, water and stir until dissolved. Urea helps the dye powder to dissolve and spread evenly across the silk fabric. Pour this solution into a large, clearly labelled screw-top jar.

Clean out the jug, and measure out 10 teaspoons of soda ash, and dissolve it in 400 ml ($^{3}/_{4}$ pint) of hot, but not boiling water, stir until the soda ash has dissolved. Each of these two solutions can be made up in advance of your painting and stored in separate, clearly labelled jars. Once again, only make up enough for the project, and keep the bulk of your ingredients in their dry form. To prepare an active fixative solution for painting with procion dyes, measure out equal quantities of the prepared urea and soda ash solutions, into a third, clearly labelled large jar. This combined urea/soda ash forms the fixative solution.

Painting with the combined dye and fixative solution on to silk viscose velvet

Using a plastic pipette dropper, put equal quantities of the prepared procion dye and combined fixative solution in a mixing palette. Once the dye and fixative solution are combined they will only be viable for three hours, and must therefore be applied to the fabric within this time to give the soda ash sufficient time to bond the dye on to the velvet fibres. Combining the fixative and dye in the palette allows working without the need for any further fixing process. The colour strength can be adjusted by diluting with water to the required shade, and then adding a little more fixative.

Silk velvet does not need to be stretched on a frame. Lay it on some polythene pile-side down using masking tape to hold it in place. If you prefer to use a frame, pin the fabric out as normal using either stenter claws or silk pins, but remember to have the fabric pile-side down.

Velvet absorbs a lot of dye, which can be applied with Chinese or foam brushes. The dye should always be applied to the reverse of the fabric, as this helps it to penetrate the pile and prevents the pattern spreading too far. The colour will spread a little, but a defined pattern can be achieved by controlling the amounts of colour released by varying the amount of brush contact given to the velvet. The tip of a brush will only release a little colour, whereas pressing down will release greater quantities of dye. The correct sized brush in combination with good brush control allows detailed patterns to be achieved without resists.

Once the velvet has been completely painted with activated dye solution, allow it to air-dry on old newspapers for several hours. It is possible to leave it overnight, but no longer, as soda ash forms a strong alkaline solution and if left for too long could damage the silk fibres.

After leaving the velvet for at least three hours, rinse out in cool water to remove any excess dye and spent fixative solution. It will take several rinses before the water runs clear. Gently squeeze out any excess water and allow the fabric to dry on clean old newspaper. Do not hang the piece on a washing line to dry, as any remaining loose dye could run down the fabric and spoil it. When the silk is still just damp, iron the velvet on the wrong side to restore the plush pile finish.

It is now possible to add devorée using a fibre etch gel, or to employ surface decoration techniques for further textural effects.

Using fibre etch gel to create devorée pattern

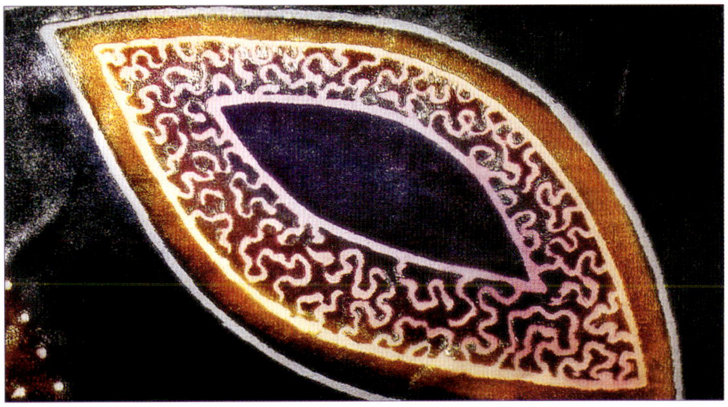

Velevet devorée on scarf - detail.

Devorée is the term given to patterns formed by a chemical etching gel that is applied to a protein and cellulose mixed fibre fabric. The fibre etch gel is usually aluminium sulphate or sodium hydrogen sulphate, which carbonises the cellulose fibre when heat is applied, creating the etched pattern. Use baking soda to neutralise the etching process should the fibre etch gel accidentally be applied in the wrong position. Fibre etch gel will work on cotton, linen, viscose and rayon, which are all cellulose or plant-based fibres. If correctly applied, it should not remove protein-based fibres such as silk or wool.

Always apply the fibre etch gel to the wrong side or backing of the silk viscose velvet. The gel is then applied at the base of the pile to ensure an effective release once the heat has been applied. Fibre etch gel can be applied to white velvet before any colour has been applied, or after the velvet has been painted or dyed.

Fibre etch gel can either be screen printed or applied direct from the applicator bottle, in a similar way to outliner. The screen can be made using a photo stencil emulsion, or with a stencil fastened to the back of a blank screen with masking tape. Pieces of masking tape stuck to the back of a blank screen can also create a very effective design that can be repeated.

How to apply fibre etch gel

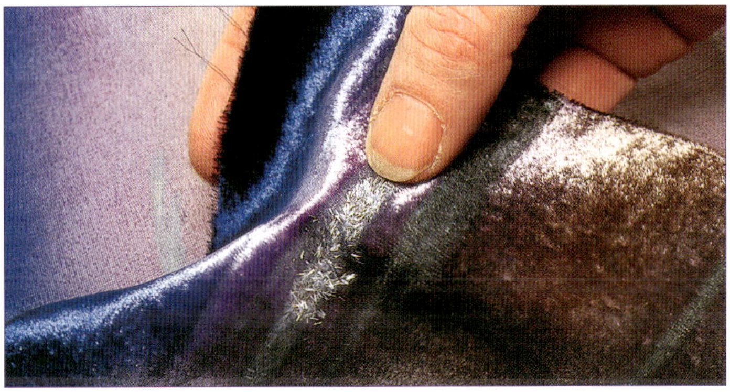

Work in a well-ventilated room. Cover the work surface with some plastic sheeting and lay the piece of silk velvet pile-side down. Tension and hold it in place with masking tape. Use a frame if you prefer.

Wear a mask and rubber gloves and apply the fibre etch gel as evenly as you can to the silk backing. Try to avoid any large blobs or areas where the gel is applied too heavily, as too much or an uneven amount of fibre etch gel can potentially create holes when the gel is activated by ironing. If you have large blobs, lift up the excess, or distribute it across the area you are working. If you are applying the fibre etch gel direct from the nozzle of the applicator bottle, remember to use light pressure. For screen printing, eight pulls of the squeegee across the mesh is usually sufficient to achieve a sharp image, with the velvet stretched on the work surface. Work a sampler on a small test piece before starting on a major project if you have not worked this process before.

Once applied to the velvet, the fibre etch gel should be dried with a hairdryer rather than letting it dry naturally. When dry, iron on the reverse of the velvet, with the iron at silk/wool setting, until the lines become pale brown, taking care not to over-heat the work so that it becomes dark brown. The fibre etch gel is colourless when dry, but the dry heat causes a chemical reaction which carbonises the cellulose fibres or treated pile of the velvet. The pale brown colour shows that the cellulose fibres have carbonised, not that the fabric is scorched, and will disappear when the fabric is washed. If you cannot easily see this colour change on painted velvet, turn to the pile side of the velvet from time to time to see whether the viscose pile in the treated areas will detach easily from the silk backing when gently rubbed with a finger.

When the whole piece of velvet has been ironed sufficiently, wash it in cool water, gently agitating the velvet to remove the pile and reveal the devorée pattern. Do not detach the pile by shaking or rubbing the velvet when it is dry, as this releases the pile fibres into the air which can cause irritation if inhaled. The fabric is quite fragile at this stage, and rubbing the silk can cause holes to develop. Once the velvet has been rinsed through and the pattern is fully revealed, gently squeeze out any excess water, and allow the velvet to dry a little before ironing on the reverse side to restore a smooth pile.

Discharge paste

This can be applied to fabric to bleach out or remove the original colour, leaving colours ranging from off-white to pale brown, depending on the dyes being used. By mixing a colorant into the chemical discharge paste, it is possible to remove the original colour and insert a new colour at the same time. The colorants can be illuminant powders, effect paints or iron-fix silk paints. Discharge paste should always be applied to the right side of silk viscose velvet to ensure the colour is effectively removed from the pile and the discharge process is activated by steaming.

How to apply discharge paste on to silk-viscose velvet

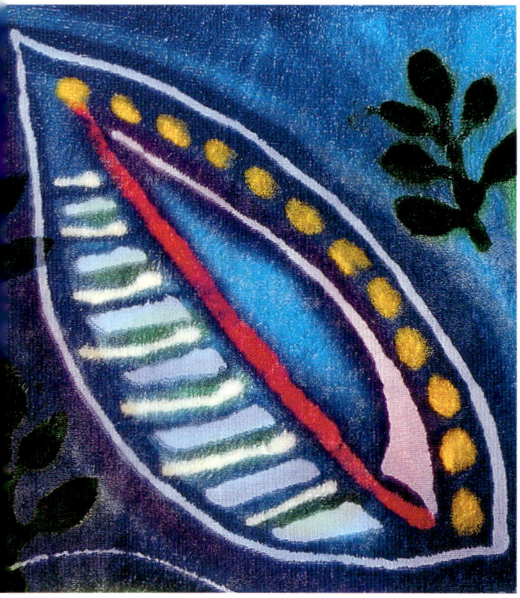

Patterns worked using discharge paste.

It is not necessary, particularly if you are working a blocked or screen printed design, to use a frame to stretch the velvet. Lay the silk velvet pile-side up on the protective plastic sheeting and hold in place with masking tape. If using a frame, pin the velvet on to the frame, remembering to have the pile side uppermost. The discharge paste, which is usually white unless mixed with colorants, can be applied from an applicator bottle, brushed on with a firm brush, applied through a screen, or printed from blocks and stamps. A screen-printing frame with a blank screen printing mesh is very useful for creating an abstract pattern. Scrunch up coloured or black velvet and place the blank screen over this fabric, then squeegee the discharge paste through this to create a broken striped effect (see the project on page 94). Apply the paste and leave it to dry, or dry with a hairdryer.

When the fabric is dry, use either a steam iron on the reverse of the velvet to activate the process, or roll up the fabric as described on page 16. Steam the parcel for between 20 minutes to approximately one hour, depending on the type of steaming equipment being used. The completed discharge or introduction of new colour will be revealed after the steaming process. The fabric should then be thoroughly washed in cool water to remove all traces of the spent discharge paste and any residue traces of colorants. Allow the fabric to dry off a little before ironing on the wrong side to restore the lie of the pile.

Silk painting and Shibori techniques fixed in a microwave

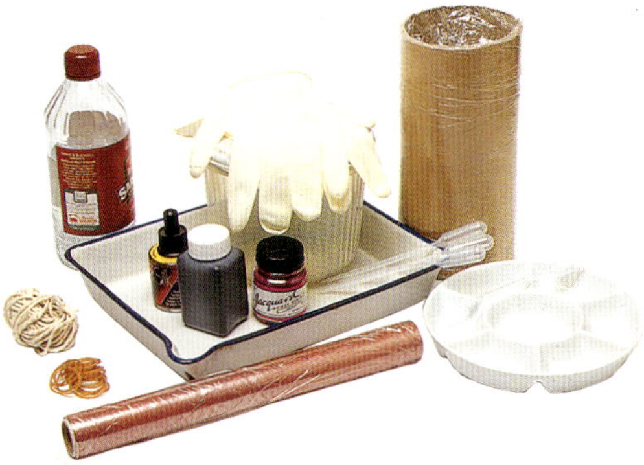

Materials and equipment used for fixing in a microwave.

Using a microwave to fix silk dyes in a range of abstract and semi-controlled patterns is a relatively new way of working that does not involve the use of any outliner mediums. This process will only work with steam-fix or acid dyes and is not suitable for working with heat-set paints. The use of vinegar is essential for acid dyes and can be included even if the steam-fix dyes you are using do not require acidic conditions to set the colour. It is great fun and is a 'hands-on' approach, that can also be enjoyed by children under supervision. It is especially suitable for Shibori work, a traditional Japanese form of dyeing that involves pleating, folding, twisting, wrapping, or stitching fabric using bindings of fine threads or string to create a range of restrictions in the fabric which influence or control the flow of the dye.

In conventional steam setting methods the dry finished work is rolled up and protected by absorbent paper or cotton fabric to prevent cross patterning during the fixing process. Fixing colours in the microwave is completely different as the work must be wet during the process to encourage colours to mix and blend until set.

Creating a range of abstract and semi-controlled patterns using a microwave

In addition to steam-fix dyes you will need the following equipment to enable you to work a selection of patterns ranging from the complete abstract to Japanese Shibori-style patterns.

Materials:

- silk fabric,
- steam-fix or acid dyes – a maximum of five colours per project is a good guide
- white vinegar
- a shallow dish
- rubber gloves
- elastic bands
- cotton string
- plastic pipettes
- water pot and mixing palette
- kitchen paper
- thick cardboard tube approx. 11 cm (4 in.) in diameter x 20 cm (8 in.) long, wrapped with cling film
- plastic sheeting to protect the work area
- microwave pot with a ventilated lid or some microwave cling film
- microwave oven

Working patterns in the microwave

Although the patterns vary, the principles for creating them remain the same. No silk painting frame is needed and the silk should be arranged into its correct formation and soaked in vinegar before the dyes are applied. Whether the vinegar is applied before or after the fabric is arranged depends on the pattern to be worked. For example, it is very difficult to neatly fold a wet piece of silk, because the silk sticks to itself. It is therefore much easier to fold the silk into neat squares before applying vinegar. See the table below to help you to prepare the fabric and apply the vinegar in the correct sequence on a selection of patterns.

Pattern to be worked	Preparation before the application of the dyes	
Softly marbled pattern	wet silk with vinegar	arrange silk in contours
Chevron pattern	twist silk dry	soak with vinegar
Folded patterns	fold silk dry	soak folded silk in vinegar
Pleated patterns	pleat silk dry	soak pleated silk in vinegar
Ruched patterns	wet silk with vinegar	ruche up the wet silk
Stitched patterns	insert threads on to dry silk	soak drawn up silk in vinegar
Knotted patterns	knot silk dry	soak knotted silk in vinegar
Arashi patterns	roll and bind dry silk on tube	roll silk into vinegar bath

Once the fabric has been arranged and soaked with vinegar, following the sequence in the above table, the dyes should be applied using plastic pipettes. Remember to spend time beforehand planning, preparing, mixing and diluting the colours selected for each project. Once applied to the silk, the colours are worked into the fabric using a squeezing, rolling or pressing action with your hands. The more the silk is handled, the more blended the colours become. The work should always be wrapped loosely in cling film or placed in a microwave pot for the cooking and fixing process.

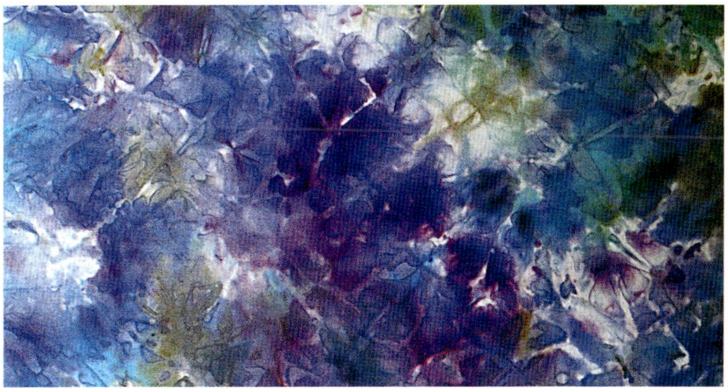

Marbled effect microwave pattern.

Chevron or feathered patterns

Twist the silk into a skein and place the skein into the vinegar. Apply the colours in bands across the skein, remembering to really press the colours through all the layers right into the centre of the skein. Carefully peek into the center of the skein to check that the colour has penetrated to the center.

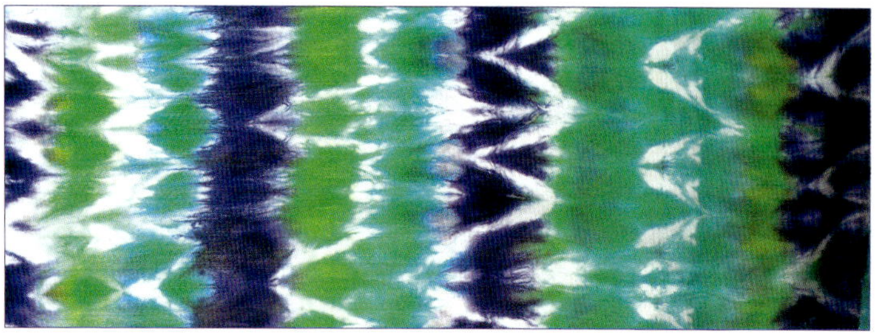

Zigzag chevron microwave pattern.

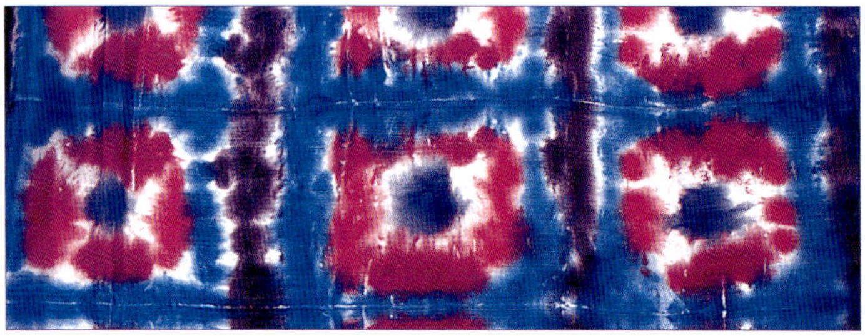

Repeated pattern from folding.

Folded patterns

Fold the dry silk into neat squares or oblongs and place it in the vinegar. Apply the colours to the top surface, then turn the silk over and re-apply the dyes to the under surface. Press the dyes down through all the layers of the silk. Check that they have penetrated all the layers before fixing.

Pleated designs

Pleat the silk using your hands, running stitches or an iron, and place it in the vinegar. Make sure you only apply the dyes along the edges of the pleat if you want to retain an un-dyed area across the middle of each pleat. Place the coloured pleat carefully into a shallow dish to avoid cross-colouring during the cooking process. Keep your work area especially clean if you want to retain some areas of the silk as white.

Interesting spripes from pleating.

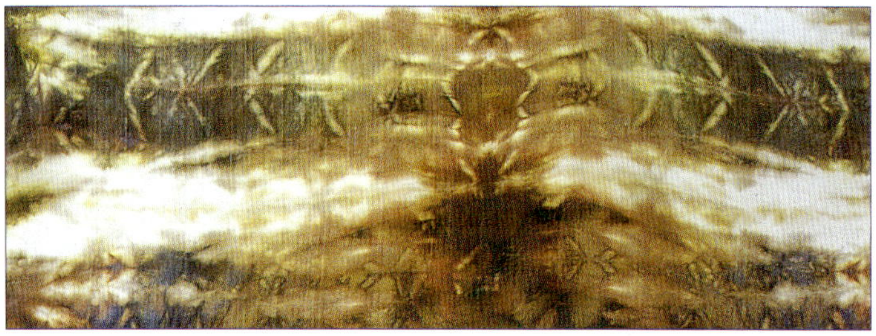

More deailed patterns formed by using string.

Pleated and bound patterns

Pleat the silk as before, but then wrap string around the pleat in a neat or criss-cross way. Dip the bound pleat into vinegar before applying the colours and pressing them through all the layers.

Ruched patterns

Immerse the silk in the vinegar, squeeze out the excess and roughly open out the silk on the plastic. Start at one end and ruche up the silk in small gathers with your fingers. Apply the colours with pipettes, but work the colour in by pressing downwards so that you do not disturb the gathers. Try to keep the silk in these gathers as you place it in the pot for steaming.

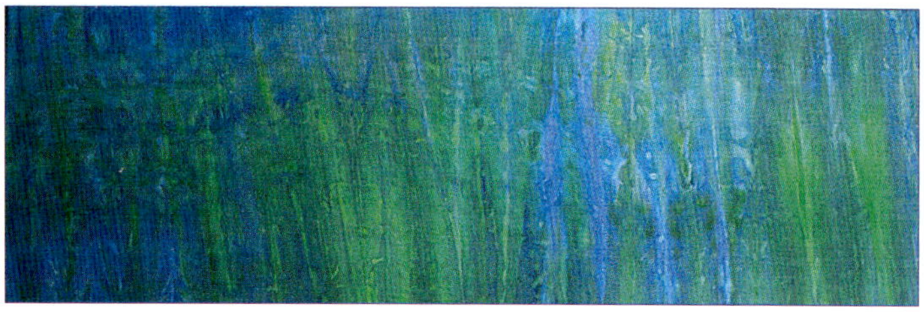

Colours softly merging along the lines of ruching.

TINY PLEATS AND STITCHED PATTERNS

While the silk is dry, insert a series of small running stitches across the work in patterns of your choosing. You can use a smocking machine to create fine pleats by inserting many threads at once if you have this specialist tool. Draw up the threads before you apply the colours. Wash the dyed fabric and allow it to completely dry before removing the threads if you want to retain the pleated effect.

KNOTTED PATTERNS

Knot the silk across the whole piece, and apply the colours to the tip of the knot, on the knot, around the knot and inside the knot to achieve coloured rings. Make sure you give the coloured knots a good squeeze to make the colours penetrate the whole depth of the knot. Do not make the knots too tight as this may restrict the movement of colour.

To set the steam-fix dyes place the work into a ventilated pot, or loosely wrap it in cling film and cook it in a microwave set at medium power for the appropriate time. Cooking times are based on the size and weight of the piece of silk. Small pieces of lightweight silk of approximately 1/4 metre in size should only need two minutes. Pieces up to approximately one metre in size will need four minutes. A silk blouse of approximately 3/4 metre will need six to eight minutes. Increase the cooking time by a couple of minutes per metre, but always ensure that the silk fabric remains wet while it is in the microwave. The dyes are set when they no longer bleed into new patterns. Keeping the silk damp throughout the cooking process prevents the silk from overheating and becoming scorched. For timings above four minutes, the additional cooking time can be given in two to three minute bursts, which allows you to check and adjust the wetness, by spraying the work with more vinegar if necessary.

Once the dyes are set the silk should be washed in warm water with a little liquid detergent to remove any traces of vinegar. Iron while the silk is still damp to remove any creases. This way of working is particularly effective on pongee, habotai, georgette, crêpe de chine and chiffon silks, and is featured in the project on page 66.

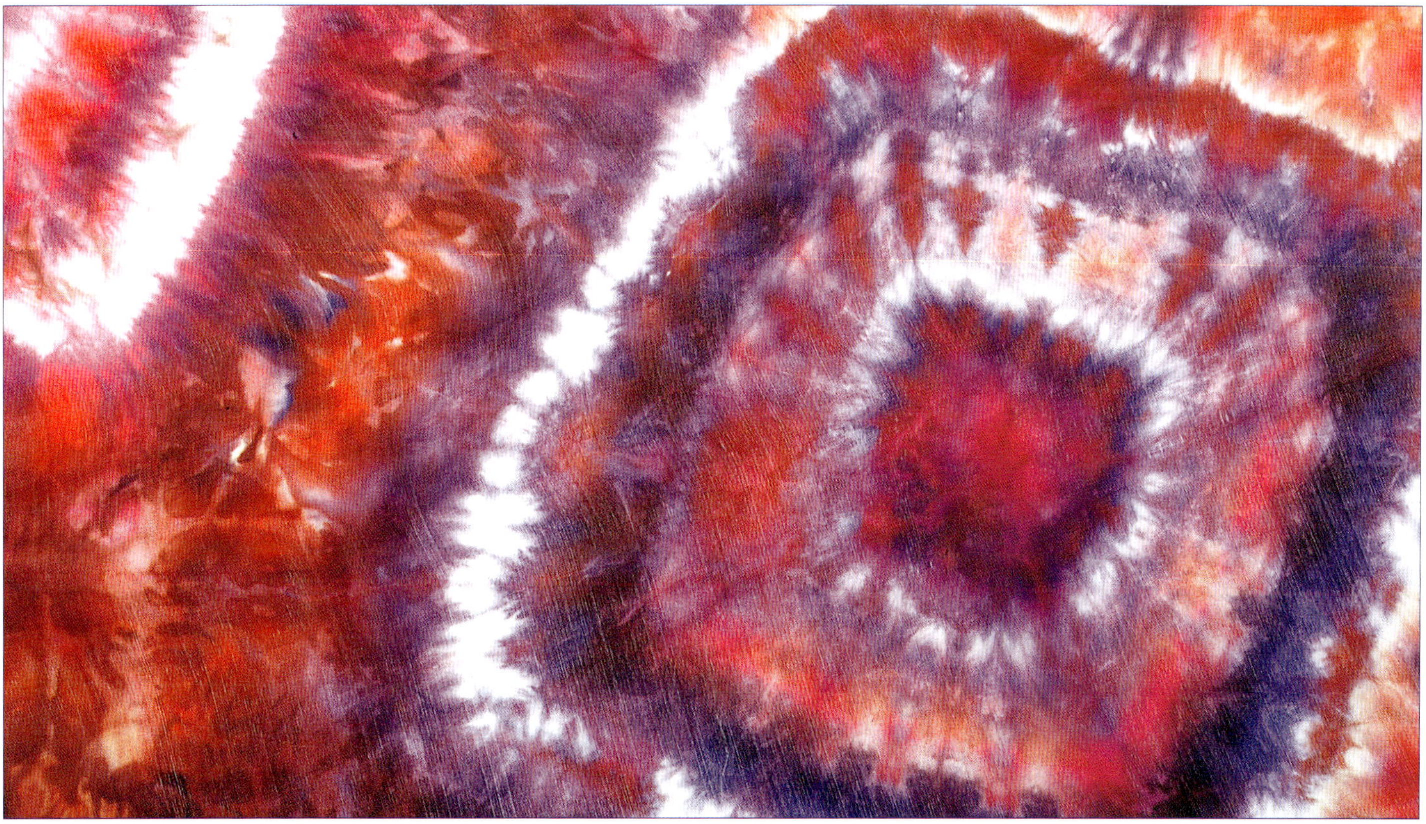

Coloured pattern rings achieved by knotting the silk.

Working Arashi patterns in the microwave

Arashi Shibori patterns are formed by wrapping or twisting fabric around a tube or pole. Arashi style can be effectively worked in the microwave using a thick cardboard tube covered in cling film. Since the arrangement of the silk influences the pattern, any fold in the fabric will give a change of direction or repeat the pattern lines created by the bindings. If the fold is on the diagonal, the finished pattern line will change direction at the fold point, creating a V shape, whereas folding the silk in half will repeat the pattern equally on each of the folded sides.

This can be useful when working a long scarf, as folding the scarf in half end to end before rolling the silk on to the tube will ensure that both the pattern and the colours will be the same at both ends. Rolling the silk on to the tube from the folded edge allows the ends of the scarf to be on the outermost surface on the tube resulting in a slightly greater depth of colour if the dyes are not worked through all the layers. Alternatively, starting at one end and rolling the silk onto the tube can give a variation of both pattern and colour strength throughout the length of the scarf. Don't roll the silk on too tightly as this makes it difficult to ruche up and bind the silk to get the whole width of scarf on to the roll. Twisting the silk on the tube also adds a variation to the lines formed, and it is worth trying different methods of wrapping and binding the silk to create a range of pattern effects.

The tightness and thickness of the string used to bind the silk can also influence the finished pattern. If the string is too fine or too loose, the dye will track under the string, leaving no obvious pattern lines. The thickness and twist of the string can also affect the pattern lines, so experiment with different types to see which produces the most pleasing effect. Variations on the pattern lines formed by the string can be made by re-using string that still contains unfixed dye in it. Alternatively, try dipping a length of string into dye and allowing it to dry, before using it to bind the work. Any unfixed dye left in the string will create darker or coloured pattern lines, whereas clean new string will create paler pattern lines.

Once the silk is wrapped around the tube, it is initially held in place with an elastic band at one end, then the tube is bound with string to form the pattern lines. Slip the string under the elastic band and bind it around the tube, placing each strand an equal distance apart before ruching up a section of about 3 cm (1¼ in.) at a time. For more dramatic, stormy pattern lines, first ruche up a section of silk, and then bind it in place, winding the string around with a much more random spacing, allowing the string to cross over itself. Continue binding around the tube, ruching up the bound section until the whole width of scarf has been worked on to the roll, holding the final end of string in place with another elastic band.

The bound silk should then be rolled in the vinegar tray, and any excess squeezed out before placing it on some kitchen paper to prevent the silk roll sitting in a puddle of vinegar and dye. The colours are applied with pipettes and worked through all the layers using gloved hands. Further colour can be applied to strengthen the depth or change the colour blends. Don't worry if the colours look as if they have all merged together. This pressing action must be thorough to ensure that the dye penetrates all the layers.

Once blended the colours are set by loosely wrapping the work in cling film and cooking it in a microwave for the appropriate time. When setting work on tubes, split the cooking time in half, so that the work can be repositioned by rotating the tube part way through the setting process. Additional patterning can be applied with decorative liners, following the contours of these Arashi patterns. (See the project on page 68 for this technique.)

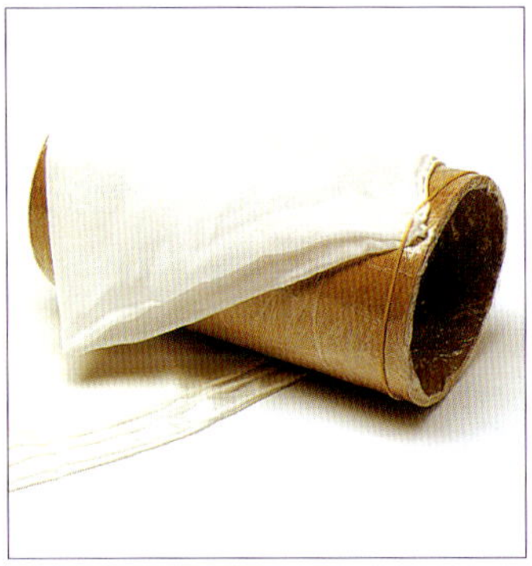

Wrap the folded silk around the tube at an angle for a chevron pattern.

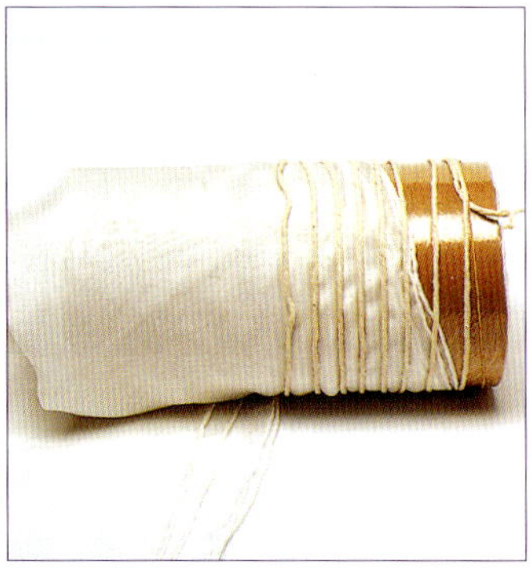

Bind the string neatly for even patterning.

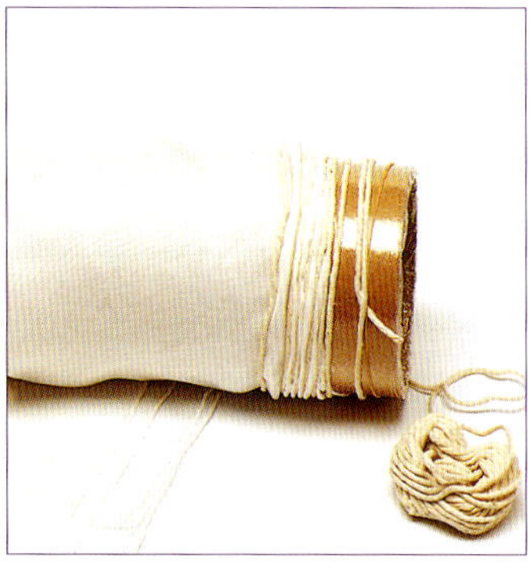

Ruche up a bound section to draw more silk on to the tube.

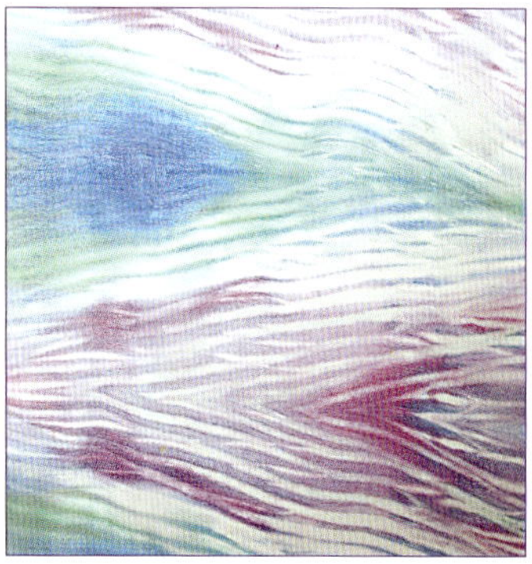

The finished Arashi pattern with a chevron directional flow.

PRIMARY COLOURS

Red, yellow and blue are traditionally regarded as the primary colours, that is colours that cannot be mixed from others, but when are themselves mixed together, produce a full spectrum. A far wider range of colours can be achieved if two of each of the primary colours are selected for colour mixing. A good selection to start with would be: a lemon yellow and a golden yellow; a magenta red and a vermilion (orange red); a cyan (turquoise) and an ultramarine blue.

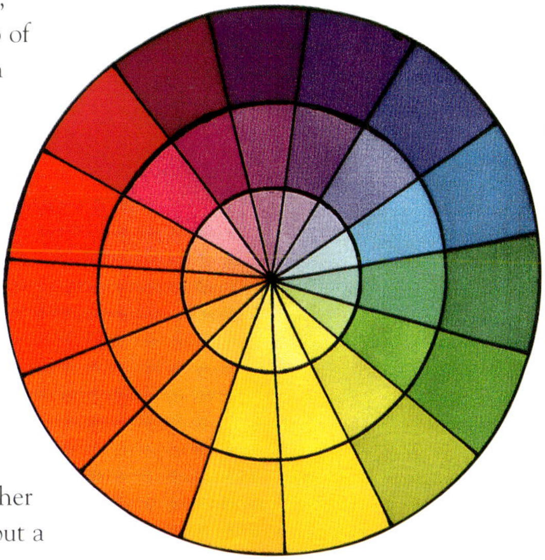

The Colour Wheel,showing spectrum of colours

SECONDARY COLOURS

Mixing together two of the primary colours in equal quantities will create secondary colours of orange, green and violet.
Yellow + red = orange   Yellow + blue = green   Red + blue = violet

Since each of the six basic colours lean towards one end of the colour wheel or spectrum, a good selection of secondary colours can be achieved. For example a golden yellow leans towards an orange in the colour wheel, whereas a lemon yellow leans towards a yellow green. This means that a richer orange will be achieved using a golden yellow rather than a lemon yellow, but a lemon yellow mixed with a cyan would be a better choice for bright greens.

INTERMEDIATE OR TERTIARY COLOURS

Mixing together a secondary colour with its nearest primary colour on the colour wheel will give an intermediate or tertiary colour. A golden yellow mixed with orange will give yellow-orange, for example.

COMPLEMENTARY COLOURS

Complementary or opposite colours are those that sit opposite each another on the colour wheel and give the greatest degree of contrast to each other.
The complementary of yellow = violet   The complementary of red = green
The complementary of blue = orange

WARM AND COOL COLOURS

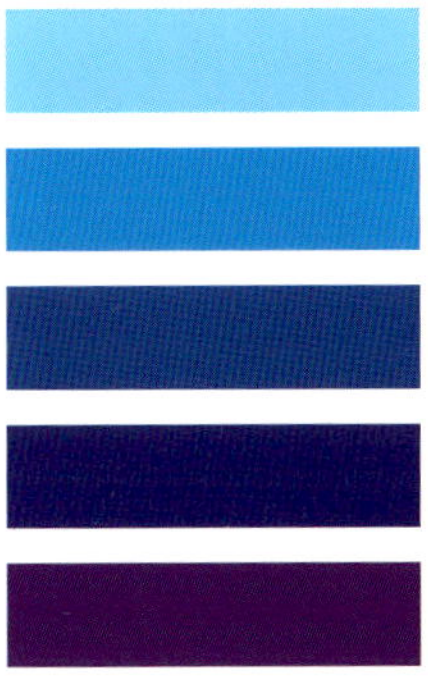

Cool colours

Colours can be grouped in one of the above categories. Reds, oranges and yellows are considered to be warm colours that appear to come forward in a design, while greens, blues and violets are cool colours that appear to retreat or recede. This optical effect can be used to add further impact to a piece of work.

The selection of a particular colour or group of colours obviously affects the appearance of a piece of work. Work a small design in a range of colours, then repeat the design, but change the colours used and compare the results. If you feel uncertain about which colours go together, start looking around you. It may be a border of flowers, someone's outfit, some packaging or an arrangement in a shop window. Take a look at how colours are used and try to analyse why they are such an effective combination.

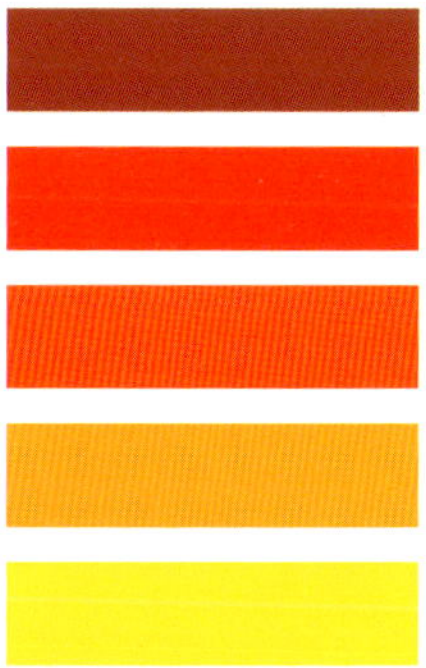

Warm colours

HUE, VALUE AND INTENSITY

Hue is the name given to a colour, for example red or yellow. Value refers to the lightness or darkness of a hue, or colour, in relation to black and white. Since there is no white dye in silk painting, add water to the colour to achieve a tint, add grey for a tone and black to achieve a shade.

Intensity refers to the vibrancy or subtlty of a colour. A pure colour or hue can be reduced or subdued by mixing a little complementary colour (the opposite colour on the colour wheel) to reduce its intensity. Adding further quantities of the complementary colour will create earth colours.

Outline control with tint and tone exercise

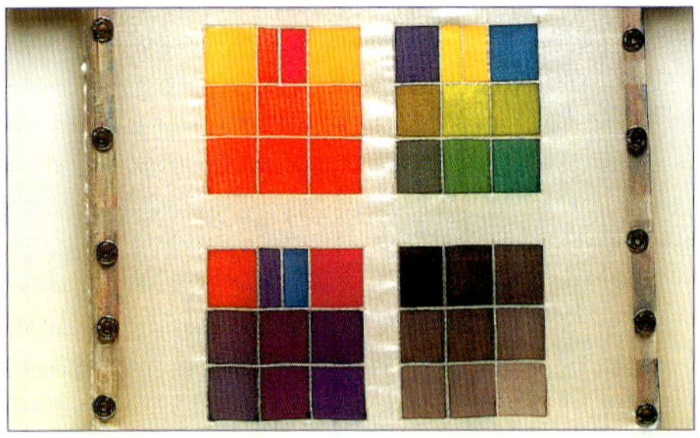

Showing tints and tones.

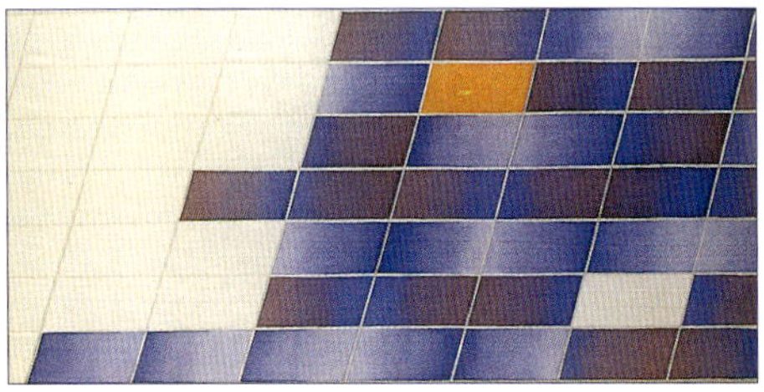

Colour filling to form tints and tones

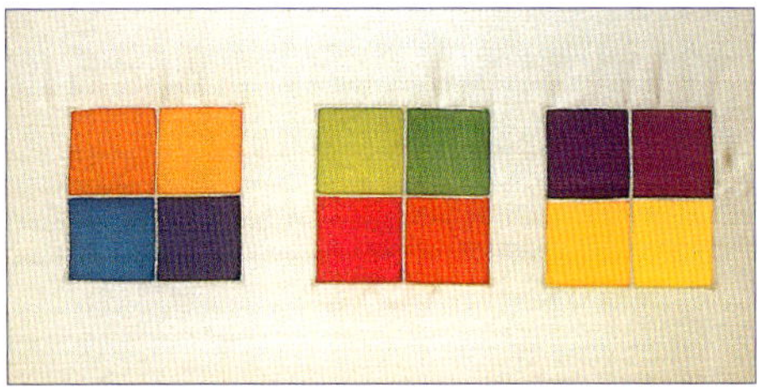

Warm and cool colours, mixed.

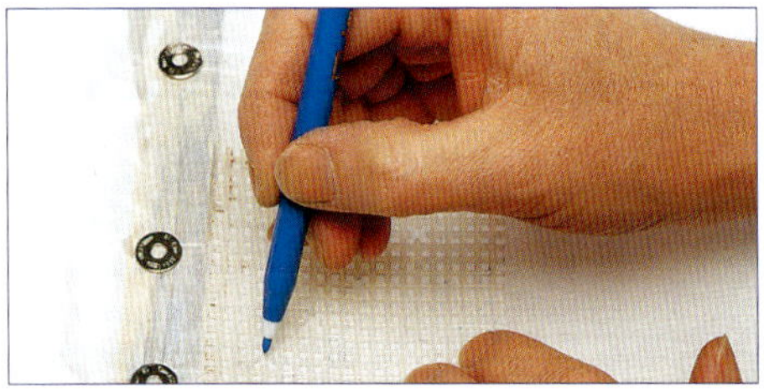

Marking out with plastic canvas & vanishing pen.

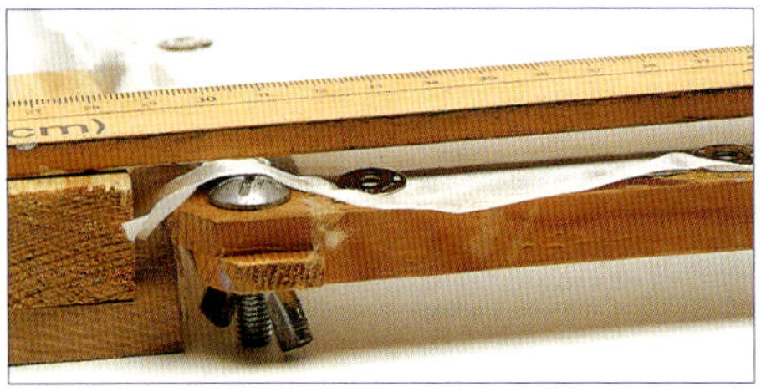

Bridge formed with wooden blocks to support the rule just above the silk.

This simple exercise can be worked purely as a sampler, or enlarged to create a lovely scarf that gently graduates from one colour to a lighter tint or darker tone creating an attractive abstract block pattern. It enables you to practise outlining and working with colour. Work this with either heat- or steam-fix dyes on a ¼ metre square of silk. Refer to the relevant sections for more informatin on any point.

1. Pin the silk on to the frame to give a taut, even surface.
2. Use a plastic canvas grid to help mark out the corner points and line spacing. Using clear outliner, carefully draw an outline around the edge of the silk to form a border. Remember to keep the end of the nozzle in contact with the silk, and to adjust the squeeze to control the outline.
3. Form a bridge with supports either side of the frame and a long metre rule. Run the edge of the nozzle along the edge of the rule to draw a series of straight lines equally distanced apart across the piece of silk. Remember to start and finish the outlines on the outside edge of the border line so that the start and stop blobs, if you have them, will not show when the work is completed.
4. Dry these horizontal lines and turn the frame 90°.
5. Repeat the outlining process, spacing the lines further apart to form an oblong block pattern. The intersecting lines can be drawn to form a brick wall pattern, set diagonally to form parallelograms or offset for a more irregular design.
6. Select one primary colour and place a measured quantity into three palette wells using a pipette dropper. Leave one well at full strength, dilute the second with an equal quantity of water, and dilute the third with three-quarters water to one-quarter of colour.
7. Mix a grey using two complementary colours, e.g. yellow and violet, and place this into a fourth palette well.
8. Select a paint brush and apply the colour in a random pattern sequence to one block at a time, working from the palest tint to the full strength colour. Always remember to dry your brush after each rinse to prevent further dilution of the colour as you work and blend the colours.
9. Repeat this process, but now work from the full strength colour to a darker tone by gradually adding a little grey as you work.
10. Continue to fill all the shapes, varying the shading from full strength colour to pale tints on some blocks and from full strength colour to darker tones on others.
11. Finally, use the complementary colour in some of the blocks to act as a highlight and add strength to the overall effect.
12. When the grid is completed allow the dyes to dry, and then fix the paints or dyes in the appropriate way. Please refer to pages 15–16 for information on the fixing process.
13. Once the work is fixed, wash the silk to remove the clear outliner, then iron it while it is still damp to restore the full sheen and movement of the silk.

Silk painting sampler

Having assembled the necessary equipment and materials, and practised mixing some colours you are ready to start your first silk painting project. This ¼ metre square sampler project uses a range of different techniques and allows you to discover the delights of silk painting while providing a good reference point for all your future pieces. It can be worked with either heat- or steam-fix colours.

This patchwork sampler is also a good way of working for a group activity with adults or children who each want to contribute a little something to the overall piece.

1. Pin the silk on to the frame to give a taut, even surface (see page 22).
2. Holding the outliner tube or applicator bottle in the correct way, draw a free-hand, double line around the edge of the silk to form a border, and then subdivide the working area into a selection of smaller shapes. They do not have to be equal in size or be a drawing of a particular shape, they just need to provide a selection of large and smaller enclosed shapes. Remember to consider using a selection of outline colours (see page 24 - drawing outlines).
3. Dry the outlines with a hairdryer.
4. Select a range of colours and place them into your palette with a pipette dropper.
5. Apply the colours with a brush of an appropriate size for the area to be filled remembering to allow the colour to spread across the silk (see page 28).
6. Try blending some colours together within a shape.
7. Try diluting some colours with water from a pure full strength colour to a lighter tint.
8. Apply spots of colour or small amounts of either alcohol or water to create further patterning on to damp coloured areas. Use a hairdryer to dry this patterning at the right time.
9. Mix a little thickener with some colour and apply this to your sampler. When dry add colour around the shape, allowing it to run up to the edge of the thickened pattern line (see page 27).
10. Apply colour to a shape and while the area is still damp sprinkle some salt effect crystals on to the wet surface. Work one shape at a time to ensure the silk does not dry too much before the salt is added (see page 34).
11. Select a slightly larger brush and apply the colour to the border area. Remember to apply paint to both leading edges of the colour, working alternatively from one side to the other so that one edge does not dry and form an unwanted watermark.
12. Dry the piece of completed work and fix in the appropriate way for the type of silk paint or dye used for this project. Please refer to pages 15–16 for details on the fixing process.

Drawing a free-hand border with a tube of outliner.

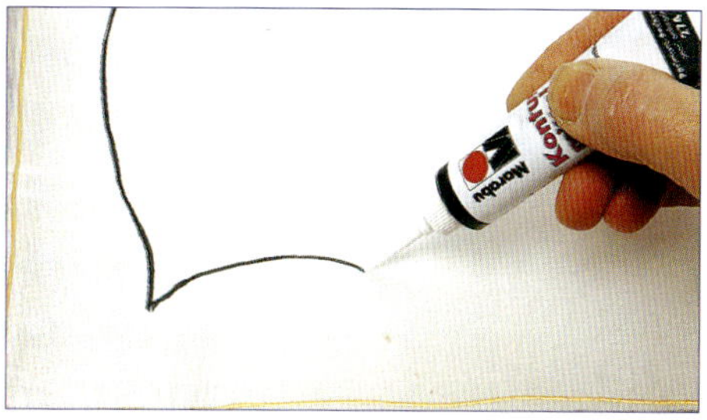

Applying the colour to the centre of the shape and allowing it to spread to the outline.

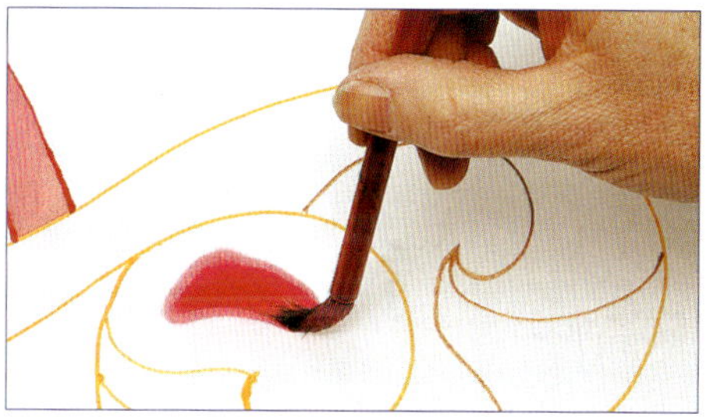

Applying spots of water on to damp silk to form patterns.

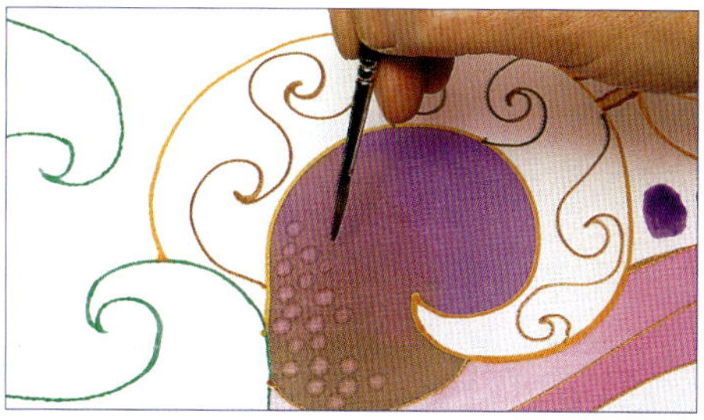

Brushing down coloured thickener to create further patterning.

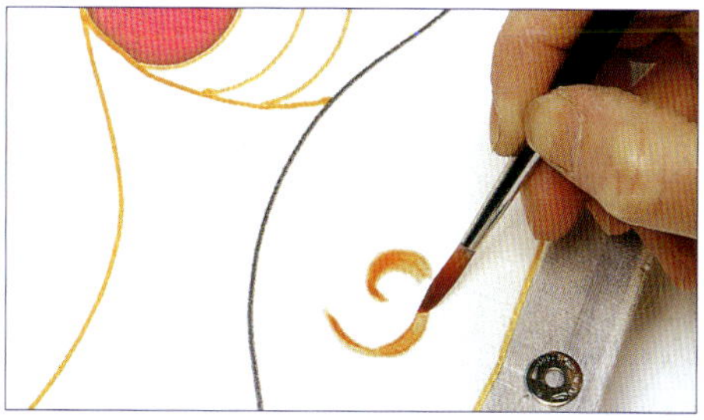

Planning a design

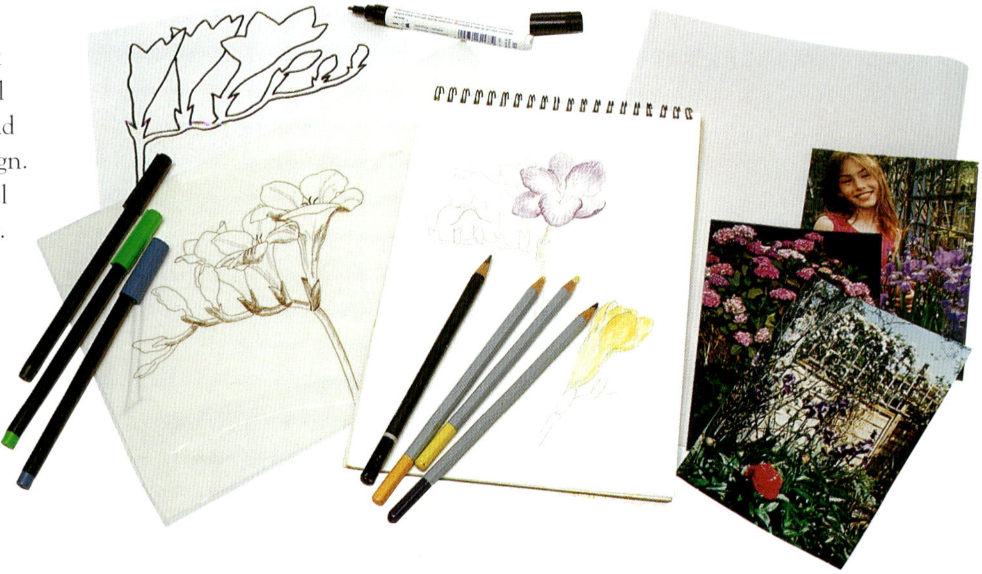

Use a variety of design source material to work up designs.

Creating an impressive piece of finished work does not just involve a high level of technical expertise in the execution of the outlining and application of dyes, it also involves good design. What makes a good design is partly a personal view, but considering certain factors can help. Borders and edges are particularly important on scarves, for example, as this is the area that will be most visible when the scarf is being worn. A border gives an opportunity to introduce another colour, possibly a complementary hue, a colour that you have already used in the piece, or a tone or shade of one of the colours already used. The border itself does not have to look like a frame mount, as it can be softened by allowing the design to spill out over or behind it. Consider using the actual pattern motifs to create a border by overlapping and placing the patterns at the edge of the work.

Achieving even colouring on large complicated background areas is often considered to be one of the most difficult facets of silk painting. Reduce the background or largest area by linking pattern shapes together to minimise the number of isolated shapes. Shapes can be joined by overlapping, making leaves or stalks touch, grouping shapes into clusters, or allowing shapes to touch the edge of the piece.

The placement of shapes is also important. Do not feel that a piece always has to have a mirror image or that you have to place an identical pattern in each corner to achieve balance. This is just one option; also consider rotating the design, working the same design at different sizes, repeating just part of the pattern, or leaving an area plain. The negative shapes and spaces have just as much importance to the design as the areas that have pattern detail or images. Achieving balance could involve using shapes or colours to create a harmony within the piece, a focal point or images that lead your eye around the whole design.

If you feel unsure about your drawing skills try using designs from pattern books, or look at nature for inspiration, experimenting with colour combinations and shapes that appeal to you. You do not need to copy these images exactly; change them slightly, or combine them with your own ideas and patterns. Try to develop your observational and drawing skills, and with practice your confidence and skills will improve.

The selection of projects featured in this book can be worked from the patterns supplied at the back of the book and by following the accompanying step by step instructions. Photocopy these designs to a size that will fit your piece of silk, and use some of these suggestions to personalise them.

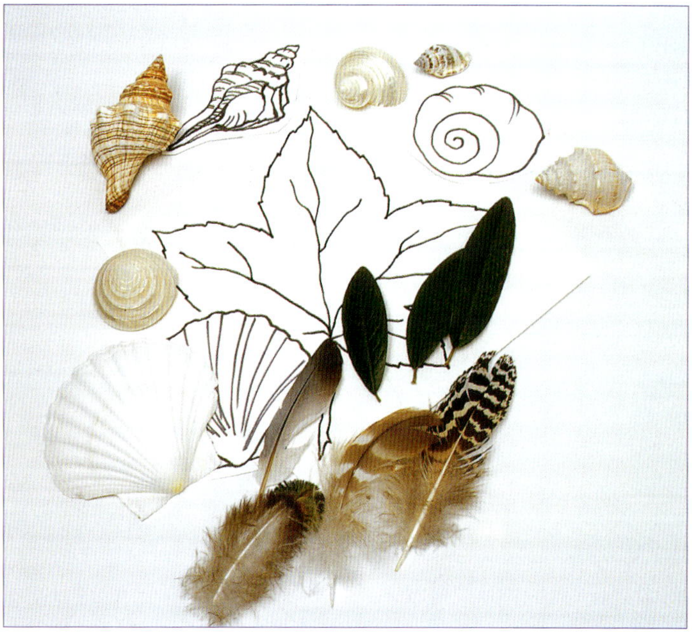

Shells, feathers and leaves provide interesting shapes.

Applying further surface decoration

Having completed a silk painting you may wish to add more embellishment or decoration, using some of the paints, decorative liners, and foils, not to mention charms, beads and sequins available to the textile artist. All of these are best applied to the projects featured in this book once the painting has been fixed and washed to allow a good bonding into the silk. Why not try adding some of these to enhance some of your projects

GLITTER LINERS

These are heat set and can be applied direct from the fine nozzle on the tube in the same way as a resist line. They appear slightly milky when initially applied, but give a glitter effect when dry. They work very effectively as a delicate highlight when applied lightly along the pattern lines of Arashi patterning to give a hint of sparkle, or used to add further interest to images formed on velvet with heat stamping.

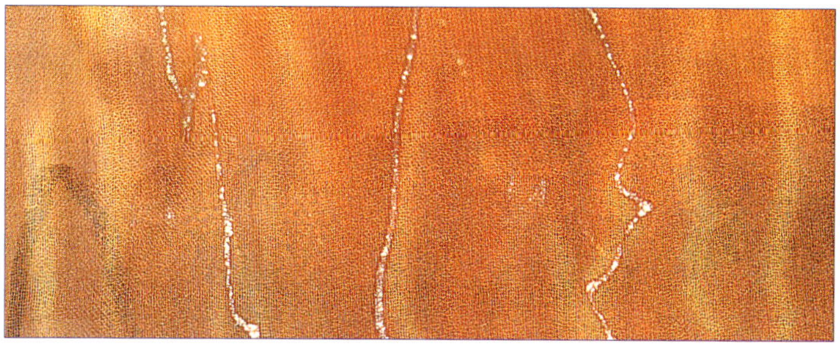

Glitter liner

PUFF LINERS AND PAINT MEDIUMS

These are applied in the same way as glitter liners, or can be brushed or sponged on. When dry they can be puffed up with dry heat from an iron, hairdryer or heat tool as appropriate. Puff liners or paint mediums can also be used to hold small beads or sequins on to the surface of the silk.

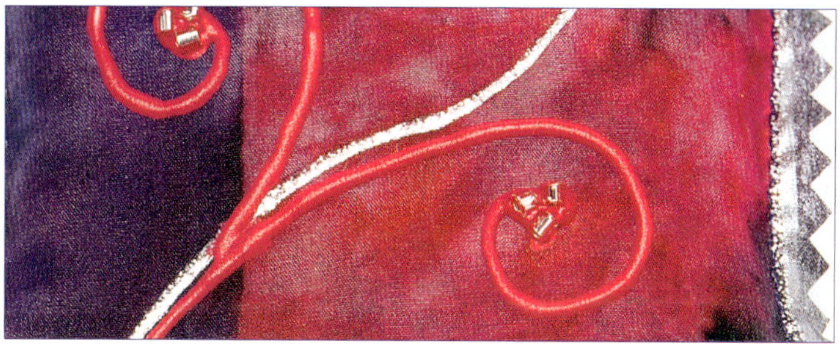

Puff liner

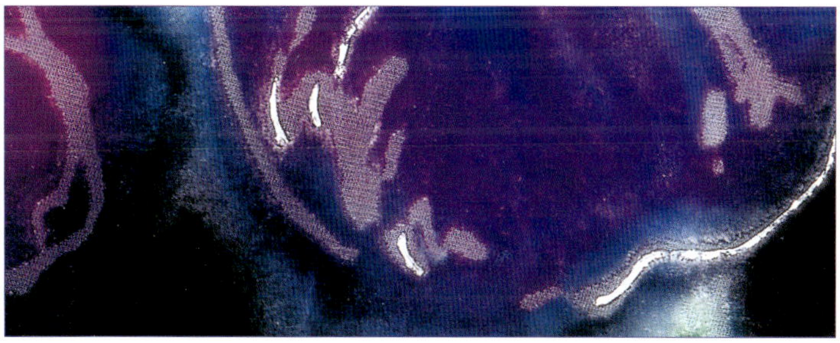

Foils on devoréed velvet

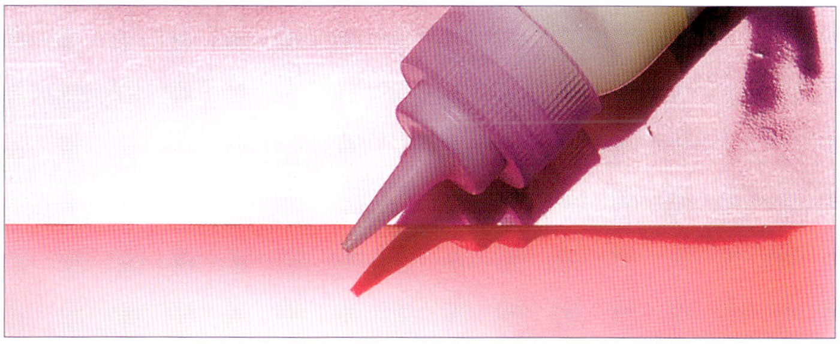

Selection of foils & plexi-glue

DECORATIVE FOILS

Available in a wide range of colours, these give a wonderful metallic finish that works particularly well as a linear highlighter on velvet, but is also effective on many other surfaces. Cellophane foils are bonded to the silk with glue or bondaweb, and give a flexible, washable finish. Special glue, either a plexi-glue or appli-glue, is first drawn on to the silk in a line from an applicator bottle. Initially, the glue appears milky, but it becomes transparent as it dries. When the glue is transparent, lay a piece of foil, colour side uppermost, on top of the glue line and press lightly with a finger to transfer the foil down on to the glue. These foils can also be applied with bondaweb for larger patches of foiling. Iron the bondaweb on to the fabric, then use the warm iron flat or the edge of the iron to transfer the foils on to the bondaweb area with a pressing action.

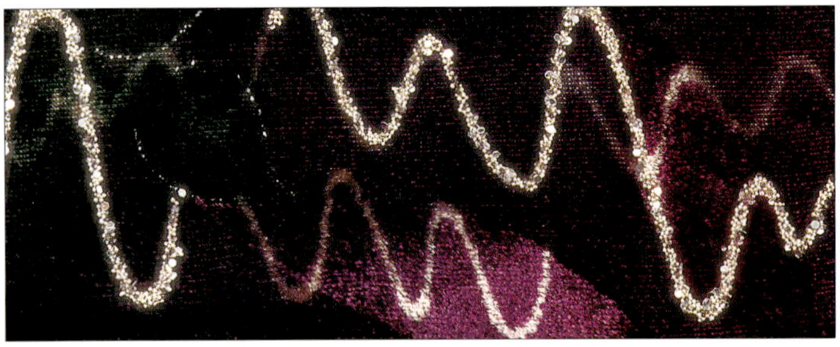

Granular beads

Granular beads

These tiny beads can be sprinkled on to wet plexi- or appli-glue and allowed to dry to give a beautiful textured finish. Any loose beads can be shaken off the fabric and returned to the pot for later use. This is more suitable for a decorative effect or on items that will only require occasional hand washing.

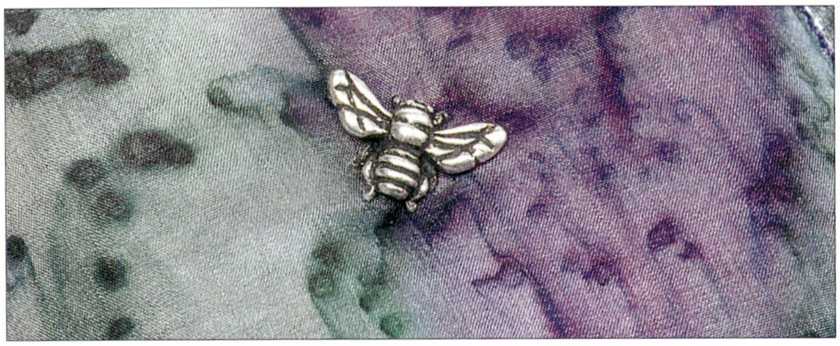

Charm 'bee'

Beads, charms, shisha mirrors and sequins

There is now a wonderful selection of these small attachments, which can add detail to the designs or along the edges or corners of work. They can be stuck with puff mediums or easily sewn on to the silk with either a fine silk or polyester thread.

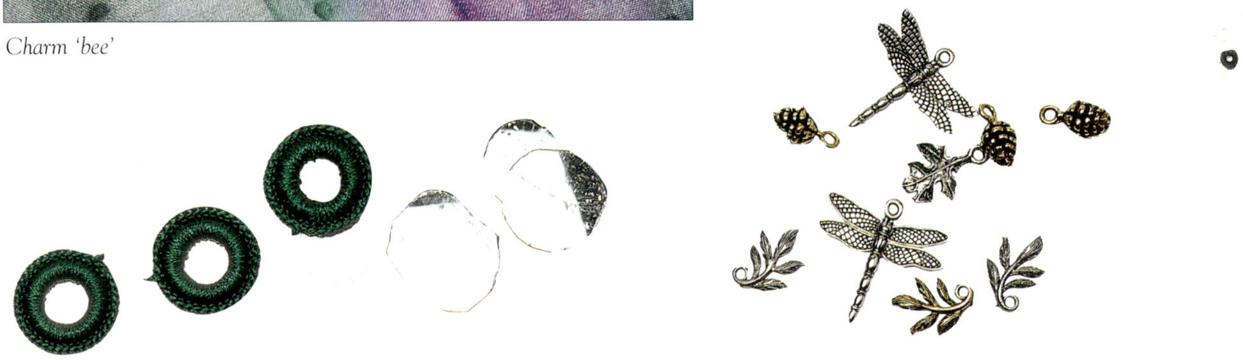

Charms, sequins, shisha mirrors

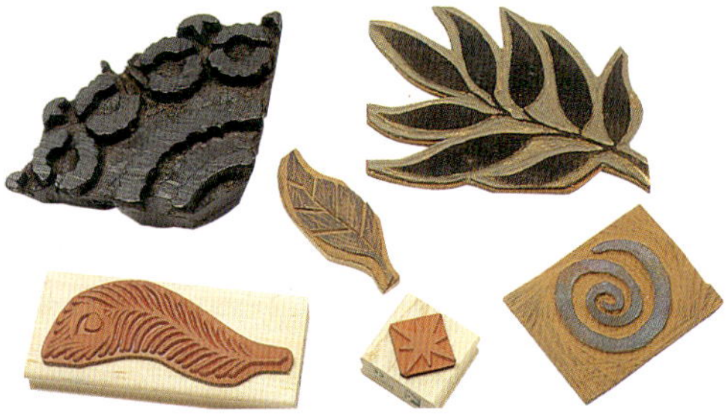

Hot stamping blocks

Hot stamping on piled fabrics

It is possible to produce some stunning effects in piled fabrics using rubber stamps or lino blocks to press the pile down and create a relief pattern in the fabric. Take a commercially available stamping block like the hot potato range, or make your own stamp by cutting a design into a piece of printing lino with lino cutting tools. Lay the block down, pattern side uppermost, and position the silk velvet pile-side down on to the block. Spray a little water on to the back of the velvet and place a flat iron down on to the backing of the velvet. (Steam irons may create hole marks from the underside of the iron sole plate on the fabric, so are not suitable.) Hold in place for 15 seconds, then remove the iron and check the pattern impression. The use of water helps to protect the fabric while it is being heated, and creates some steam which helps to form the impression. Patterns worked with this method provide a decorative effect that will not withstand washing, as the pile will revert back to its original position.

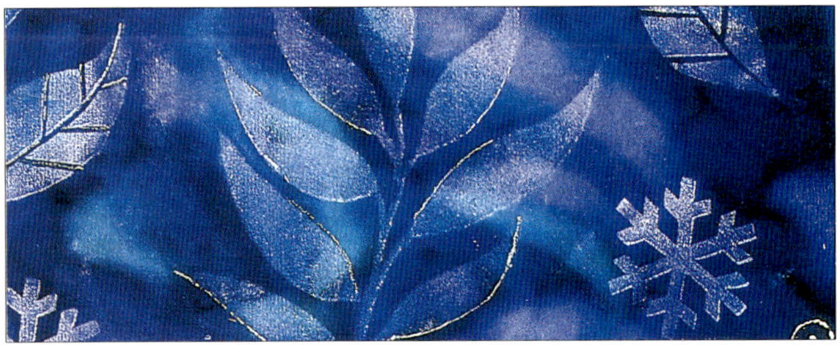

Hot stamping - sampler

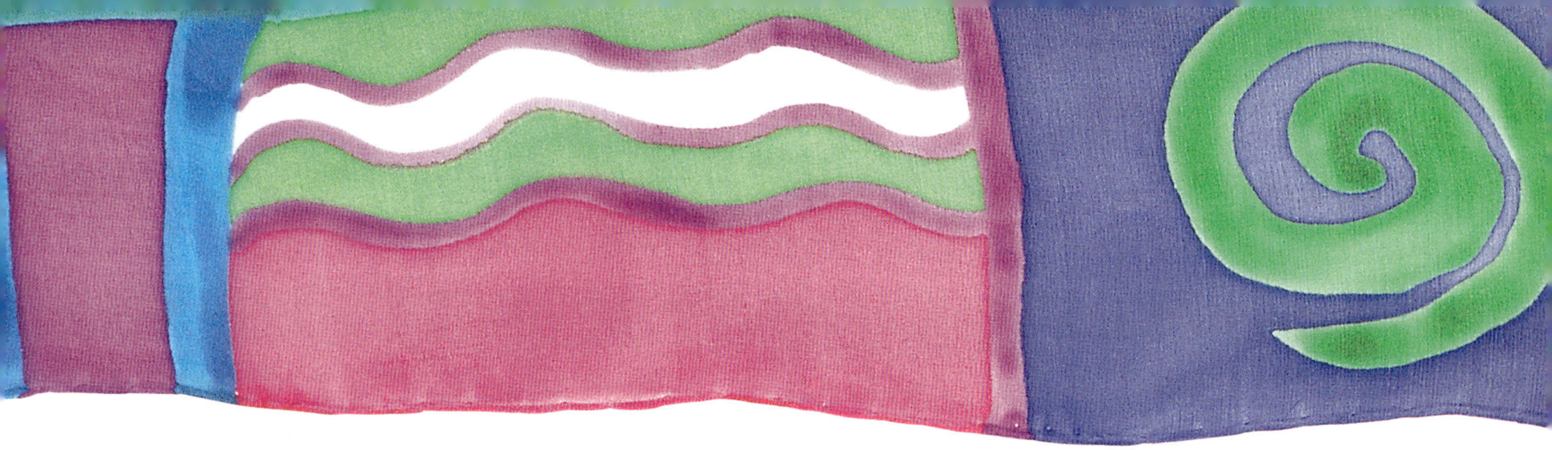

Silk Painting Projects

These projects cover a range of skill levels, using a selection of silk painting techniques, paints and dyes. The most simple projects are at the beginning and they progress to more challenging works, allowing you to develop your silk painting skills. It is usually possible to substitute a different dye from the one featured in the project if you wish, but remember to take into account any changes needed, particularly in the fixing process.

The step-by-step instructions provide the sequence of working, but if you need further information or clarification refer to the earlier chapters which describe the materials and techniques in detail.

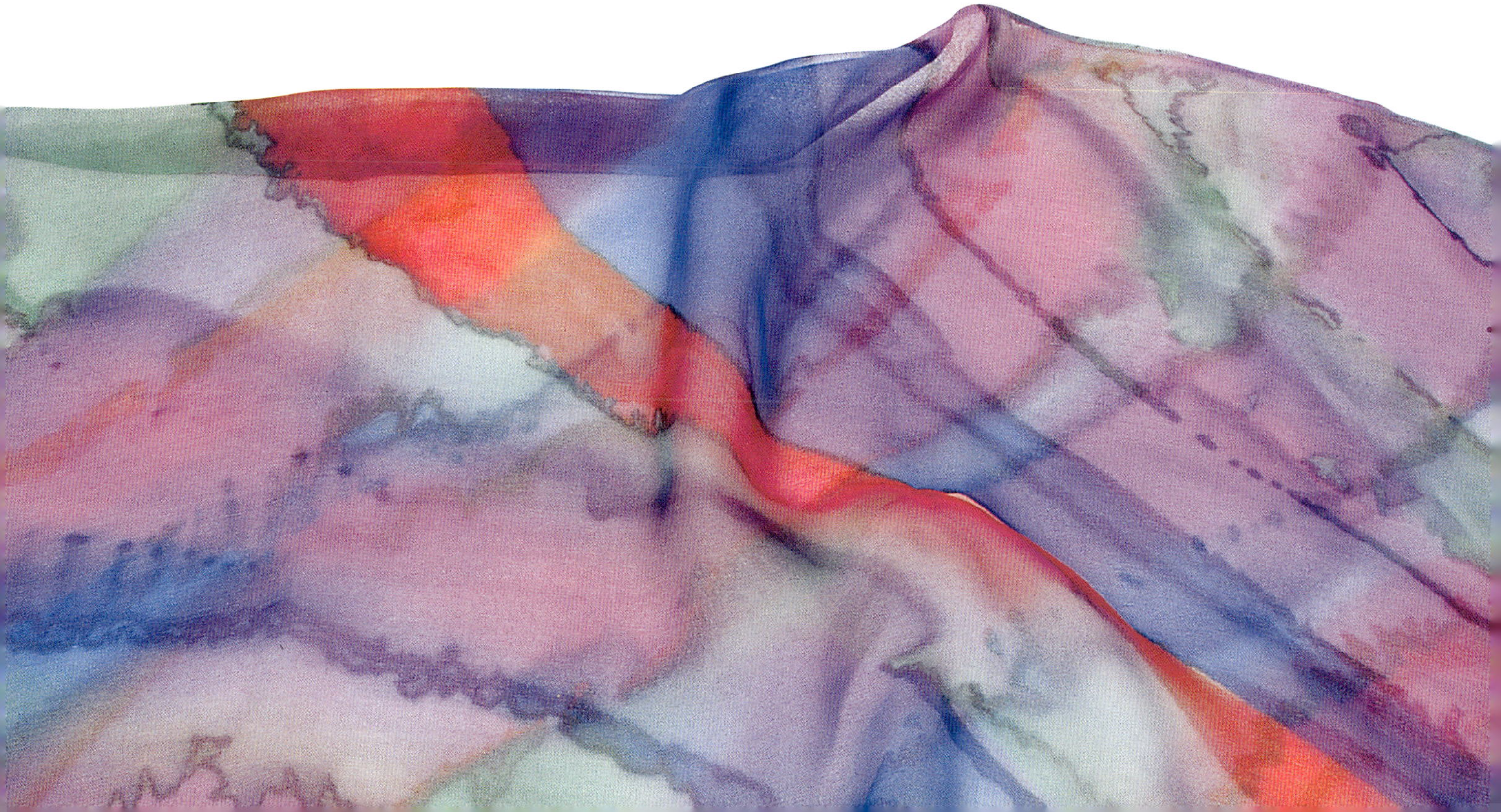

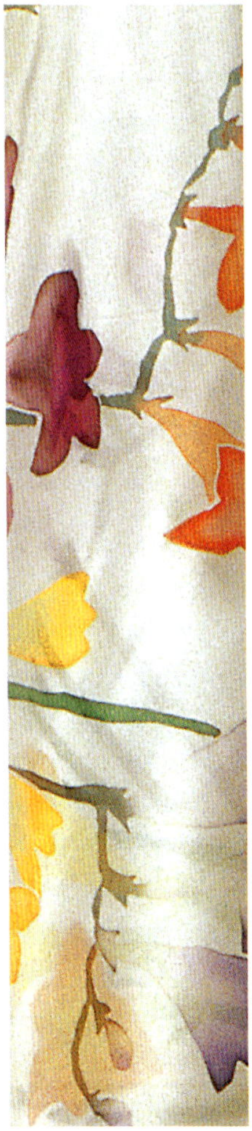

Freesia scarf

This is a lovely project that can be painted successfully and with confidence by novices. The outlining is completely worked with a clear resist and the background is left unpainted. This ensures that any thick outlines or blobs accidentally formed as the lines are drawn do not show in the completed piece. Painting the freesias provides good practice at mixing and applying tints, and gives the completed piece a delicate and realistic feeling that will inspire you to continue.

Equipment and materials

- Ready edged pongee or habotai scarf or piece of silk
- Heat-fix dyes
- Clear heat-fix outliner
- Frame and silk pins
- Paint brushes
- Mixing palette and water pot
- Kitchen paper
- Iron for setting the paints
- Template p102

Tip: Remember to hold the tube at about 45° and keep the nozzle tip in contact with the silk while applying very light pressure to control the flow of the outliner.

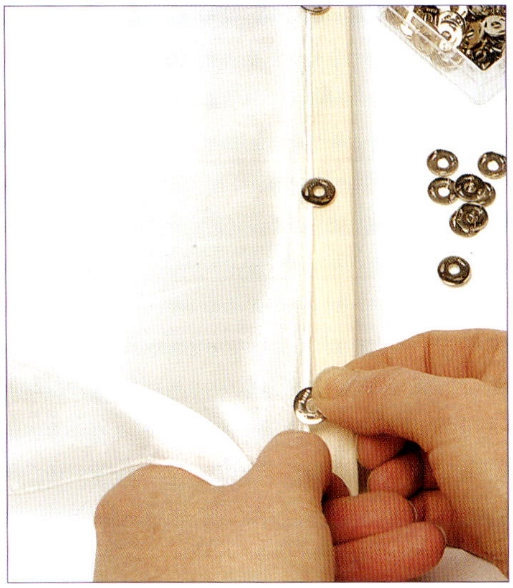

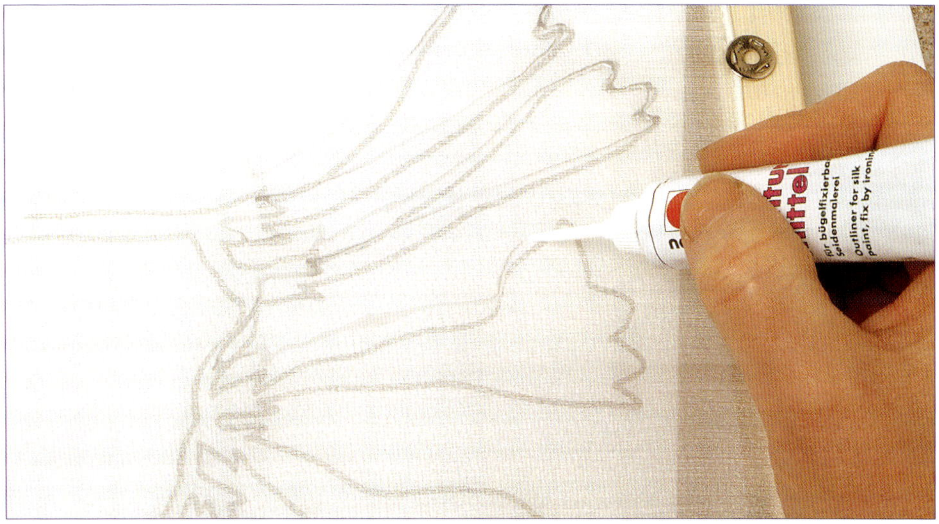

1. Assemble the frame to fit the piece of silk, and fasten the fabric to the frame with silk pins.

2. Place a selection of the photocopied patterns under the silk, moving them around until you create a pleasing arrangement. Try overlapping, grouping or fanning out the shapes to fit the piece of silk. Look through the silk to follow the patterns and trace out all the freesias on to the silk using the clear outliner. Only use light pressure to squeeze the tube and keep a piece of kitchen paper handy to wipe the nozzle tip.

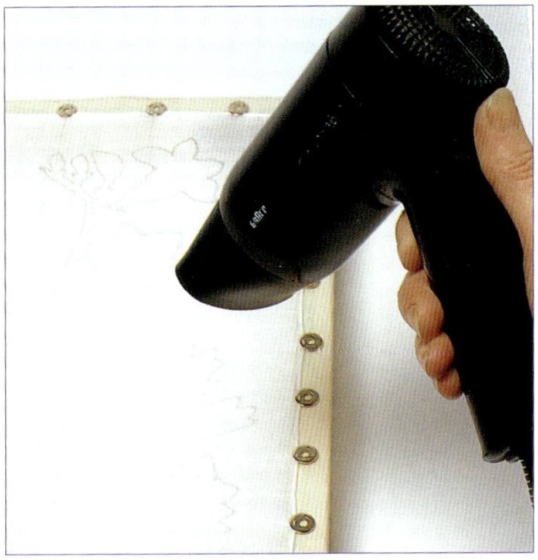

3. Use a hairdryer to dry the outliner. Remove all the photocopied patterns from under the work frame.

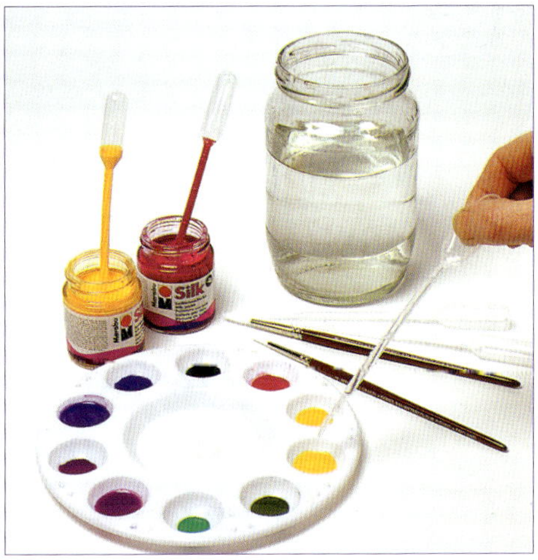

4. Using pipettes, select a range of colours, and prepare a few tints by diluting some of the colours with water.

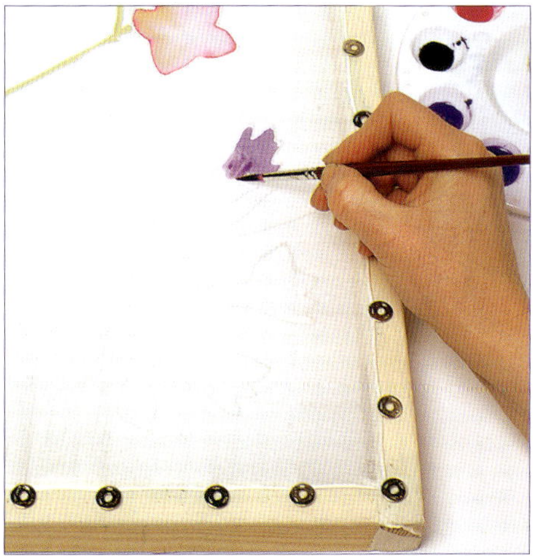

5. Use a brush to apply the colour, allowing the paint to run to the outline. While the colour is still damp add a little water to push the colour to the outline to give halo shading, or blend a lighter tint with the deeper colour to give blended shading.

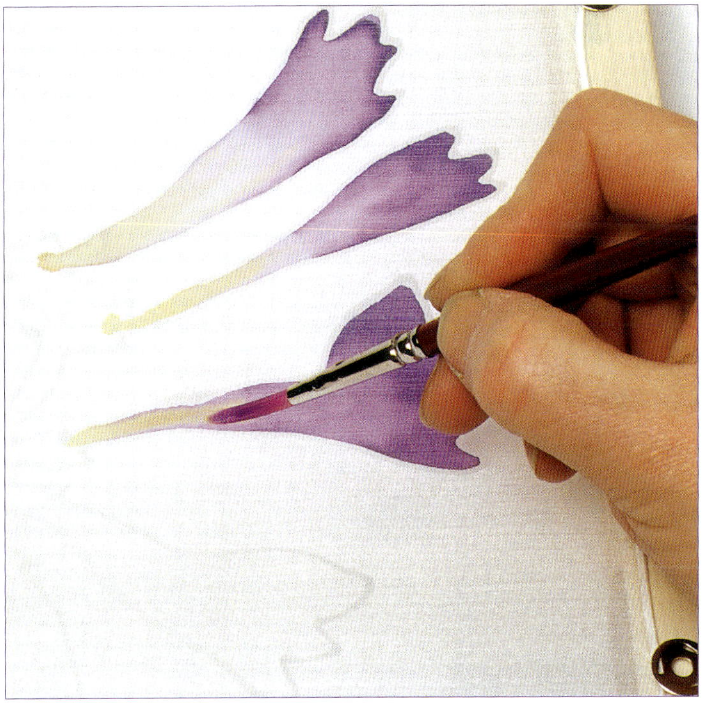

6. Continue painting-in all the flowers, one stem at a time, then add a little green for the stalks.

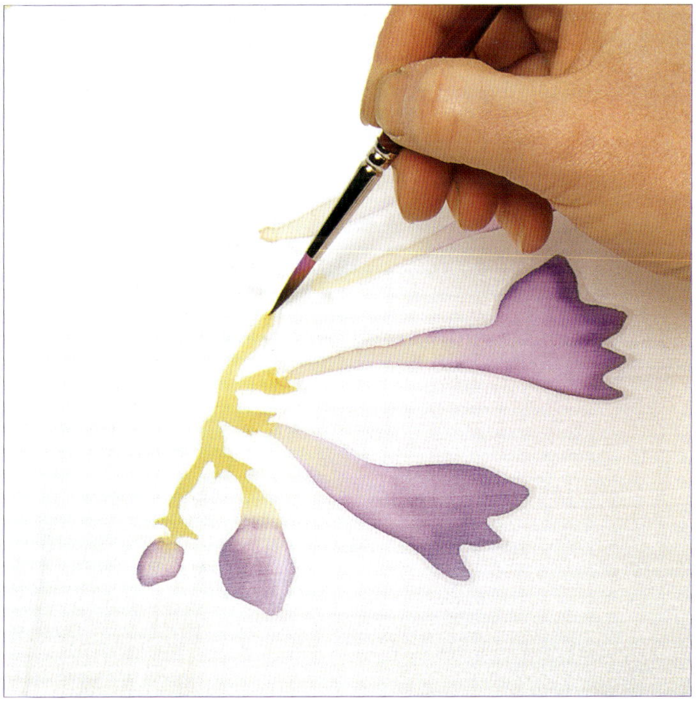

7. Use a fine brush and remember to allow for the spread of the paint, to ensure that the green does not run into the flower heads too much. Remember not to paint in any of the background.

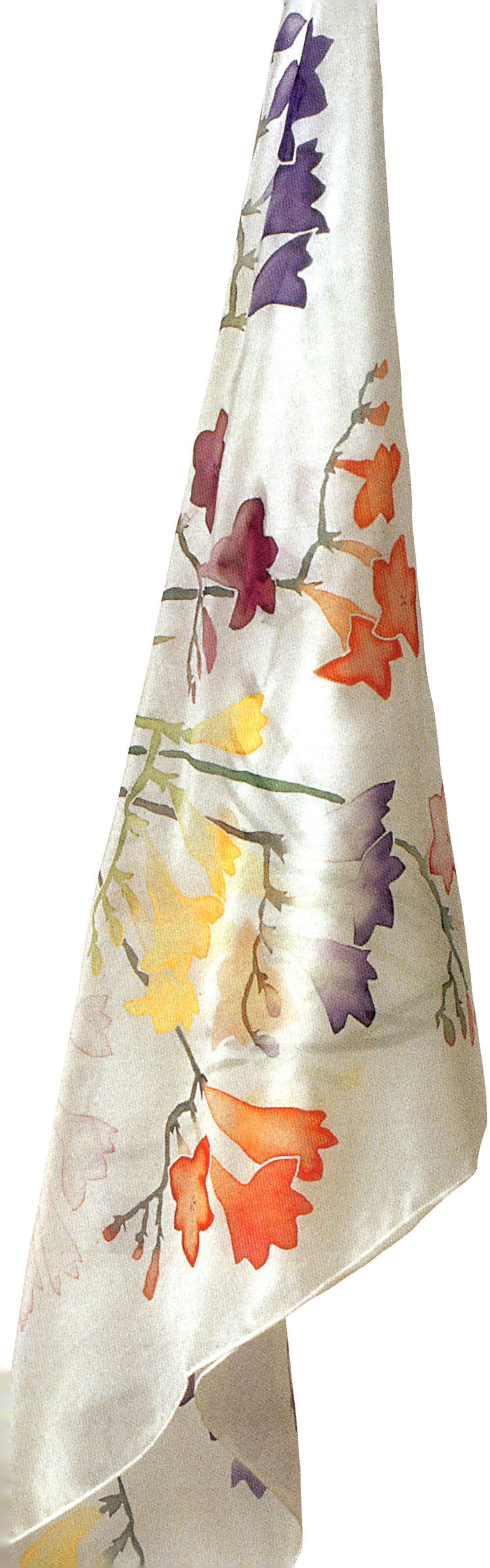

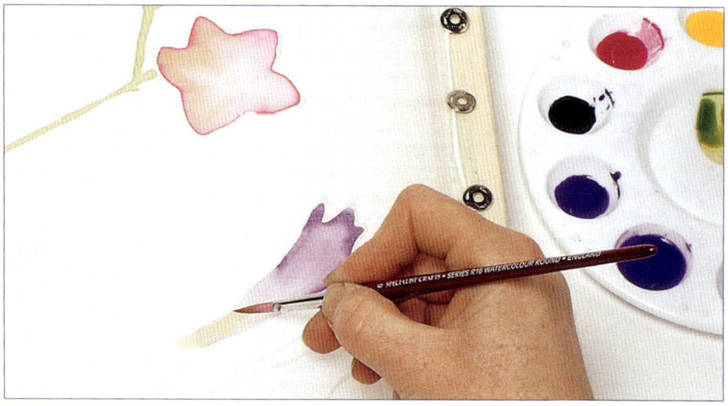

8. Create natural shading with tints.

9. Create halo shading using water.

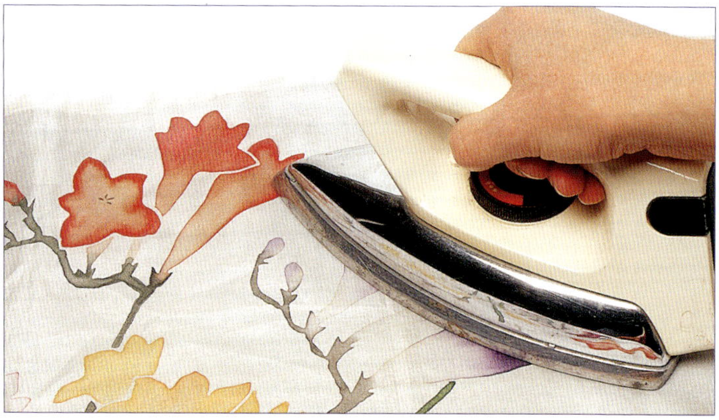

10. When the painting is complete, allow the work to dry. Before unpinning the work, check that the table underneath the frame is clean and that there are no drops of paint. Fix the work with an iron on wool setting, ironing on the reverse side of the silk for about three minutes across the whole piece, or fix in the appropriate way if other paints are used. Wash the fixed piece in warm water with a little liquid detergent to remove the clear outliner. Re-iron the silk while it is still damp to bring out the full sheen of the silk and give a beautiful finish to your completed scarf.

Silk painted cards

Equipment and materials

- Heat-fix paints
- Frame and silk pins
- Piece of silk
- Water pot and mixing palette
- Selection of brushes
- Pattern motifs
- Iron to set the colours
- For mounting:
- Window aperture cards or quality cartridge paper
- Craft knife
- Sharp scissors
- Stick adhesive
- Double-sided tape
- Wadding for padded cards
- Silk outliner or metallic pen
- Template p103

Cards are a lovely way of developing skills as they can incorporate many techniques on a smaller scale which makes everything less daunting. Heat-fix paints are the ideal choice for cards because they are so easy to fix. The patterns featured at the back of the book can be used to make a selection of greetings and occasion cards, and there are suggestions for mounting to provide a variety of ways of presenting the finished work.

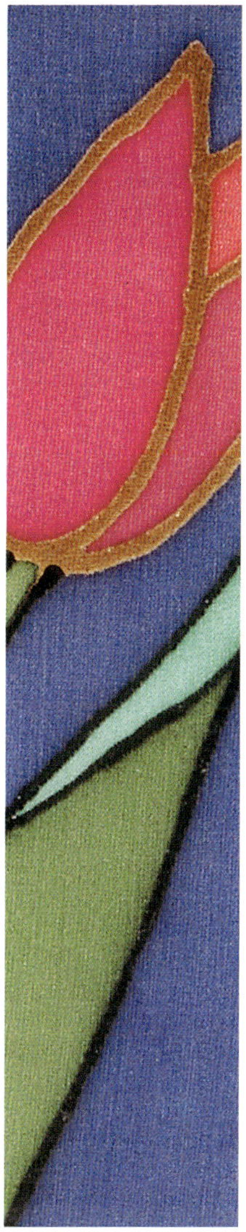

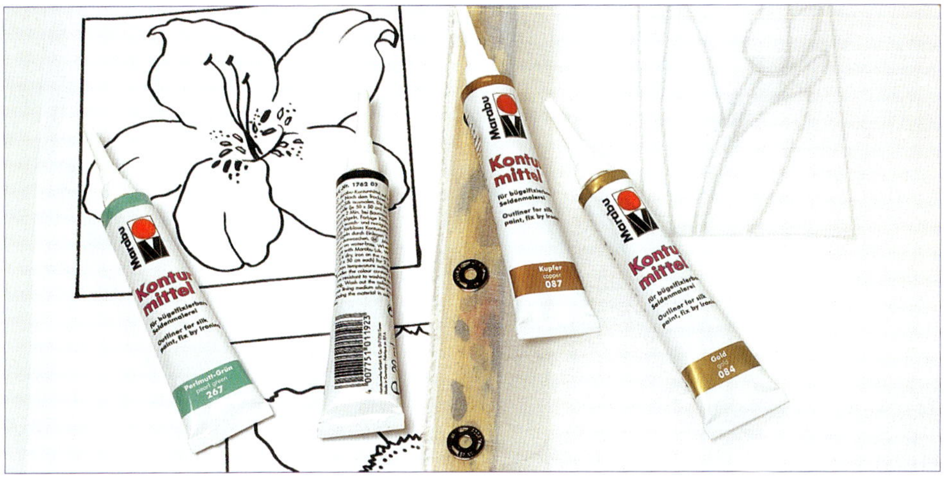

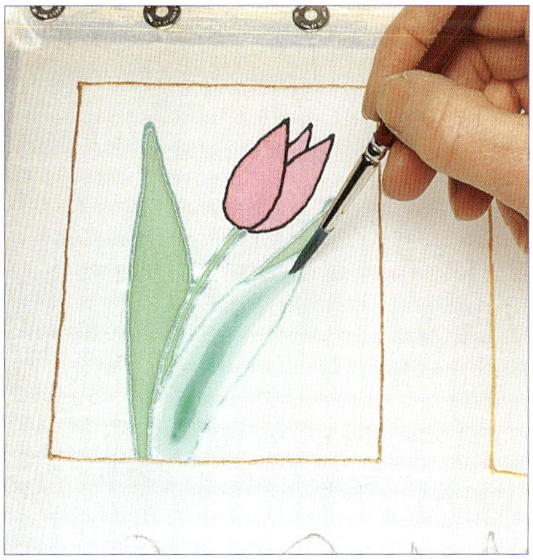

1. Assemble the frame, pin out the silk, and place the selected pattern under the work as described in the freesia project. When working cards it can be helpful to divide the area of silk into boxes using the outliner, to allow several cards to be worked from the one piece of silk. This prevents the colours from one card running into another card design which is being worked alongside.

2. Draw out the outlines in a selection of outliner colours. Allow them to dry and remove the pattern sheets before starting to paint in the flower.

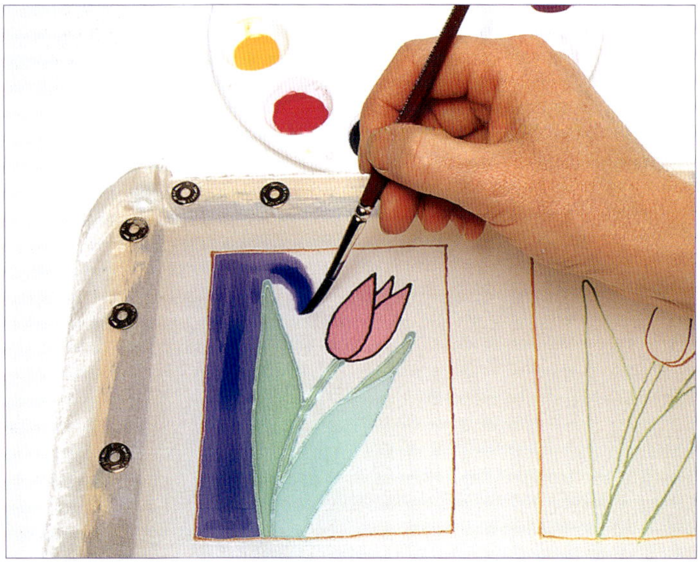

3. When the flower has been completed, paint in the background. Start at one corner and work across to the opposite side.

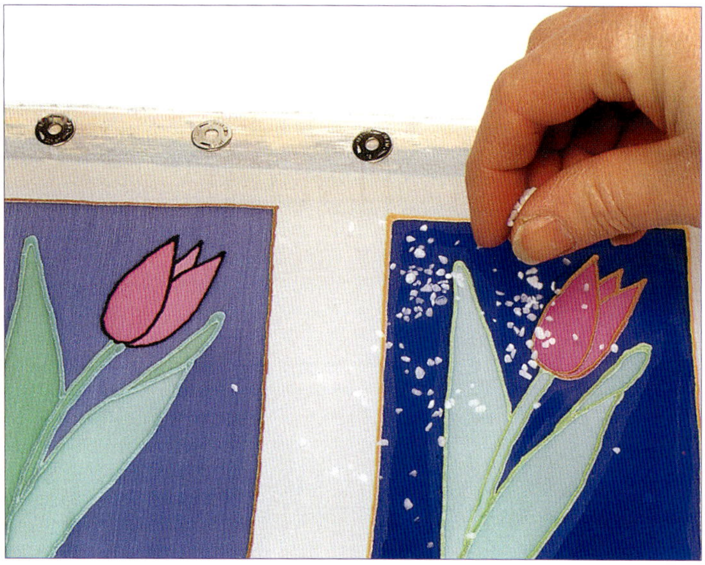

4. Lightly sprinkle salt crystals on to the wet silk paint if you want to create texture patterns.

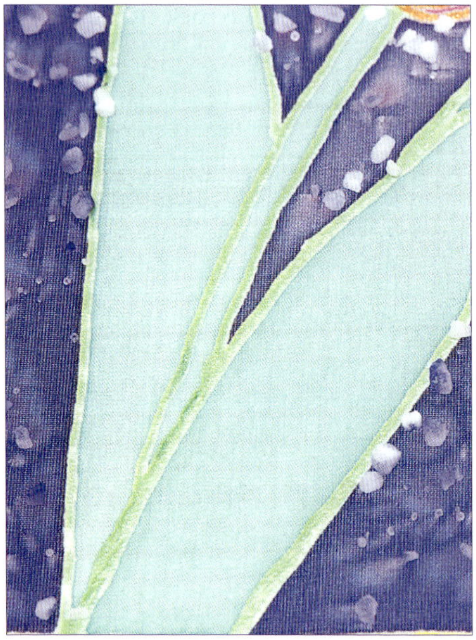

5. Leave the work to dry naturally to allow the salt patterns to form.

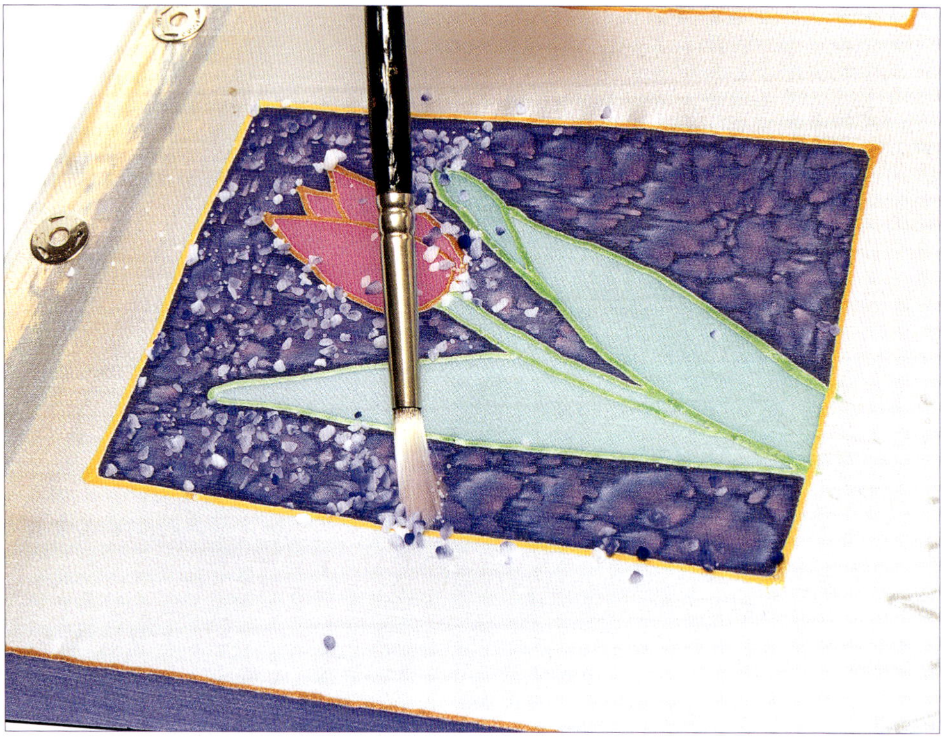

6. Brush off the salt crystals, iron the work on the reverse side to fix the designs, then wash and re-iron while damp to restore a smooth, flat finish ready for mounting.

Surface mounting

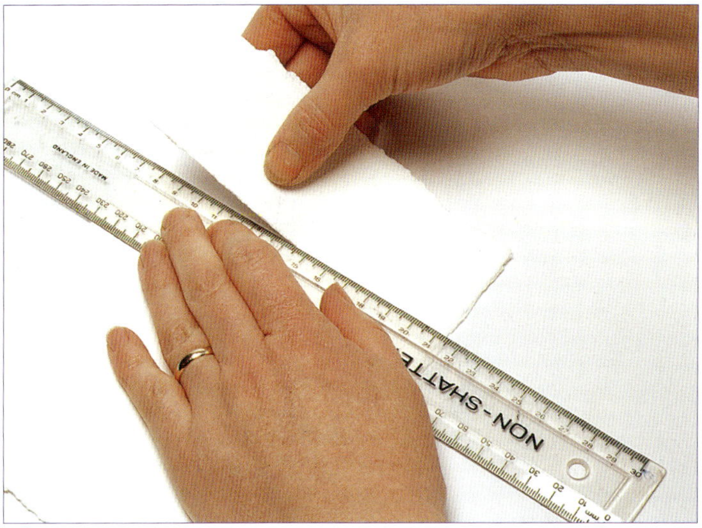

1. Take a good-quality ready-folded greetings card or a piece of heavyweight cartridge or watercolour paper and cut or tear it carefully into a rectangle of your chosen size. Fold the rectangle in half, pressing along the folded edge to form a folded card. Tearing the edges gives a more interesting edge, but they can be cut with a craft knife if a smooth edge is preferred.

2. A silk design that is to be surface-mounted can be trimmed ready for mounting on to the card front in the following ways to give a variety of finished edge effects:

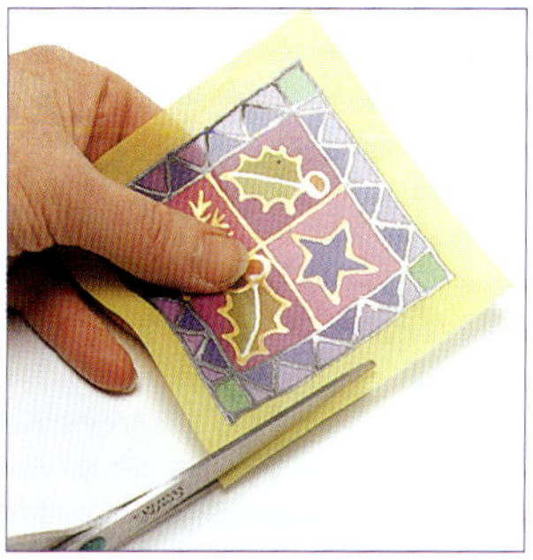

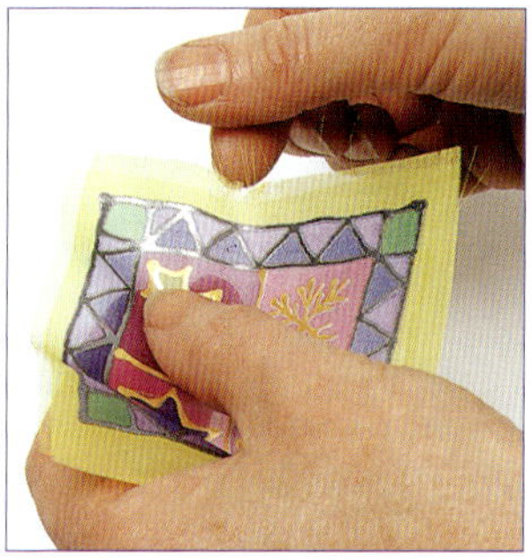

- If the design has an outline around the edge the silk can be cut along this line giving a neat no-fray edge.
- The silk can be trimmed just inside an outlined edge and then carefully frayed back for about $^{1}/_{2}$ cm ($^{1}/_{4}$ in.) to give a fringe effect along each of the edges.
- The silk can be trimmed just outside the outlined edge and then carefully frayed back to the outliner edge, which will prevent any further fraying.

Tip: TIP: Make sure your card will fit into a standard envelope.

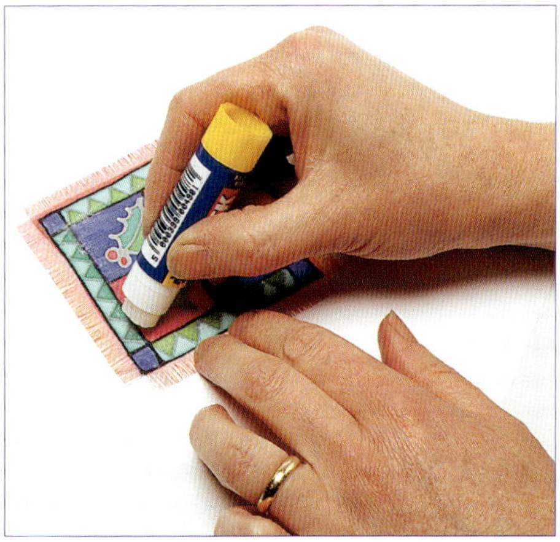

3. Apply a small amount of stick adhesive on the wrong side of the piece of silk, cut to size in one of the above ways. Take special care not to get any glue on the fringe or front of the design.

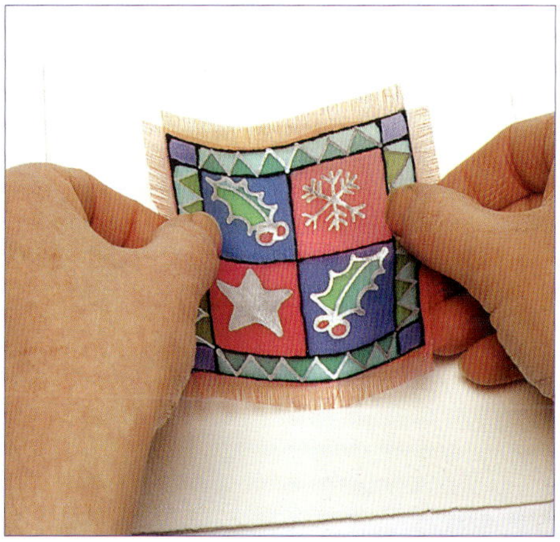

4. Position the silk over the card front, then carefully lower into position and secure by pressing firmly across the surface.

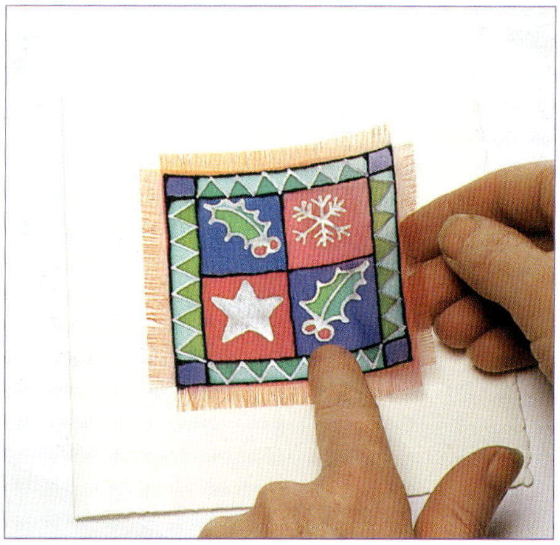

5. Allow to dry, before adding any further detailing or wording with the heat-fix outliners or a metallic pen.

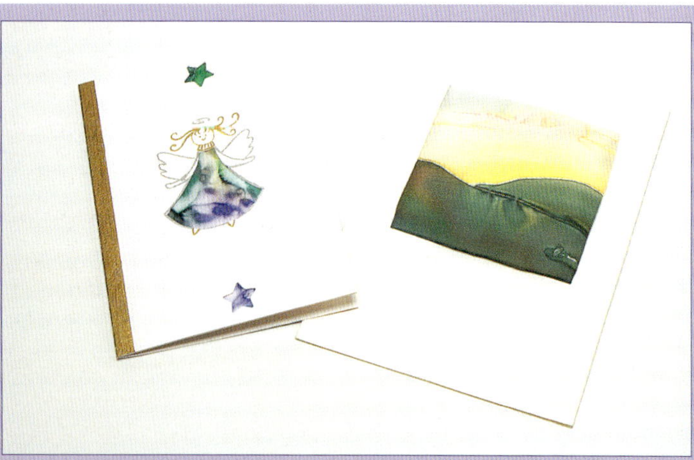

Variations: Surface-mounting techniques can be applied to other shapes beside the basic square and rectangle. Any shapes with a heat-fix outliner edge can be cut out along the outliner edge, which seals the edge and prevents further fraying.

The no-fray edging technique can also be scaled up and used to finish a scarf or sarong without the need for any sewing. It can be effective to add a little wadding to pad out your finished design. Follow the steps for window aperture cards, but add a little extra allowance when cutting out the silk to accommodate the wadding. Cut the wadding the same size as the window and place it behind the silk to pad out the design when the card flap is stuck into position.

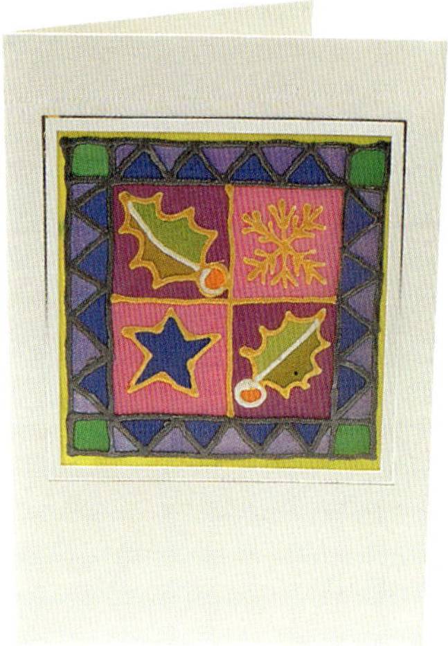

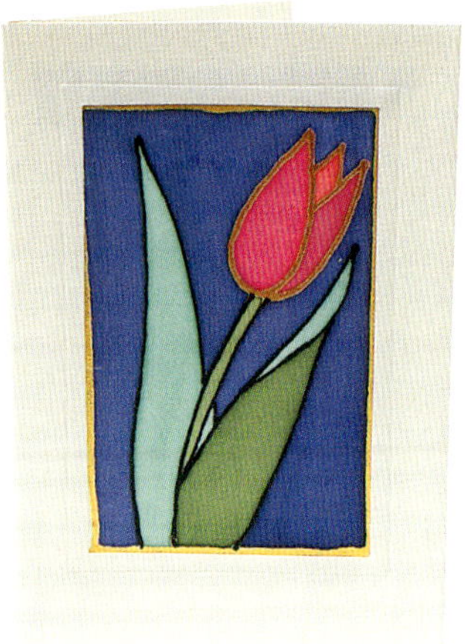

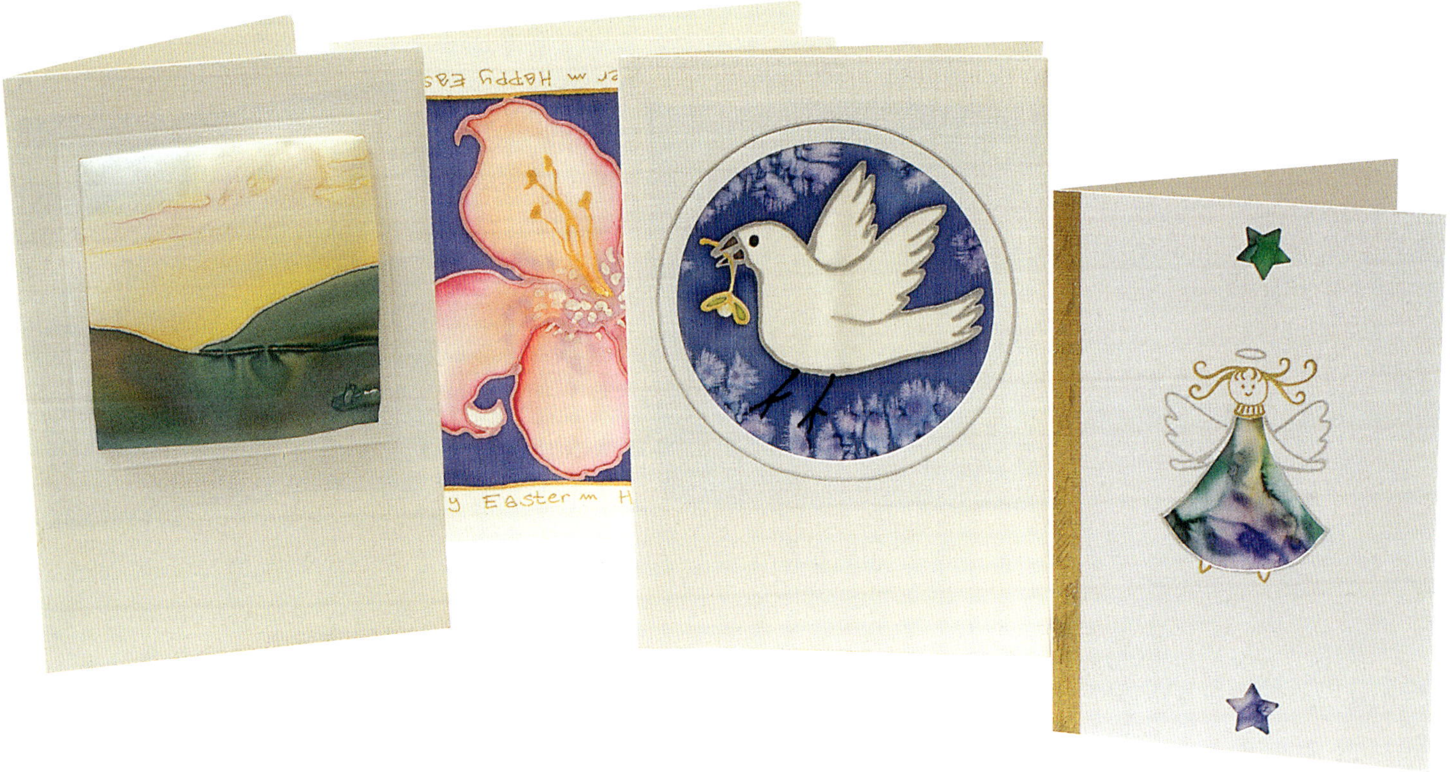

Silk beaded necklace

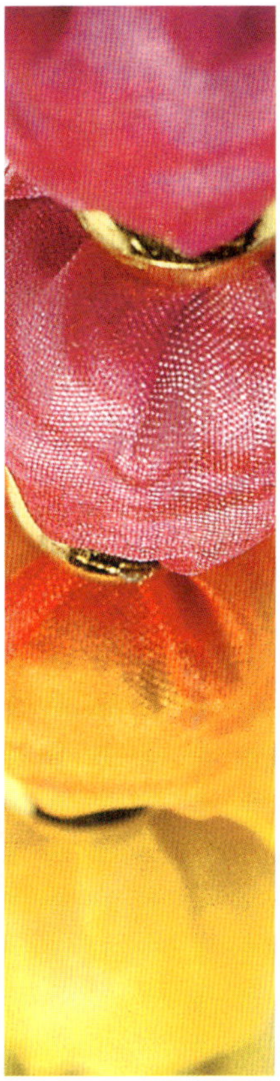

Equipment and materials

Piece of silk
Frame and silk pins
Heat-fix dyes
Large paint brushes
Water pot
Salt effect crystals
Iron for heat-fixing the paints
Pressed cotton fibre beads
Pony beads
Sewing equipment

This very simple but effective way of making a necklace can be worked in any colour combination to make jewellery suitable for any occasion. The simplicity of the project and the use of salt to create the beautiful textural patterns lends itself to working with children, or as a clever way of using up small strips of silk or samplers.

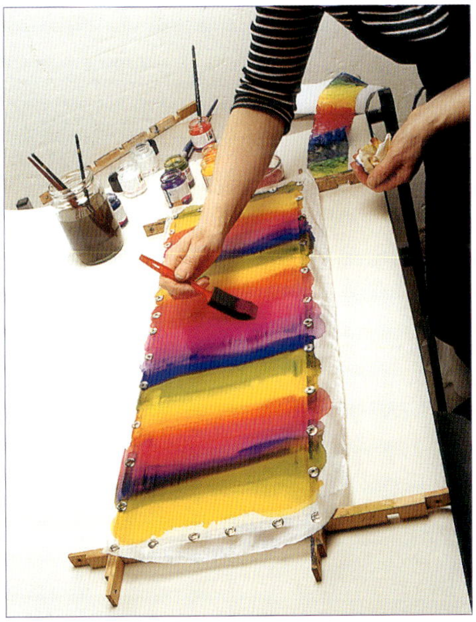

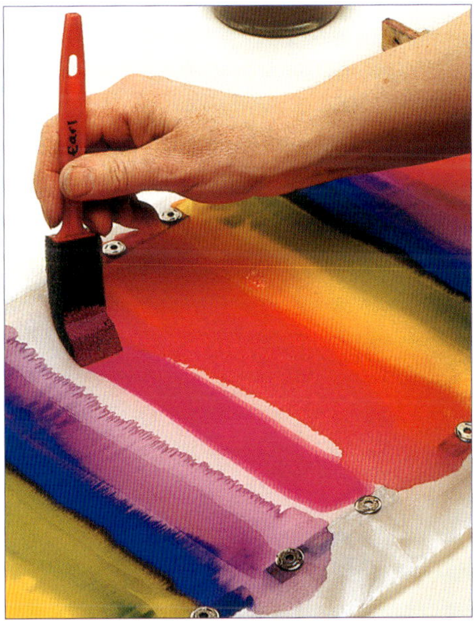

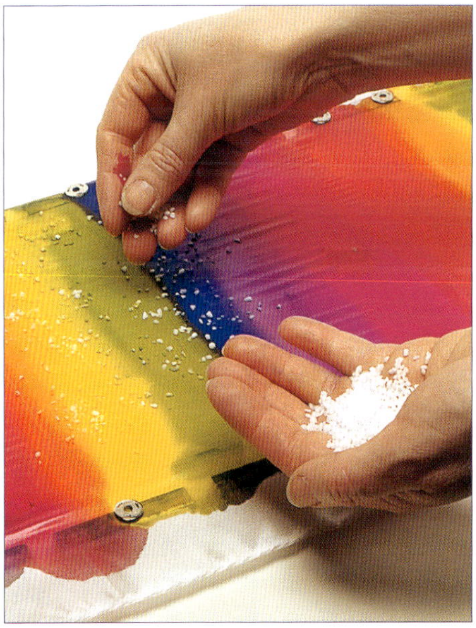

1. Assemble the frame to fit a piece of silk, approximately 75 cm long (30 in.), and fasten the fabric to the frame with silk pins. Select a range of colours and place them in the mixing palette. Use a large Chinese brush or sponge brush to apply the colour in stripes across the silk.

2. Space the stripes so that they just overlap as they spread out. Work quite freely to ensure the whole piece has plenty of colour to prevent quick drying.

3. Check that the silk is still wet before sprinkling salt crystals over the whole piece. To ensure maximum patterning, do not overcrowd the salt.

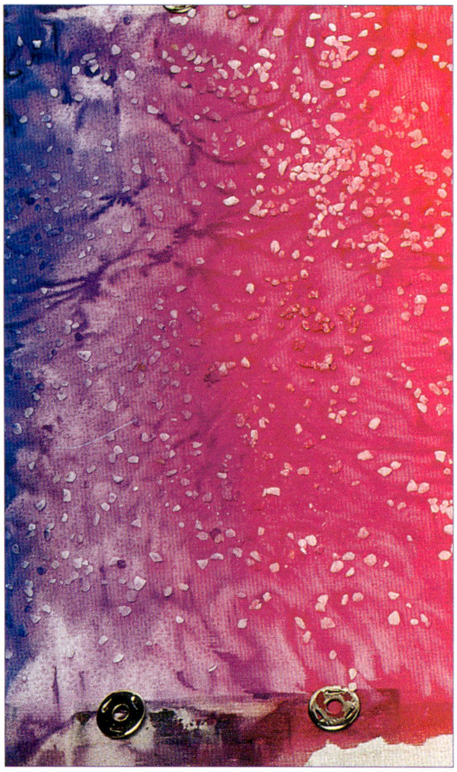

4. Allow the work to dry naturally, then brush off all the salt crystals and unpin the silk from the frame.

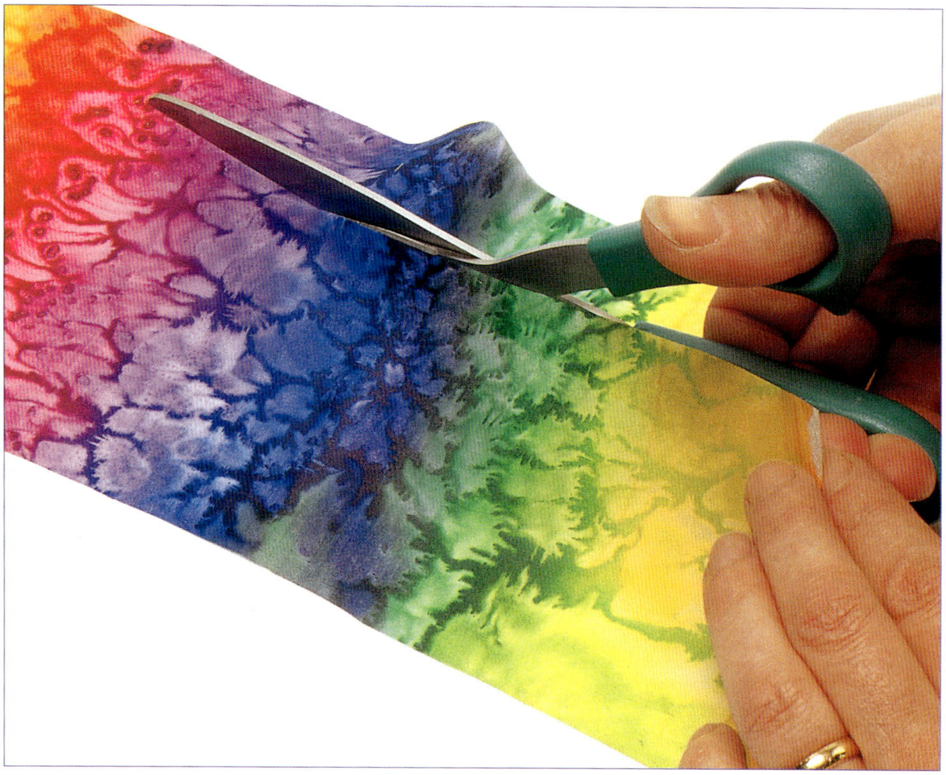

5. Use an iron to set the colours. Wash the silk in warm water to remove any excess colour and salt deposits. Allow to dry and re-iron. Cut the silk into a strip about 70 cm (28 in.) long. The width is determined by the size of the cotton fibre beads. Measure the circumference of the bead and add a little extra for a seam allowance.

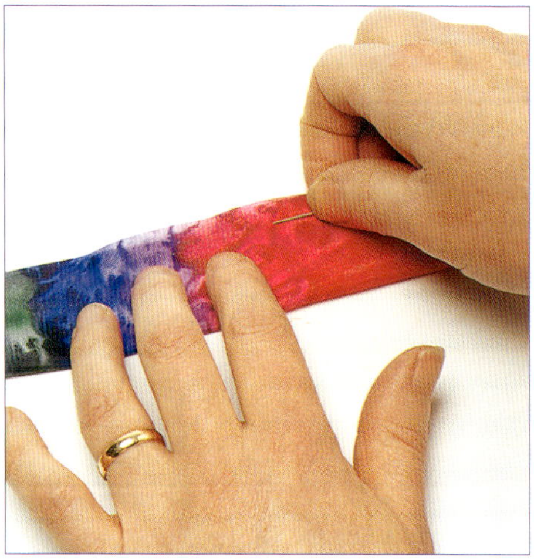

6. Fold the strip into half lengthways. Pin and tack along the long edge, before sewing it up, but leave both ends open.

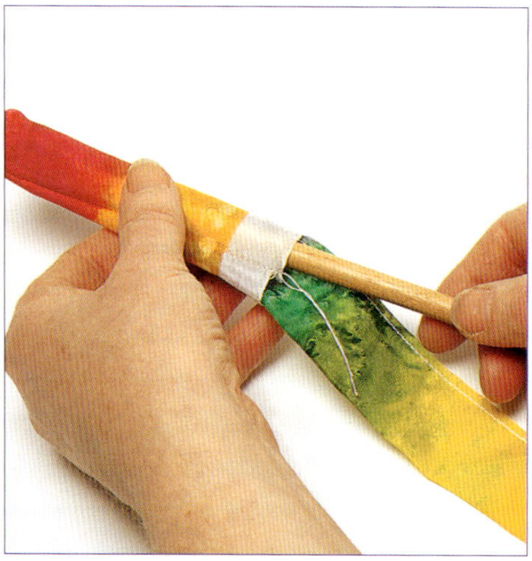

7. Turn the tube inside out. You might find a knitting needle helps.

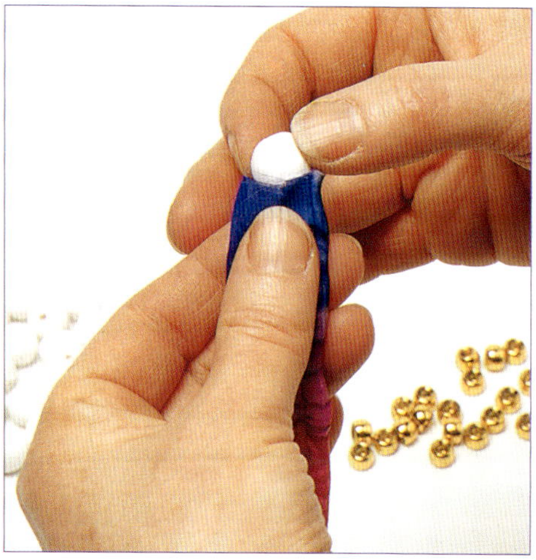

8. Take one of the cotton fibre beads and insert it down the tube.

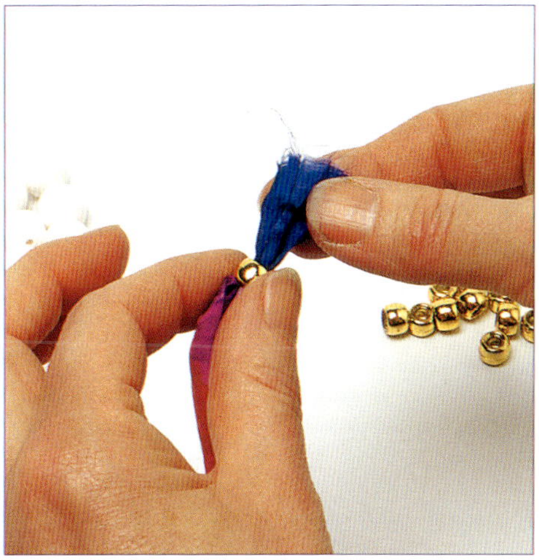

9. Thread one of the small spacer pony beads on each end of the tube, and push these along until they sit next to the covered bead.

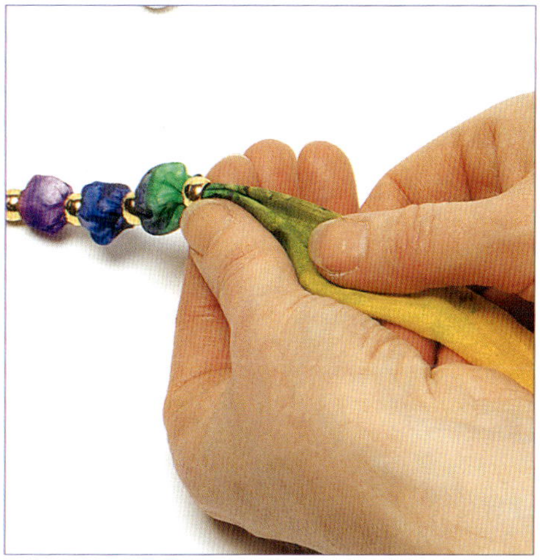

10. Continue inserting cotton fibre beads and threading spacer beads along the necklace until it is the length you want.

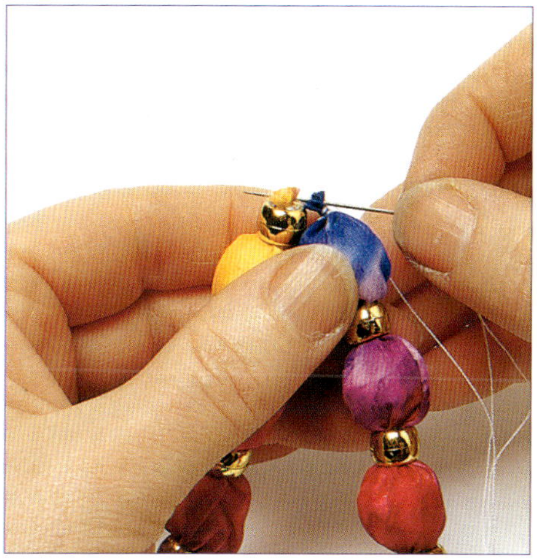

11. Join the open ends of the tube together with a few stitches to complete the necklace.

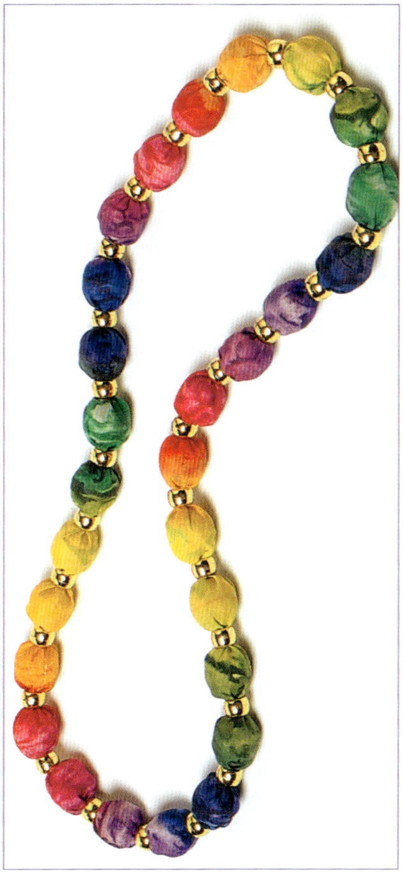

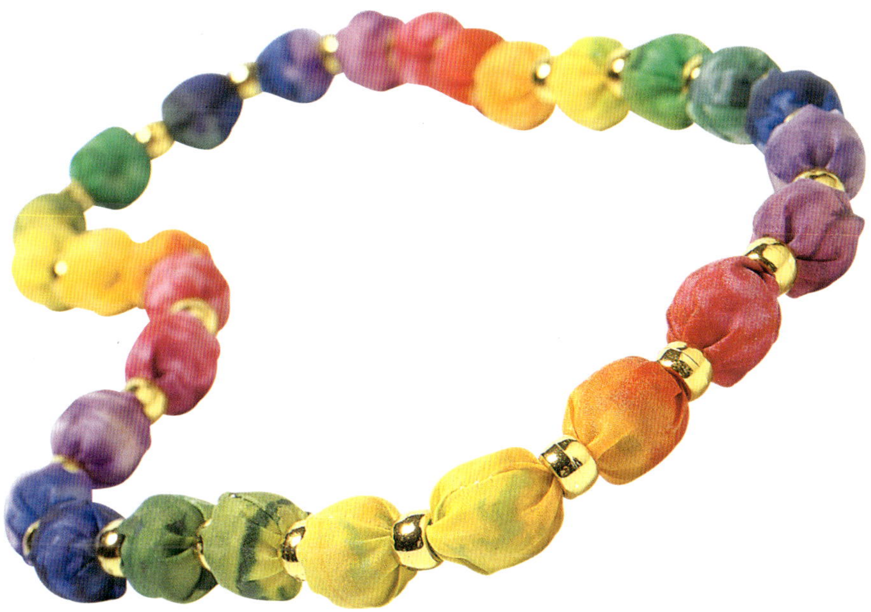

Silk pot-pourri or lavender sachets

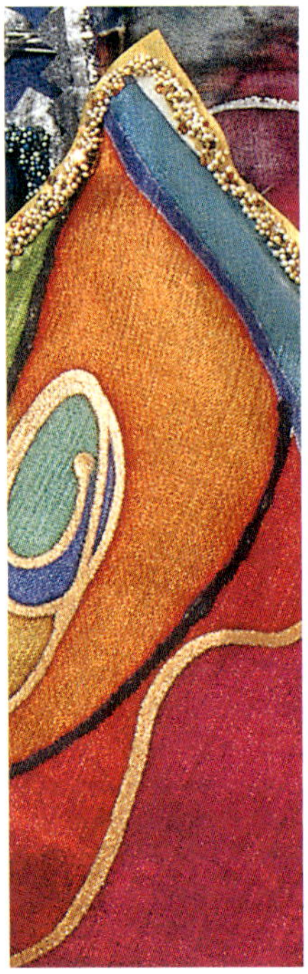

As you practise the various techniques you will inevitably produce a few samplers and test pieces, some of which you will not want to keep for reference. Why not use them to make some scented sachets to hang in your wardrobe or place in your clothes drawers. The variation of finishing details is endless and helps to make each sachet an original piece of work.

Equipment and materials

A completed, fixed and washed piece of silk
Frame and silk pins
Selection of heat-fix outliners (not clear)
Sewing thread and needle
Selection of beads, charms, sequins or ribbons for decoration
Pot-pourri or lavender
Sharp scissors or pinking shears
Metre rule or yard stick
Water-soluble or disappearing pen
Baking or greaseproof paper
Iron for setting the outliners

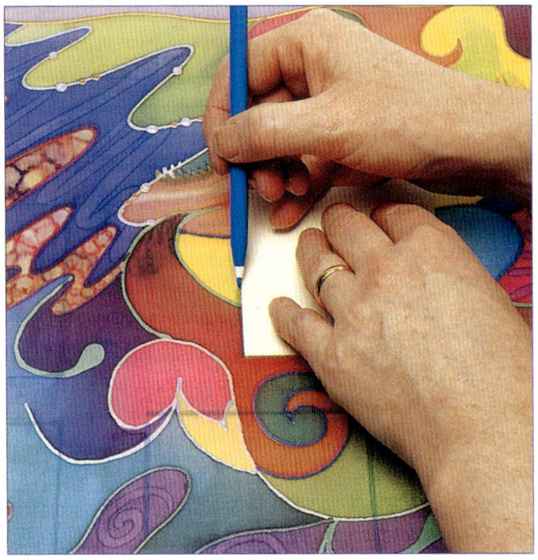

1. Re-stretch the finished piece of coloured silk back on to a frame, securing it with silk pins. Use the disappearing pen to mark out half the fabric into squares of about 9 cm ($3^1/_2$ in.).

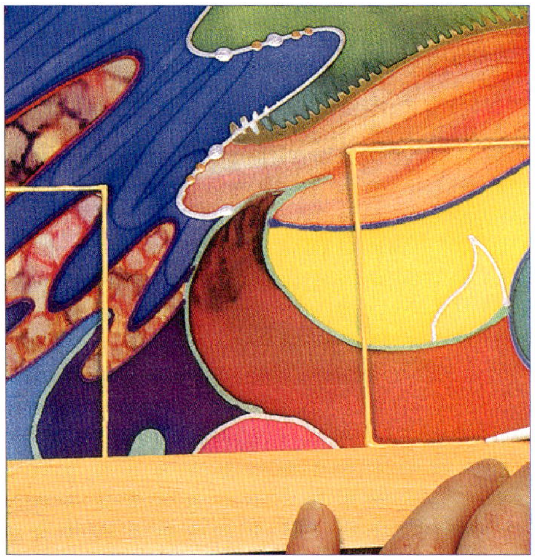

2. Make a bridge with the metre rule, using some supports to lift the rule just above the silk, and draw out the squares using a heat-fix outliner.

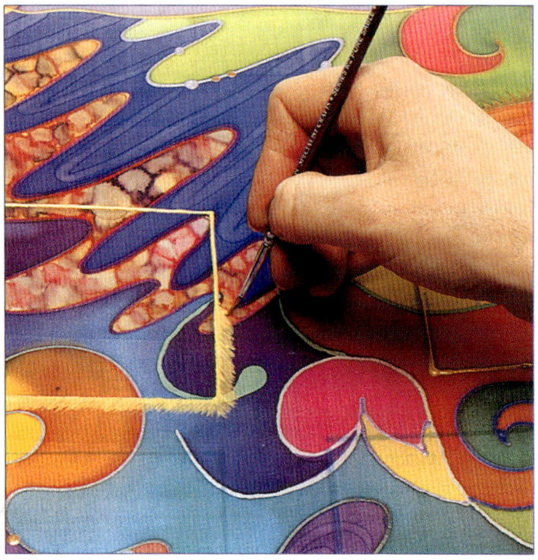

3. Use a brush to spread out the outliner, and don't worry if the lines look untidy, as the edges will be trimmed after sewing up.

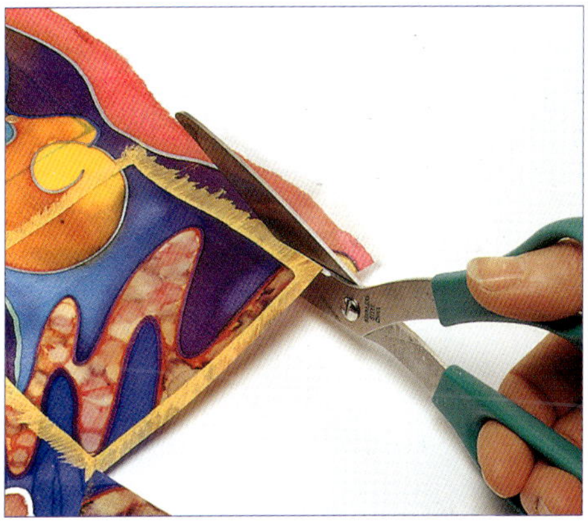

4. Dry the outlines, unpin the dry silk and cut out these squares and the remaining fabric, all slightly oversize to make it easier to sew the squares together.

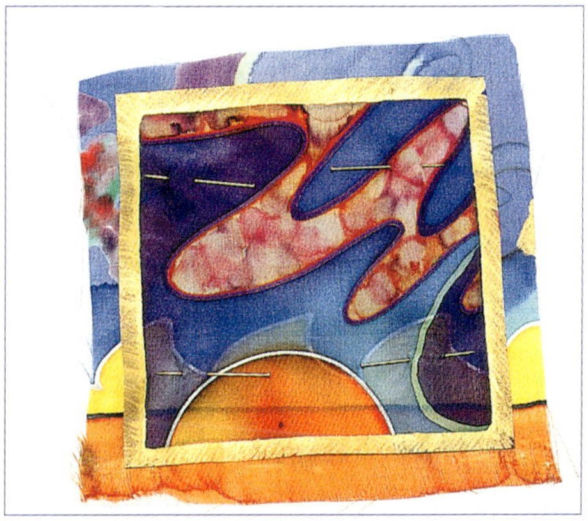

5. Pin an outlined square on to another unmarked square of silk and carefully sew around all the sides with a small running stitch (or use a sewing machine), leaving a small gap to insert the pot-pourri. Sew just inside the dry outliner.

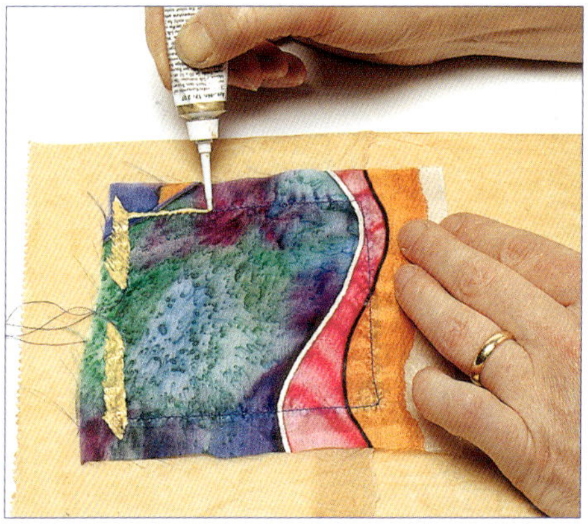

6. Lay the sachet on to some baking paper, and using the sewing line as a guide, re-outline the other side, and allow to dry. This will seal the two squares neatly together. When dry, use a sharp pair of scissors or pinking shears to trim the edges.

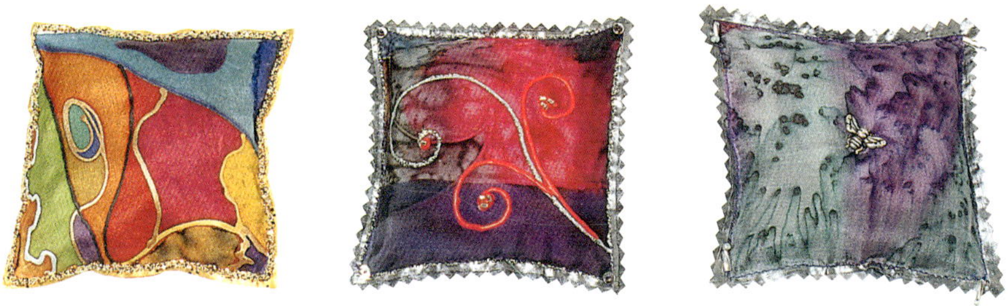

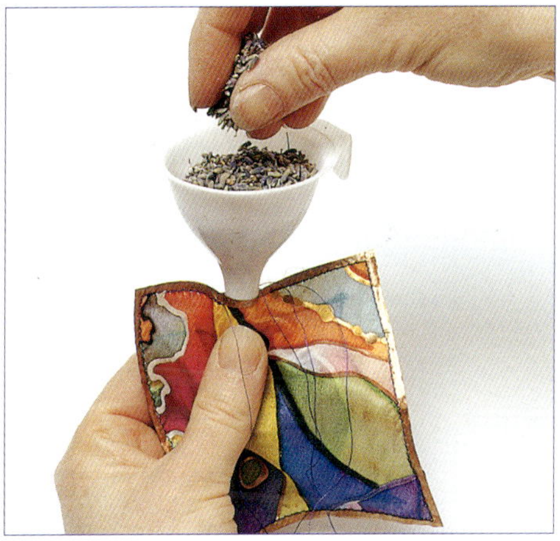

7 Fill the sachets with lavender or pot-pourri, then close the hole with a few more stitches.

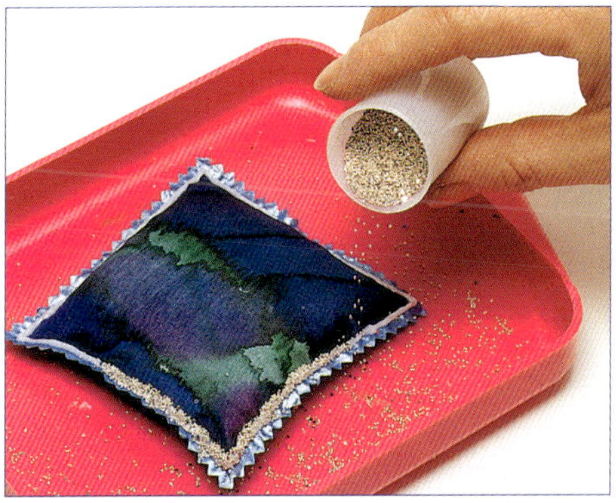

8. Add further decoration with glitter liners, puff liners, beads, sequins, ribbons or charms.

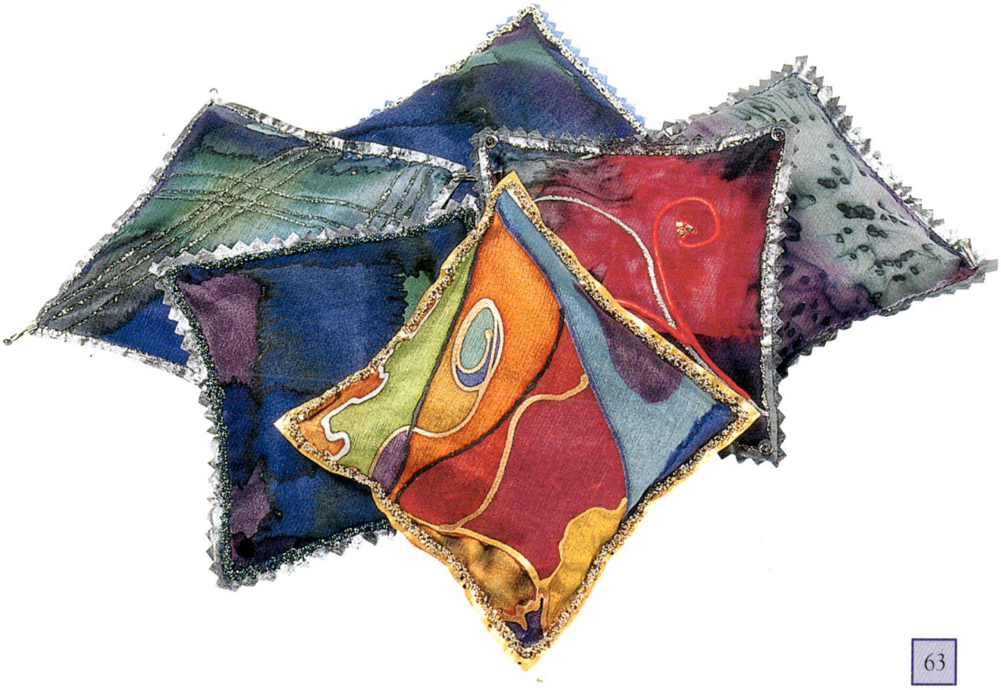

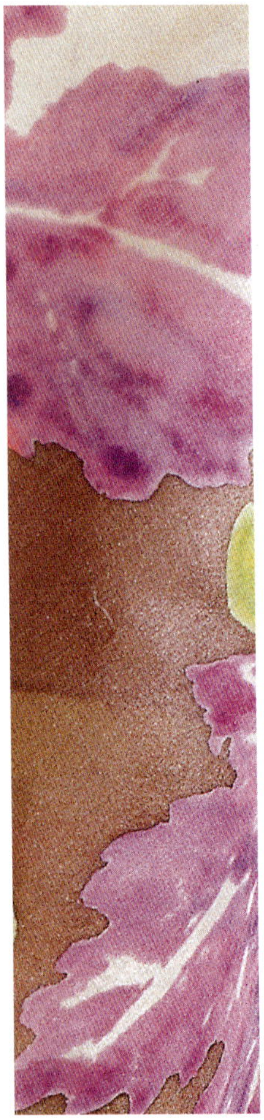

Printing with silk paint thickener

Using silk paint thickener to form a simple printed design works very well, and is especially suitable for children or anyone who finds it difficult to achieve fine brush control. The printing can be worked from commercially available sponge stamps, or you can make your own very effectively from thin polystyrene, which can be cut with scissors or a craft knife. If the background is to be a pale colour it is possible to paint this in as an overall wash first, before printing the shapes on top. For darker backgrounds it is better to print the shapes, then paint the background in around them.

Equipment and materials

Ready-edged scarf or piece of silk
A frame and silk pins
Heat-fix paints
Heat-fix silk paint thickener medium
Water pot and mixing palette
Paint brushes
Ready-made sponge stamps or your own print blocks
Iron for setting the colours

Tip: Make sure that you thoroughly mix the paint and thickener together, otherwise the paint may run and spoil the design.

1. Assemble the frame to fit the silk and fasten it to the frame with silk pins. Place a small amount of thickener into a well of the mixing palette. Add an equal amount of silk paint to the thickener, and thoroughly mix the two together. Repeat this with as many colours as you want to use in your design.

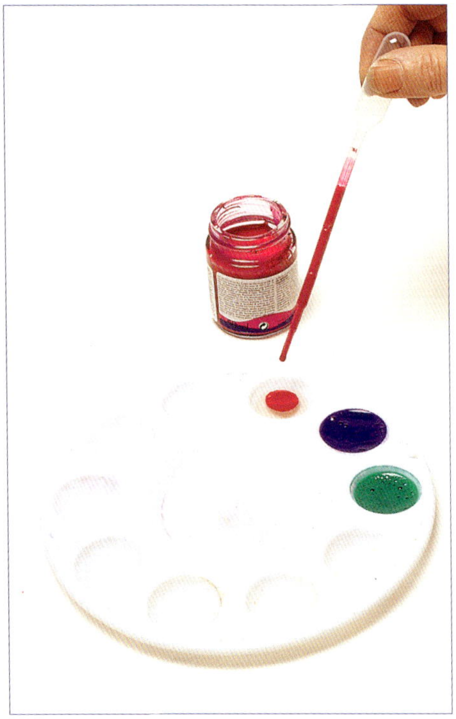

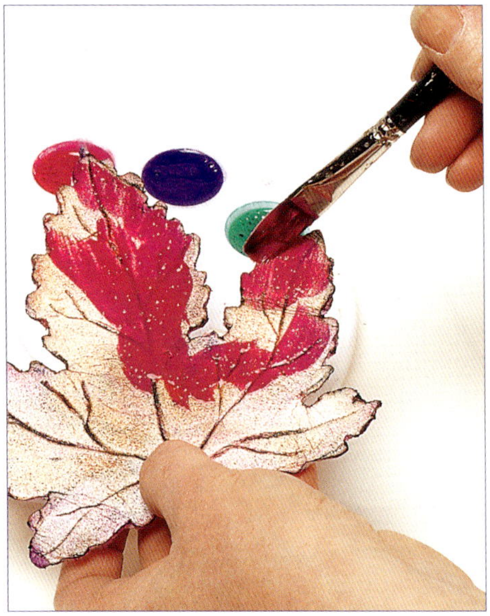

2. Take a stamp and apply the coloured, thickened silk paint medium to the stamp.

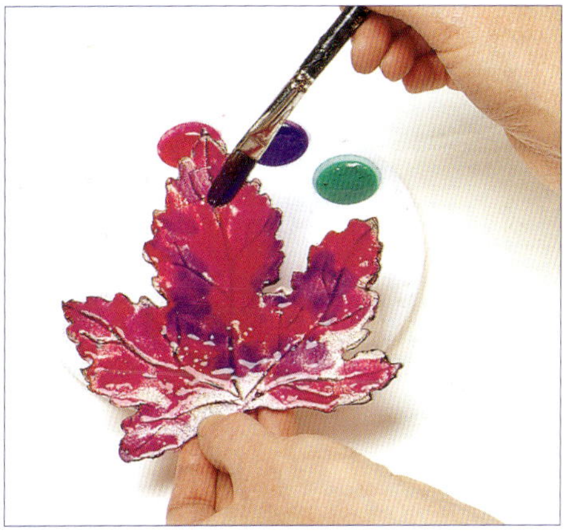

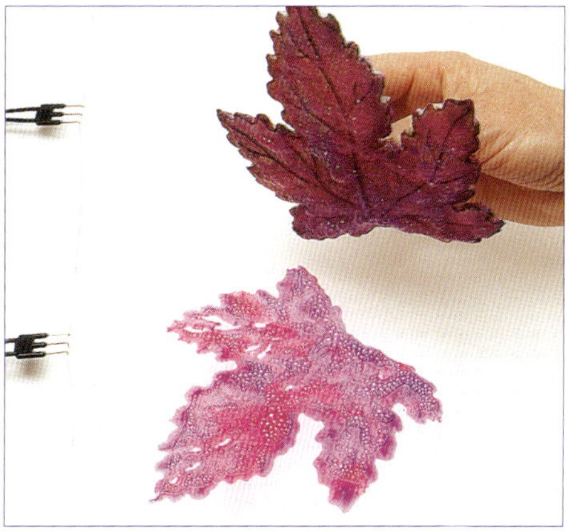

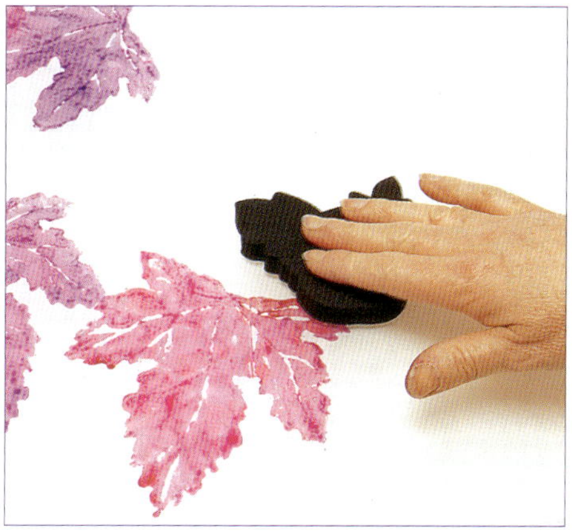

3. Several colours can be applied to one stamp for multi-coloured prints.

4. Carefully press the stamp down on to the stretched silk to achieve a good print. Re-apply the thickened colour and continue.

5. Here the pattern is applied using a commercial stamp block.

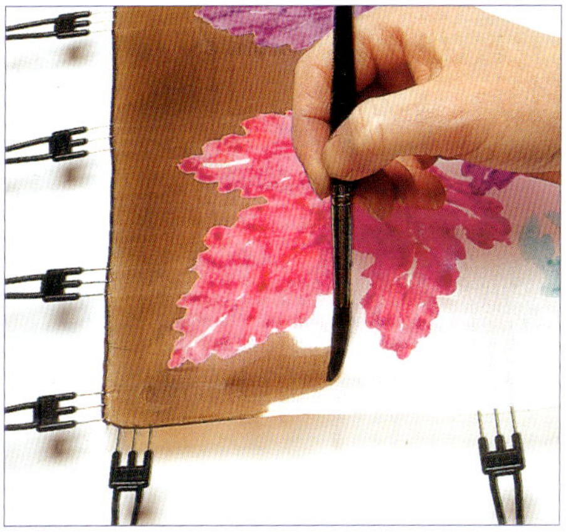

Variations: it is possible to add further detail by using a heat-fix outliner in and around the printed shapes. Do not, however, apply the outliner over the top of any of the thickener, as the outliner will not be able to bond directly with the fabric, and will come away at the washing stage. Alternatively, after fixing and the final wash, which removes the thickener, re-stretch the silk on to the frame and then apply outliner as surface decoration. You can also substitute steam-fix dyes if you prefer, following the instructions on page 16 for steam-fixing.

6. Allow the work to dry before painting in the background colour. Use unthickened silk paint to paint the background, but still leave a little spreading distance, and allow the paint to run up to the printed shapes. Select the best starting place and paint outwards, working around the shapes as you go.

Allow the work to dry, remove from the frame and fix by ironing. Wash the fixed work in warm water to remove the water-soluble thickener and any excess colour. Allow to dry a little before re-ironing to give a lovely finish to the silk.

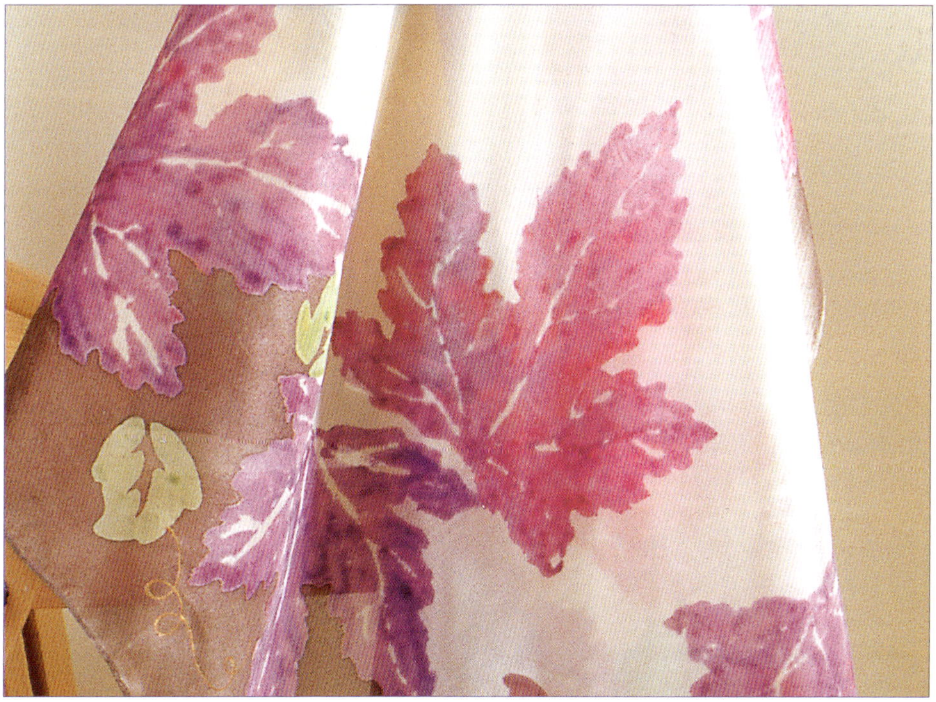

Abstract patterns fixed in a microwave

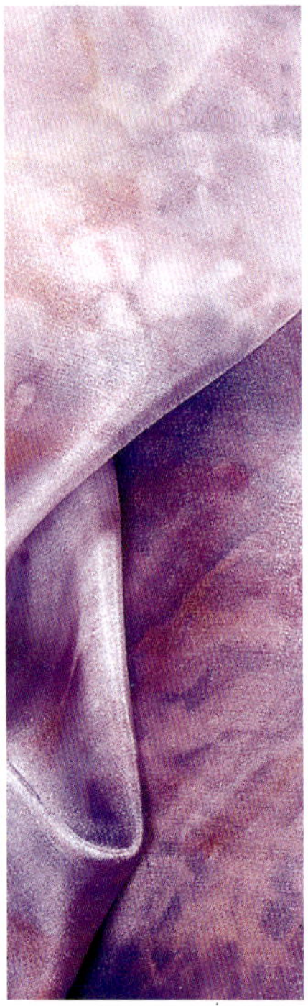

The lovely soft marbling produced in this technique is easy to work especially on pongee and habotai silk. As the dyes will mix to produce other colours, remember to choose hues that mix well together and consider introducing a contrast element by using colours of varying tonal strengths.

Equipment and materials

Ready-edged scarf or piece of lightweight pongee or habotai silk

Steam-fix dyes (maximum of four or five colours works best)

White vinegar to help set the dyes (essential if using acid dyes)

Shallow tray

Mixing palette

Plastic pipettes

Plastic gloves

Piece of plastic to protect the table (clear or white plastic is preferable)

Ventilated microwave pot or bowl and cling film

Microwave

Tip: Take a little time arranging the fabric without compacting it too much, as the 'hill and valley' contours form the marbled pattern in the silk.
Tip: To avoid tiny dot splash marks, refill the pipette with more colour rather than trying to squeeze out the last drop. Tiny splashes of dye can be difficult to blend out and can spoil the completed work.

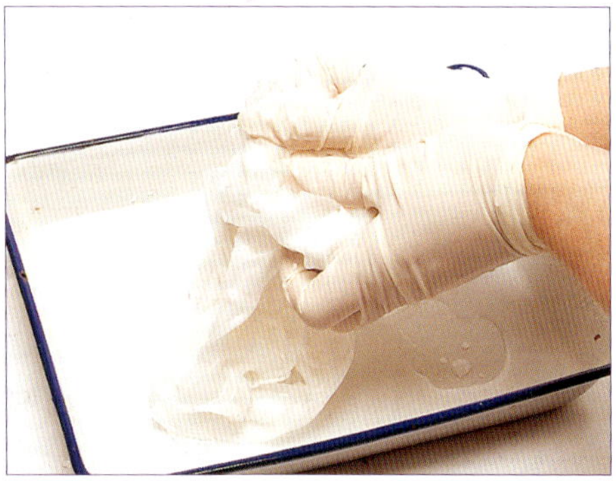

1. Cover the table with the plastic sheeting. Wearing plastic gloves, pour some vinegar into the shallow tray and immerse the silk. Squeeze out the excess vinegar and place the wet silk on to the plastic.

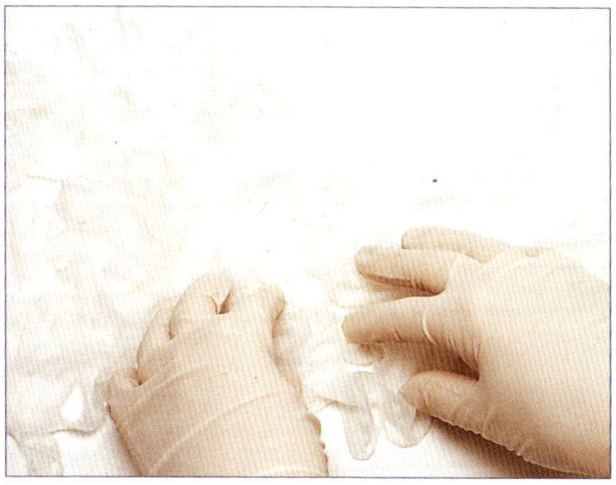

2. Arrange the wet silk into some interesting hill and valley contours. The silk will stay in the arrangement you create as it is wet and will cling to itself or the plastic.

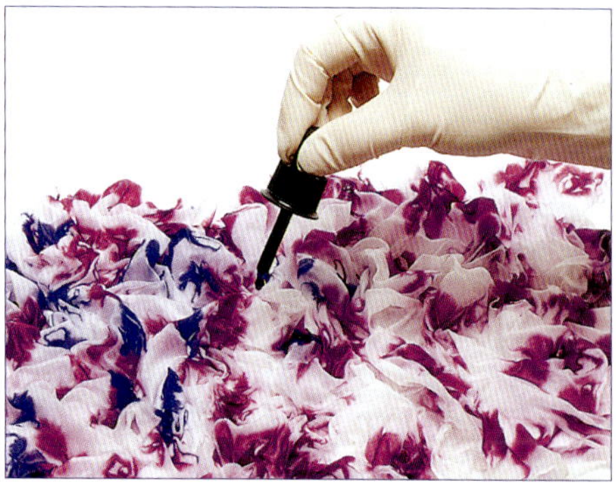

3. Use a pipette to lift up the colours and drizzle the dye on to the silk.

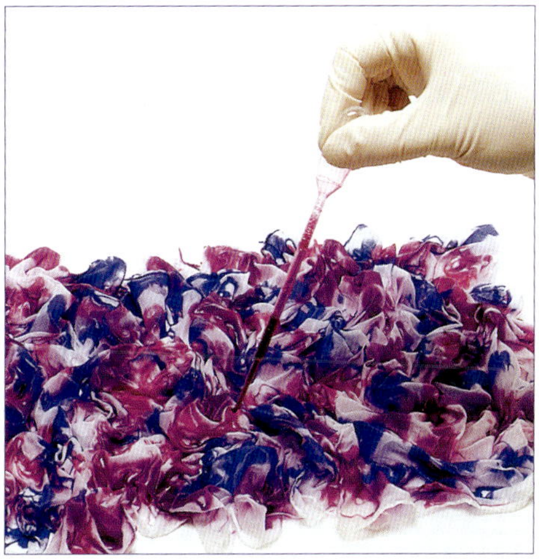

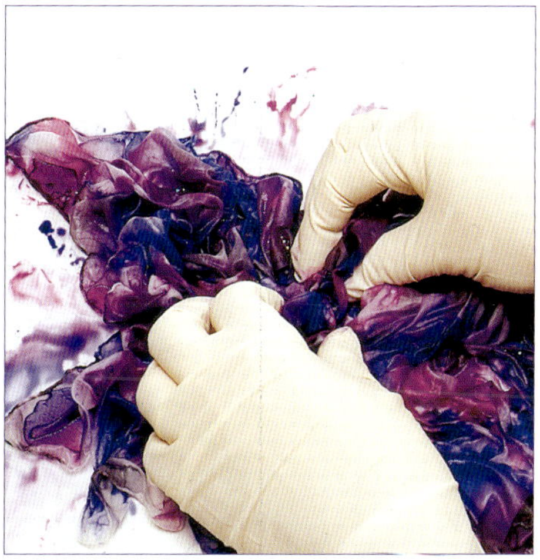

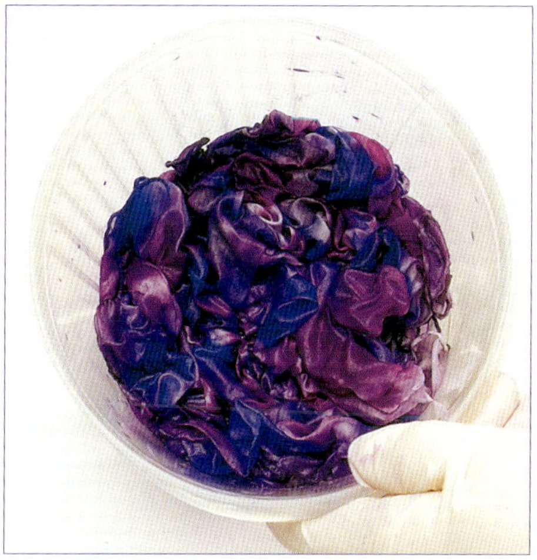

4. Try to distribute the colours evenly across the silk, using light pressure on the bulb of the pipette to release a controlled amount of dye.

5. When all the colours have been applied, blend them using the tips of your fingers. Try to keep the contours of 'hills and valleys'. The more you handle the work, the more blended the colours become.

6. Draw the wet silk together, lift it up and place it in a plastic container, keeping the silk well down in the base of the container, cover with a ventilated lid and place the container on the microwave turntable.

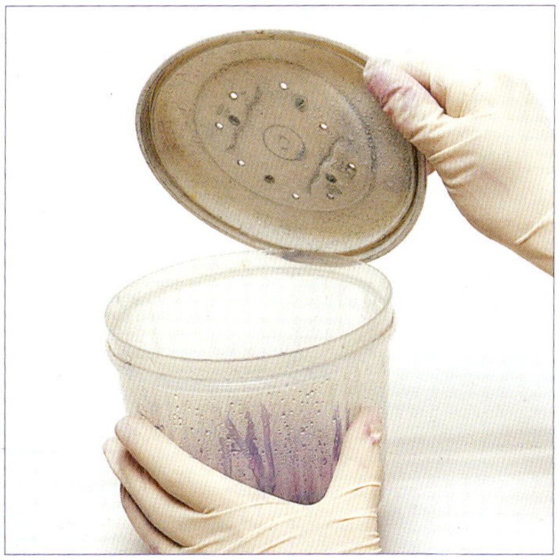

7. Turn the microwave to medium power setting, and cook for four minutes. Remove the container and carefully open the lid to allow the hot vinegary steam to escape.

8. Remove the silk and rinse in warm soapy water, to remove any traces of vinegar or excess dye. Iron the silk while it is still damp to remove any creases and give a beautiful finish.

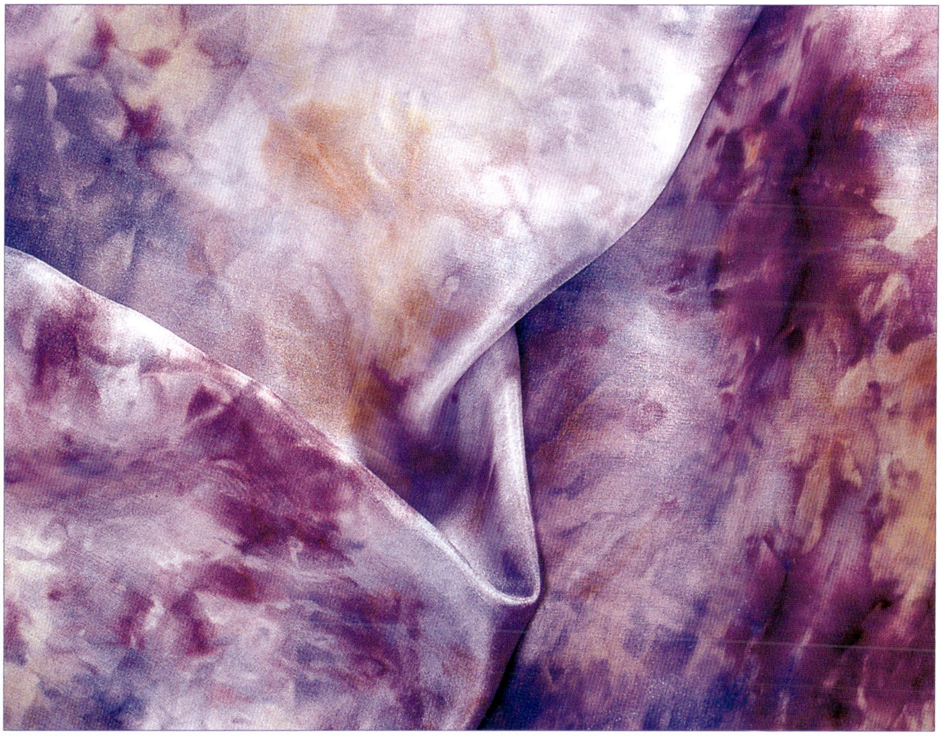

Variations: see page2 42–43 for information on how to create other informal patterns using a microwave to set the steam-fix dyes.

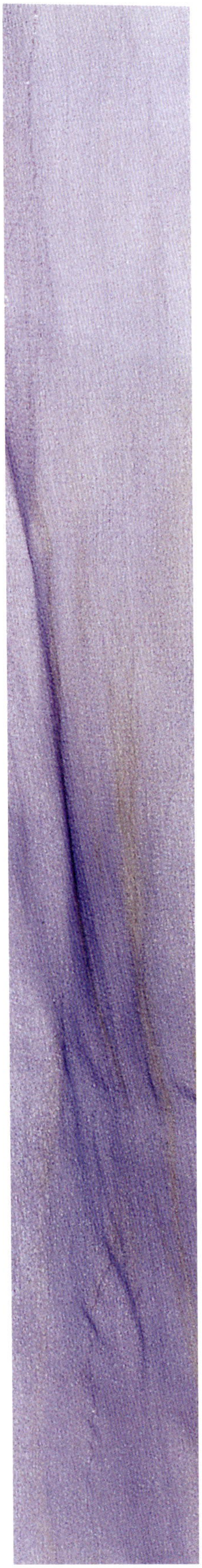

Arashi Shibori patterns fixed in the microwave

The beautiful translucent qualities of a light pongee, or chiffon silk are very well suited to Shibori work; the depth of colour and patterns are greatly enhanced from the layering effect as the silk softly drapes back on itself. Finally, further embellishment can be added by attaching small shisha mirrors or fine glitter lines for a little sparkle or evening elegance.

Tip: If you would prefer the stripes to run across the width of the scarf, fold the scarf in half lengthwise, twice, and start wrapping the folded silk around the tube from the ready rolled edges.

Tip: If you prefer stormy pattern lines, work the binding and wrapping much more freely by pushing up the silk before binding it in place with the string. Taking the string back over itself forms lozenge shapes. The more carefree the binding, the more stormy the resulting pattern becomes.

Equipment and materials

Long ready-edged scarf or piece of chiffon or mousseline silk

Steam-fix silk dyes (maximum of four or five colours works best)

White vinegar (essential if using acid dyes)

Shallow tray (a roasting tin slightly wider than the length of the tube)

Mixing palette

Plastic pipettes

String (new or already coloured from previous dyeing)

Elastic bands

Kitchen paper

Plastic gloves

Piece of plastic to protect the table

Approx. 20 cm (8 in.) length of thick card tube (carpet roll tube is ideal)

Cling film

Microwave

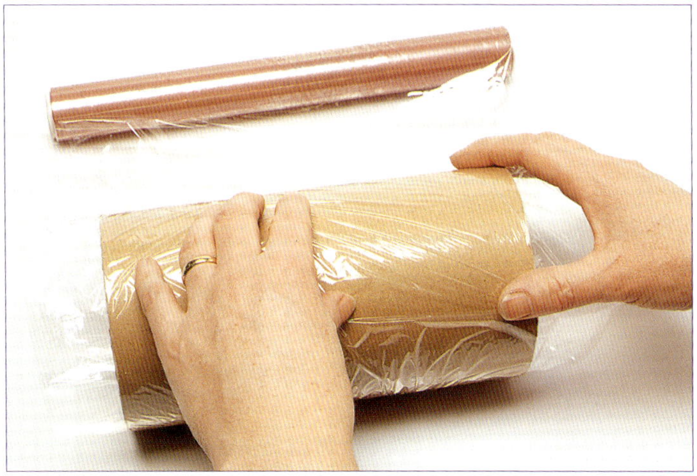

1. Cover the table with the plastic. Wrap some cling film around the cardboard tube to prevent the dyes from staining or wetting the cardboard.

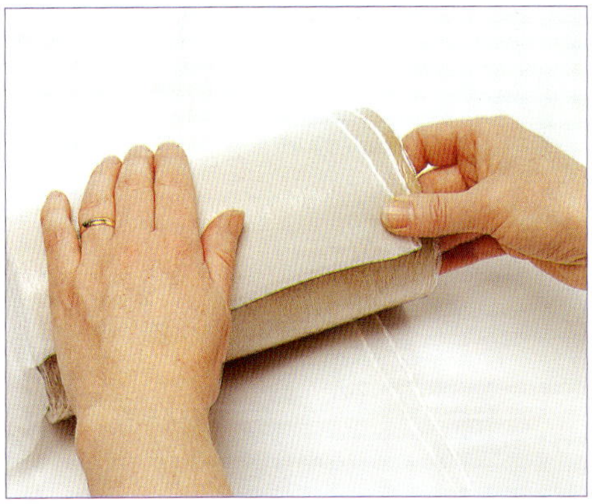

2. Fold the chiffon in half end to end for a mirror image. Wrap the folded silk around the tube, starting from the folded edge. This will give pattern lines that run the length of the scarf.

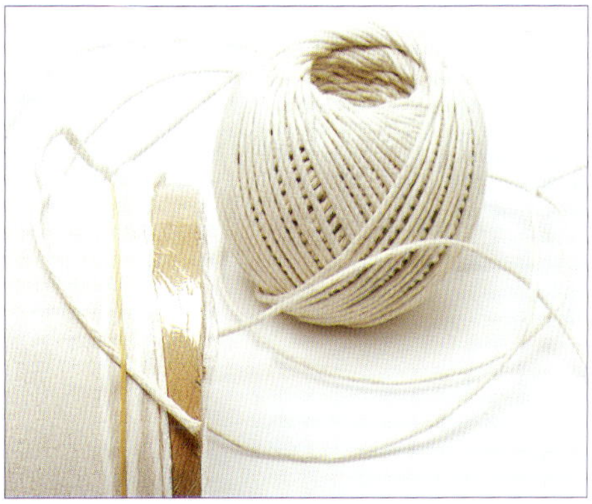

3. Place an elastic band around one end of the tube to hold the rolled silk in place. Slip the end of the string under the elastic band and start winding the string around the tube.

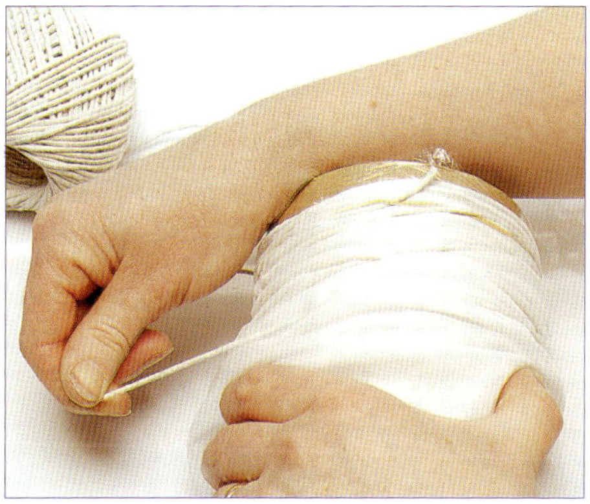

4. If you want neat, evenly spaced lines, wrap the string evenly around the tube for about 8 cm (3 in.) then push this section together to draw the loose end of the silk on to the tube. Continue binding in this way until the silk is completely wrapped and bound around the tube, then secure the end of the string with another elastic band.

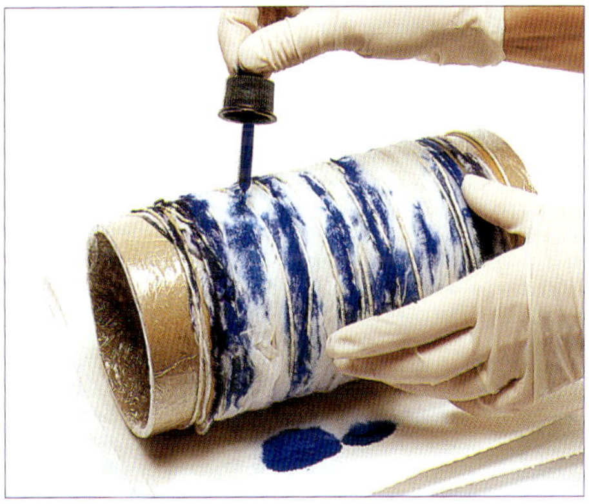

5. Wearing plastic gloves, pour some vinegar into the shallow tray. Roll the tube with the wrapped silk in the vinegar. Squeeze out any excess and place the wet silk on some kitchen paper. Use pipettes to apply the steam-fix dyes. Drizzle the dye around the silk following the direction of the string, until the colours have been evenly distributed. Keep the tube on some kitchen paper to soak up any excess puddles of liquid.

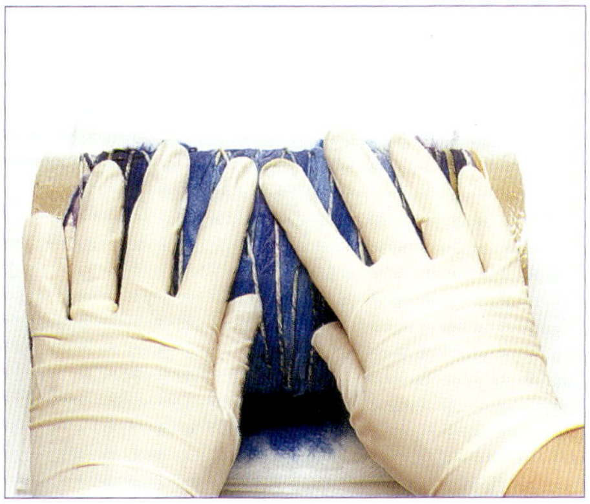

6. Press and roll the tube to push the dye down through the layers of the chiffon silk. It is very important to press firmly, even if it looks as if all the colours have merged together too much. Have confidence, as inadequate pressure will result in undyed or poorly patterned areas in the finished work.

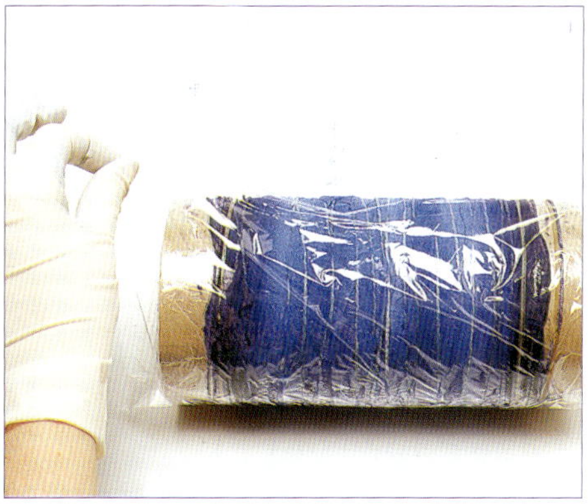

7. Loosely wrap the dyed, wet silk roll in cling film, and place on the microwave turntable. The length of the card tube is dictated by the diameter of the turntable of your microwave.

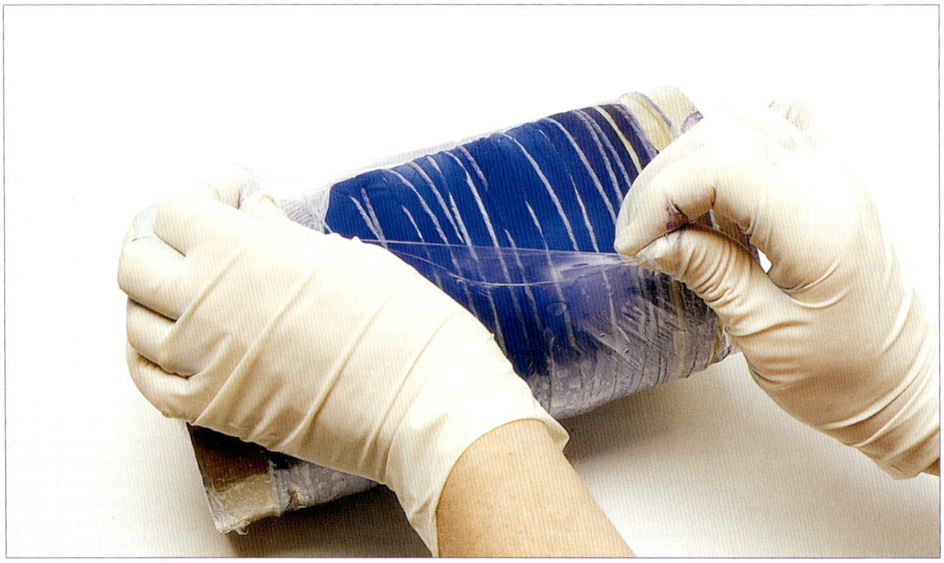

8. Cook the silk for two minutes on a medium heat setting, open the microwave, rotate to reposition the covered tube, and cook for a further two minutes on medium setting. This time is suitable for a long thin or square scarf of approx. 1 sq. m. When cooked, remove the silk tube from the microwave and carefully unwrap the cling film, allowing any steam to escape. Be careful as the silk will be hot.

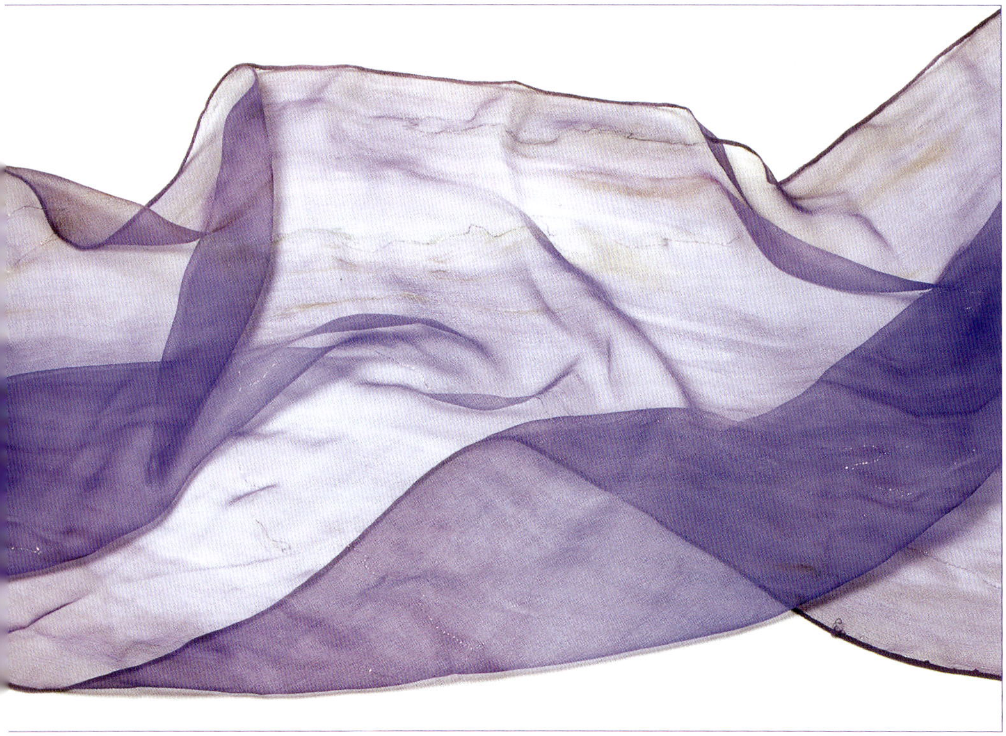

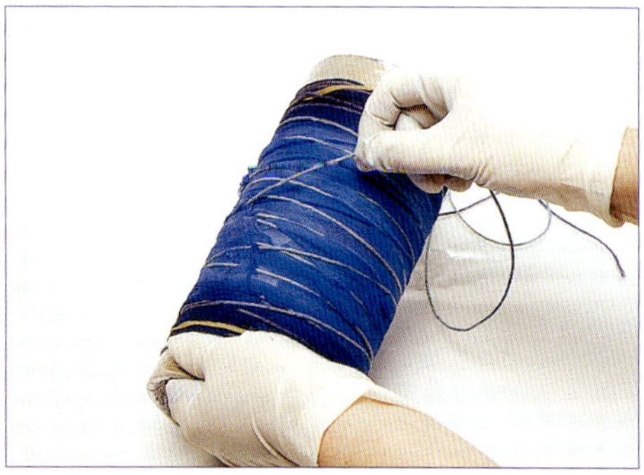

9. Remove the elastic bands and unwind the string. Check that the dye has penetrated through the layers properly.

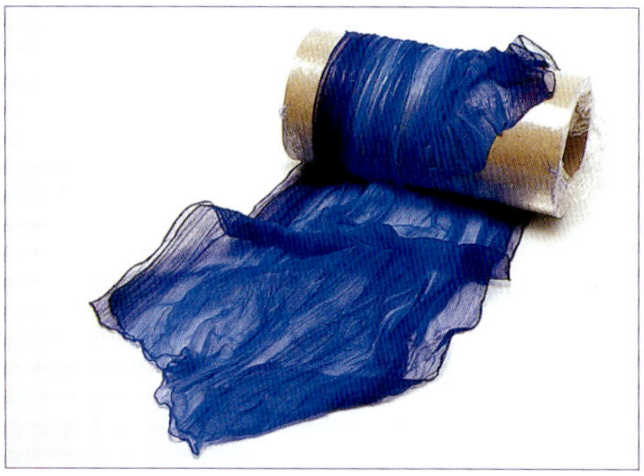

10. Then wash the scarf in cool, soapy water to remove any excess dye and vinegar. Keep the string for re-use in further projects. Iron the silk while it is still damp to restore the shape and softness of the chiffon.

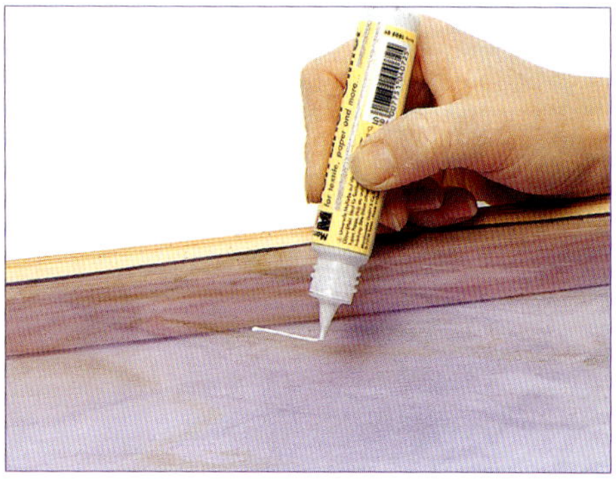

11. If you wish, add a little heat-set glitter liner along the pattern lines or sew on some shisha mirrors for a little added sparkle.

Velvet drape for a table or sofa

Equipment and materials

Long length of white silk viscose velvet

Selection of procion dyes made up into liquid dyes (see page 37)

Jam jar per colour.

Soda ash

Large shallow tray (marbling tray, cat litter tray or motor oil tray is ideal)

Rubber gloves

Pipettes

Synthrapol (optional)

Some old newspapers

This velvet drape will give a touch of luxury to any table or sofa. The simple method of dyeing in a tray gives lovely results and is an easy introduction to working with procion dyes. Once finished, the drape can be further embellished with any of the decorative media or finished with some tassels at each corner.

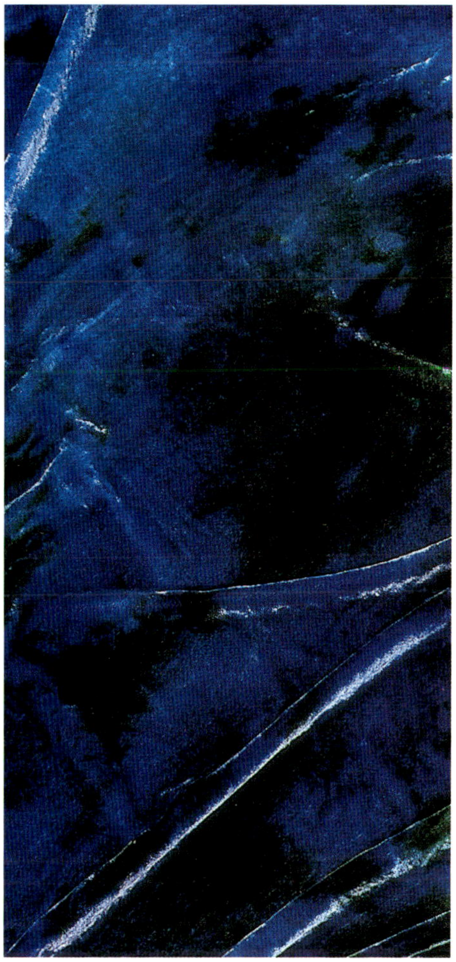

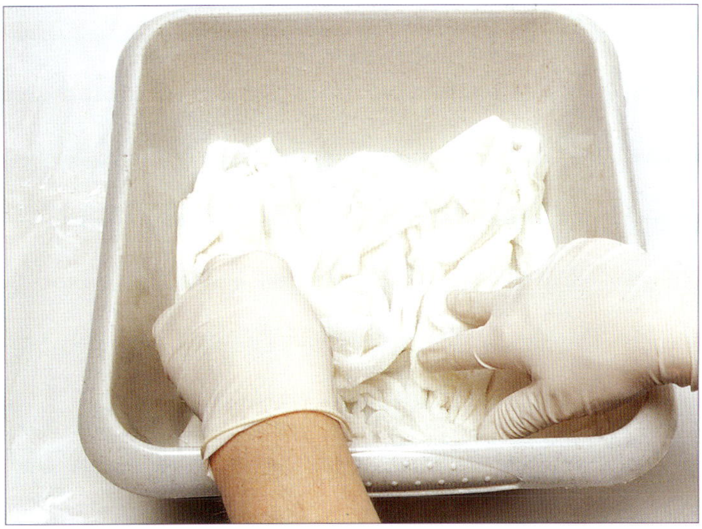

1. Wet the piece of silk velvet in water, and squeeze out the excess so that it is just damp. Loosely arrange the velvet in the tray, to create some interesting contours.

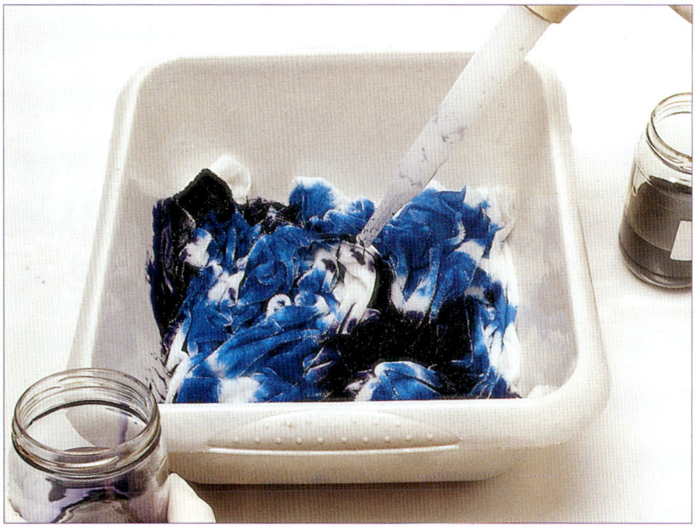

2. Wearing the rubber gloves, apply the liquid dyes one colour at a time, using either a pipette for controlled application, or just sloshing the colour on for a more random effect.

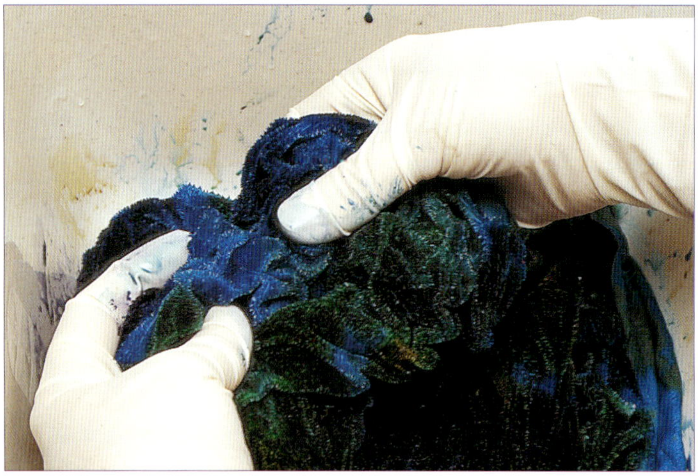

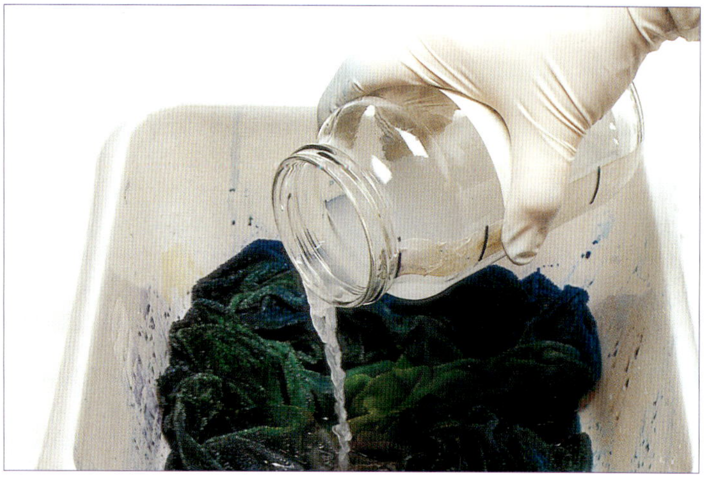

3. When all the colours have been applied, use your hands to lightly blend the colours together. Then carefully tip away any excess colour to prevent the fabric sitting in dark pools of dye. Leave the velvet for at least 30 minutes to allow the colours to blend. The longer the velvet is left and the more it is handled the more blended the colours become.

4. Mix up the soda ash to make the fixative solution (see page 37), and pour it all over the velvet. Leave the fixative to work for approximately one hour.

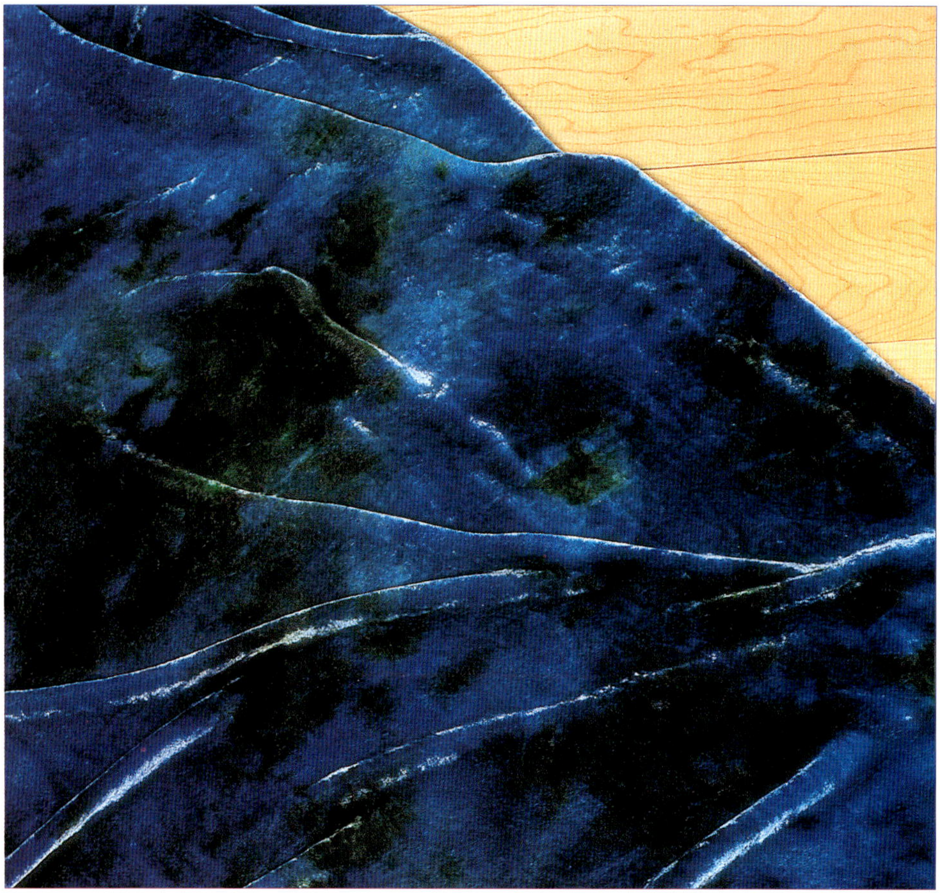

5. Tip away the spent fixative solution and dye, then rinse the velvet in cold water. Keep rinsing until the water runs clear. It will take several rinses to achieve this, or use Synthrapol to help rinse out surplus dye. Squeeze out any excess water, and then spread out the dyed velvet on newspapers to dry.

6. When the velvet is still just damp, iron it on the wrong side to restore the plush sheen. For a crushed velvet look, allow the velvet to dry completely before giving a quick ironing on the reverse, or tumble dry on a cool setting.

7. Finish the edges by hand or on a sewing machine, adding any embellishment or tassels if you wish.

Chiffon silk scarf with overlaid colour and watermark patterns

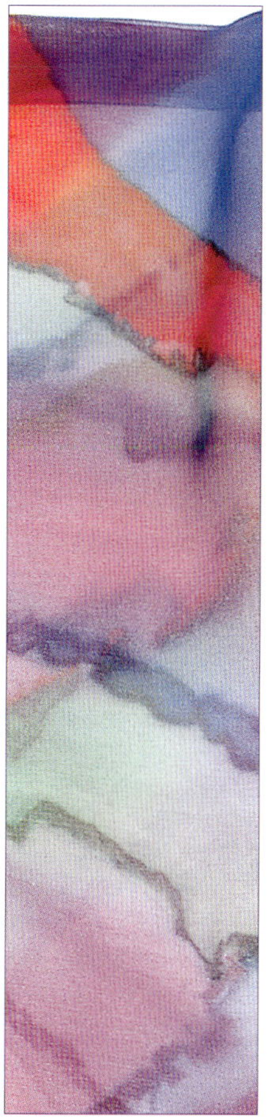

Equipment and materials

Two long silk chiffon or mousseline ready-edged scarves or pieces of chiffon silk
Frame and silk pins
Steam-fix dyes
Large brushes
Water pot and mixing palette
Hairdryer
Steam fixing equipment

This scarf is worked as a double layer of translucent chiffon to give a beautiful overlaid pattern that is finished with a decorative edge of small beads. Choose colours that will work well together when layered, and consider varying the patterns for different effects.

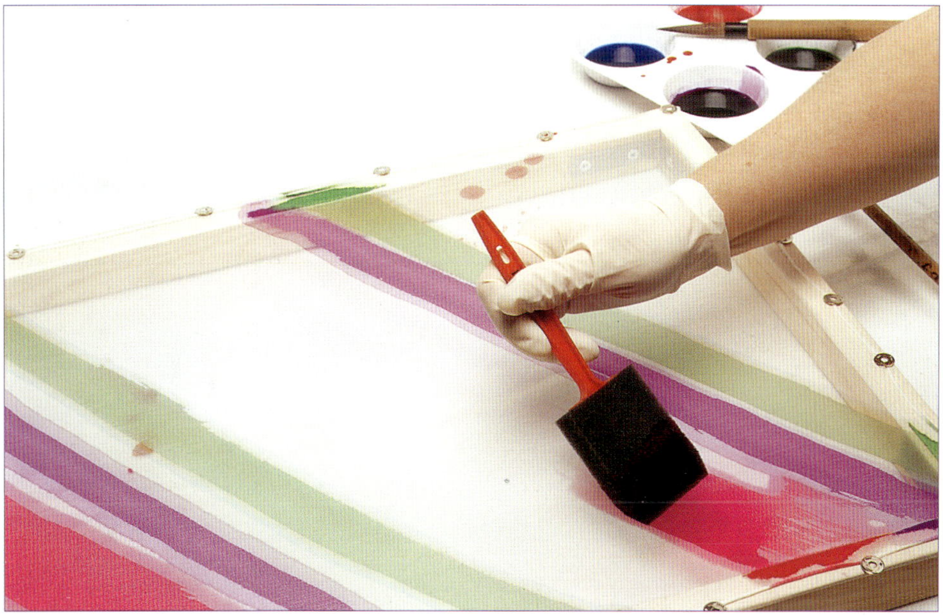

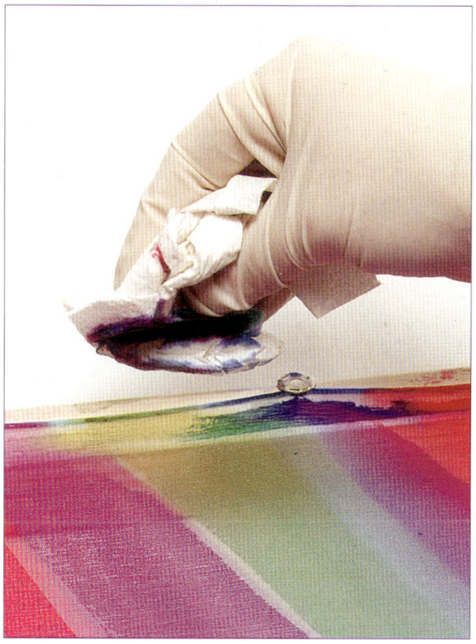

1. Pin out the silk using the silk pins. Place the selected colours into the mixing palette, diluting if necessary with water. Apply the dyes to the silk in a diagonal stripe, using a large brush to release a wide band of colour. Vary the amount of contact the brush makes with the silk to control the spread of the dye.[

2. Dab the wet edges of the scarf with kitchen paper to prevent the dyes from flowing back.

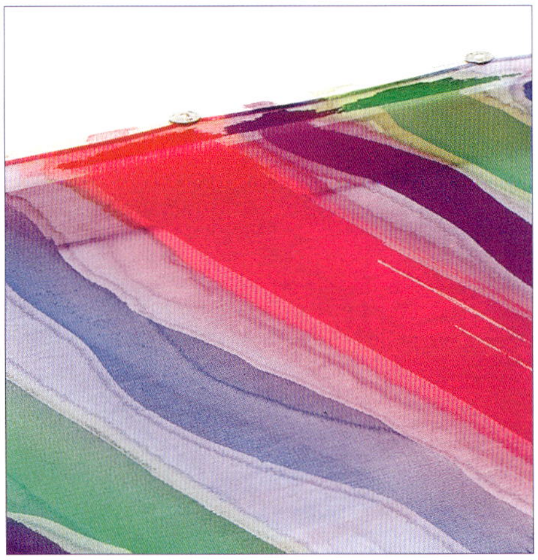

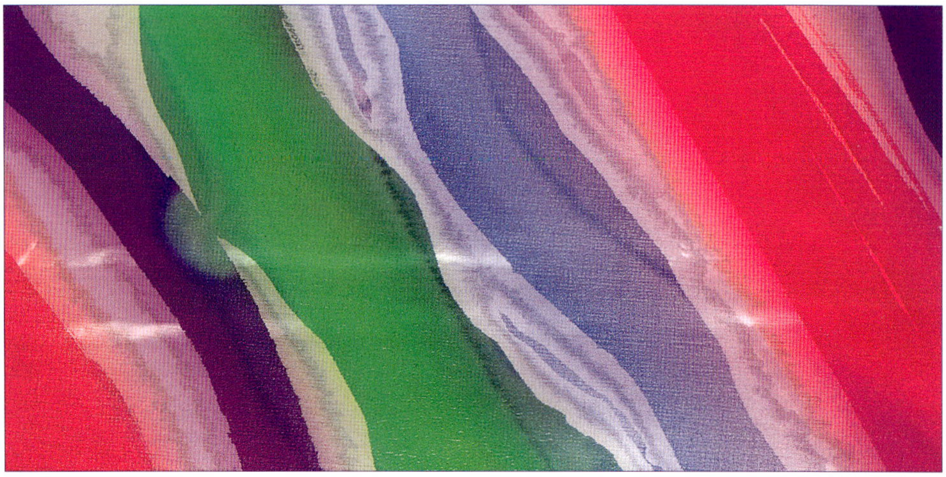

3. Dry the first layer of colours when each of the stripes has merged with its neighbour in a pleasing way. Repeat the application of dye, or use water for a lighter effect.

4. This second application of liquid will create some beautiful watermarks. Leave to dry naturally or use a hairdryer for more dramatic patterns. Repeat this colouring process on the second scarf, using different colours. Steam both scarves to set the dyes (see page xx). Wash and iron the scarves.

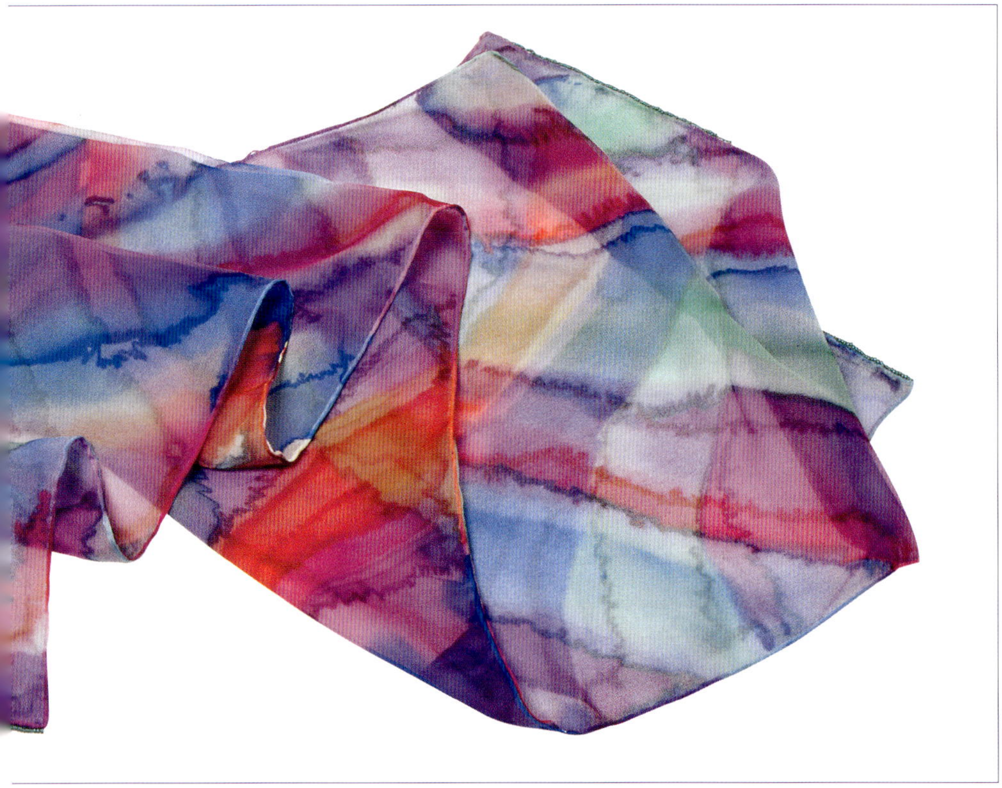

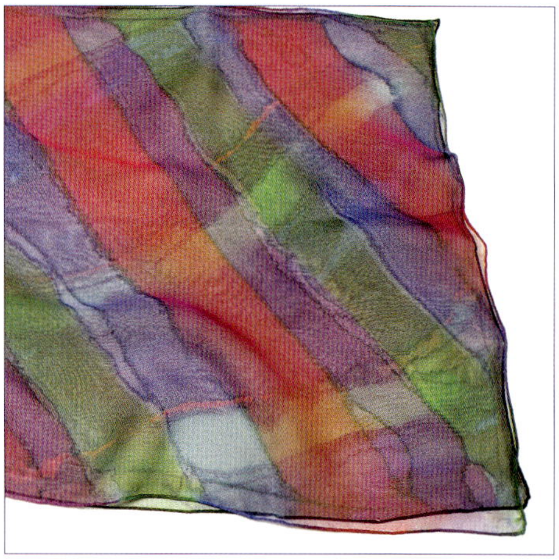

5. Lay one scarf on top of the other to see the cross-over patterns formed. Try all the pattern overlay possibilities by moving the scarf around before deciding which one works most effectively.

6. Sew the two scarves together along the rolled edge with a fine thread.

7. Finish the scarf with a line of beads along each bottom edge to add a little sparkle and weight to the completed item.

Variations: try sandwiching some frayed silk organza shapes between the layers, or add outliner or glitter liner to decorate the scarf further.

Silk sarong

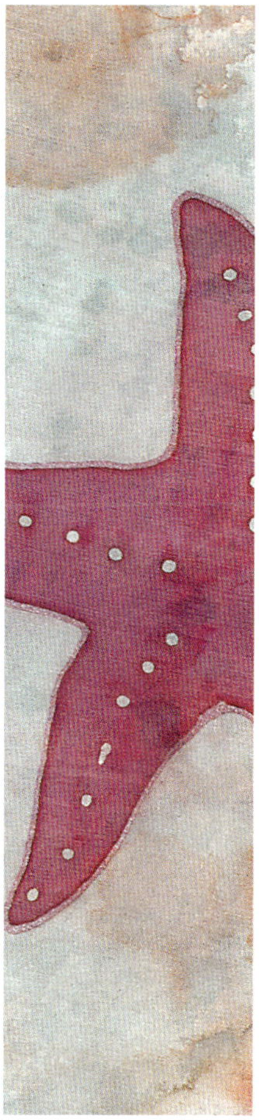

Equipment and materials

Two long bamboo garden canes slightly longer than the length of the sarong
Two bamboo garden canes slightly longer than the width of the sarong
Reel of masking tape
Clothes pegs
Regular frame and silk pins or a large embroidery hoop
Heat-fix silk paints (three or four colours works well)
Three or four pump action spray bottles, one per colour
Heat-fix outliners
Heat-fix silk paint thickener
Piece of natural sponge
Paint brushes
Mixing palette and water pot
Hairdryer
Pattern motifs
Plastic sheeting or newspaper to protect the floor
Iron to set the colours or dry cure in an oven
Template p104

This project shows how easy it can be to work a large length of silk without the need for a specialist frame. The silk is pegged on to garden bamboo canes taped together and supported on chairs, table ends or saw horses, worked either outside on a sunny day, or over a floor area protected by plastic sheeting. Working a much larger piece is good practice, great fun and helps to give spontaneity to the work. The paints are sprayed on in this project, with the patterns formed using thickener and outliner. The completed project makes a lovely sarong or silk wrap.

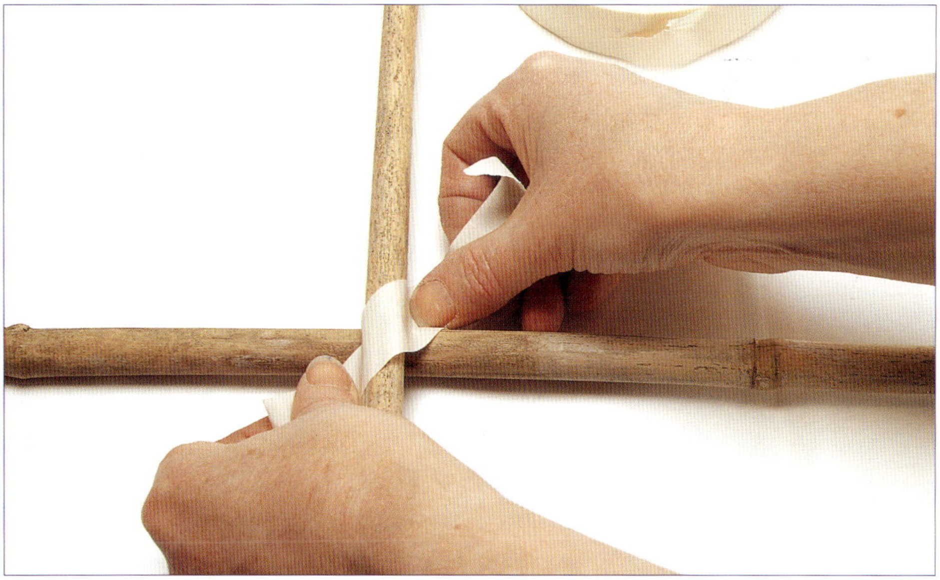

1. Assemble the bamboo canes into a frame large enough to take the piece of silk, crossing over the ends of the canes and taping them securely together with masking tape. Support each end of the assembled frame on suitable supports (as suggested above) and cover the floor with plastic if you are working indoors.

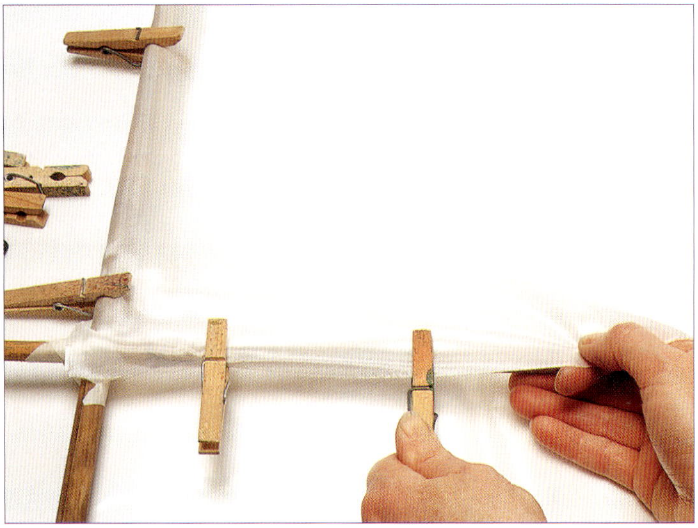

2 Start at one corner and fasten the silk on to the canes using clothes pegs. You should be able to achieve a reasonable tension, and it does not have to be as tight as you might normally work.

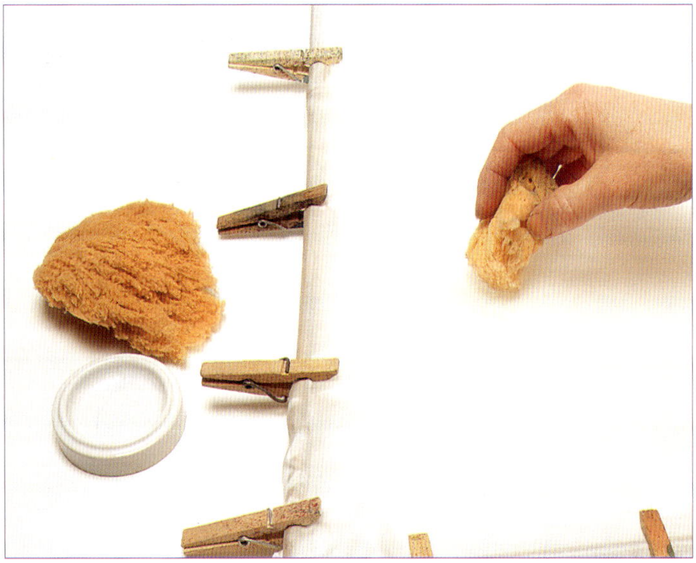

3. Place some silk paint thickener into a large palette well and dip in the sponge. Lightly sponge the thickener on to the silk in arc patterns to form waves. Do not sponge too heavily or you will have solid areas of thickener. Dry the thickener with a hairdryer or allow to dry naturally while you mix-up the paints.

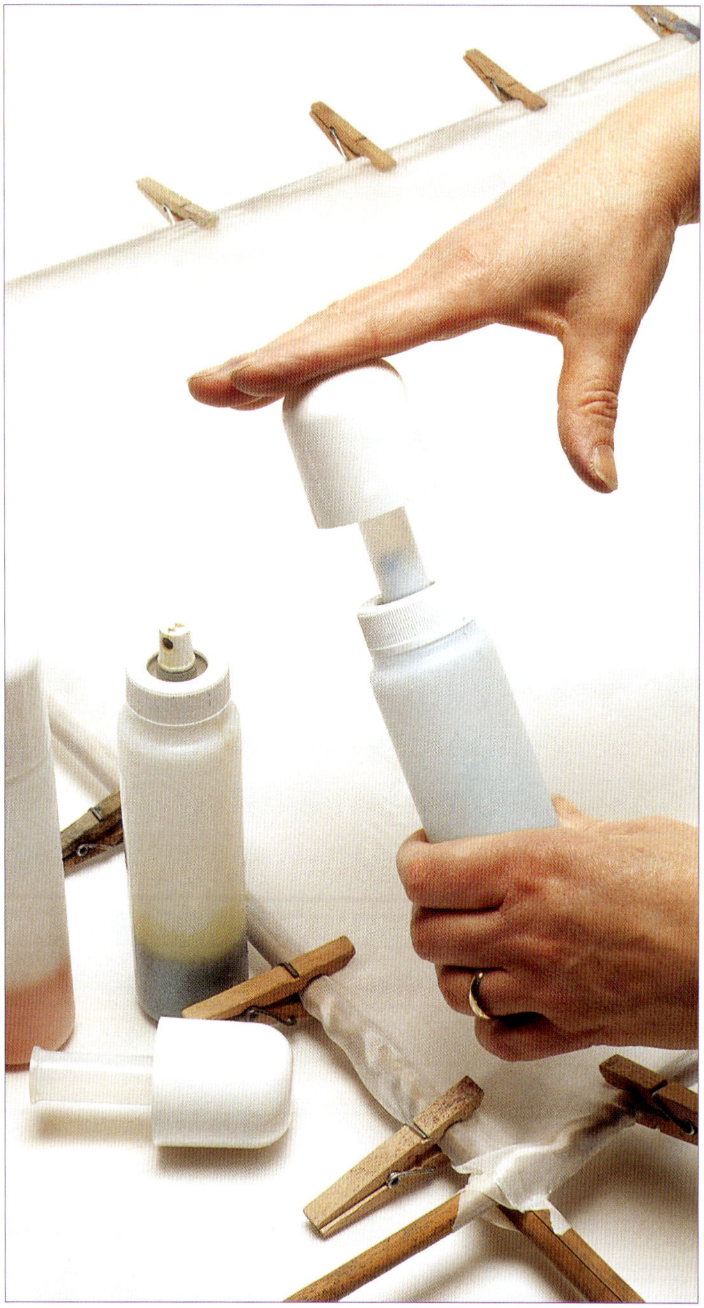

4. Prepare two of the pump action bottles using 10 pipettes of colour for the two dominant colours in the project. Prepare the remaining pump action bottles using five pipettes of colour for the accent colours. Dilute each of the bottles with a good quantity of water and test the depth of colour on a scrap of silk. Adjust if necessary, but keep the colours pale to mid-strength so that the colours of the motifs applied later will still show.

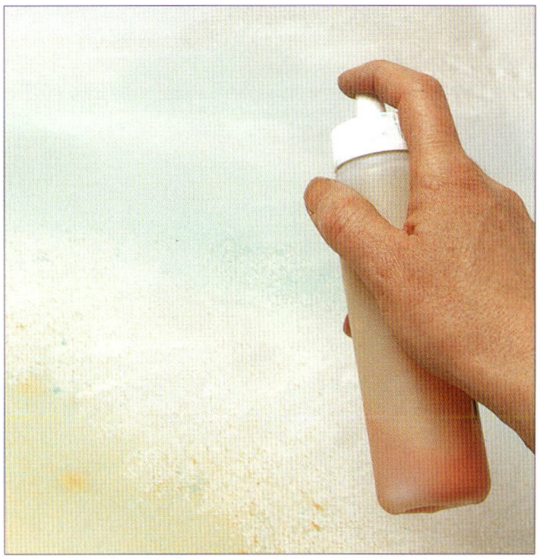

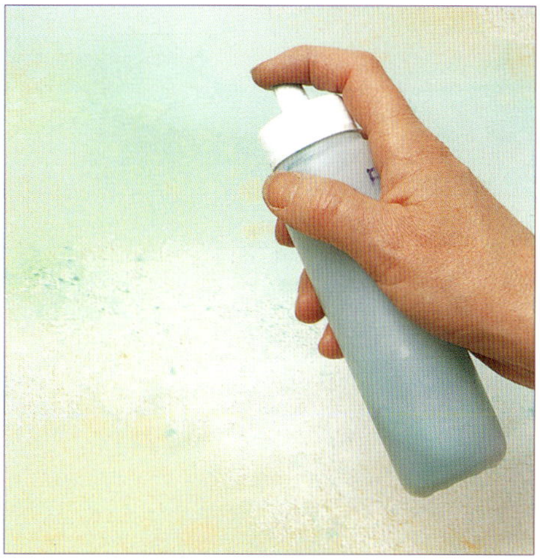

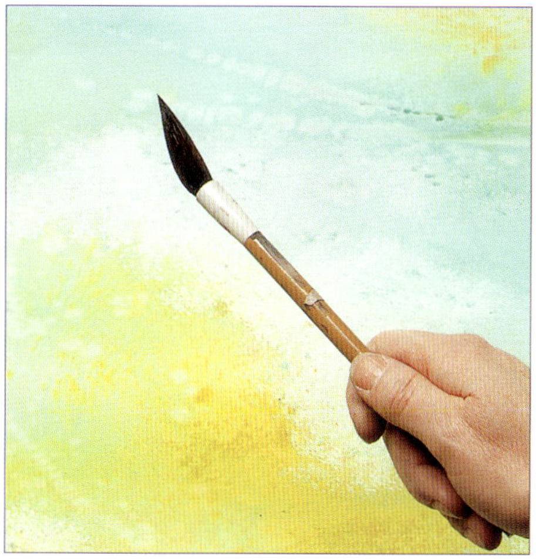

5 Spray the colours on to the silk, initially spraying around the thickener shapes to allow the paints to flow up and into the printed waves.

6. Change over the colours as you spray, wet on wet to give a blended effect, and then lightly spray over the printed waves to pick out the open textured detail. Work freely, and quite quickly until the whole area is coloured.

7. If the paints are still damp, drizzle full strength colour from a pipette or flick water from a brush to give further patterning.

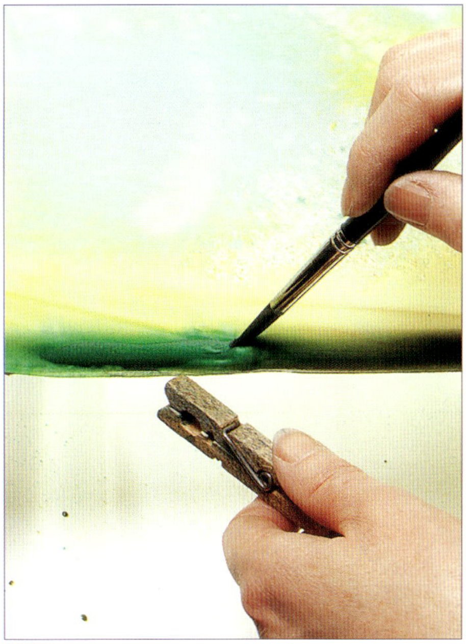

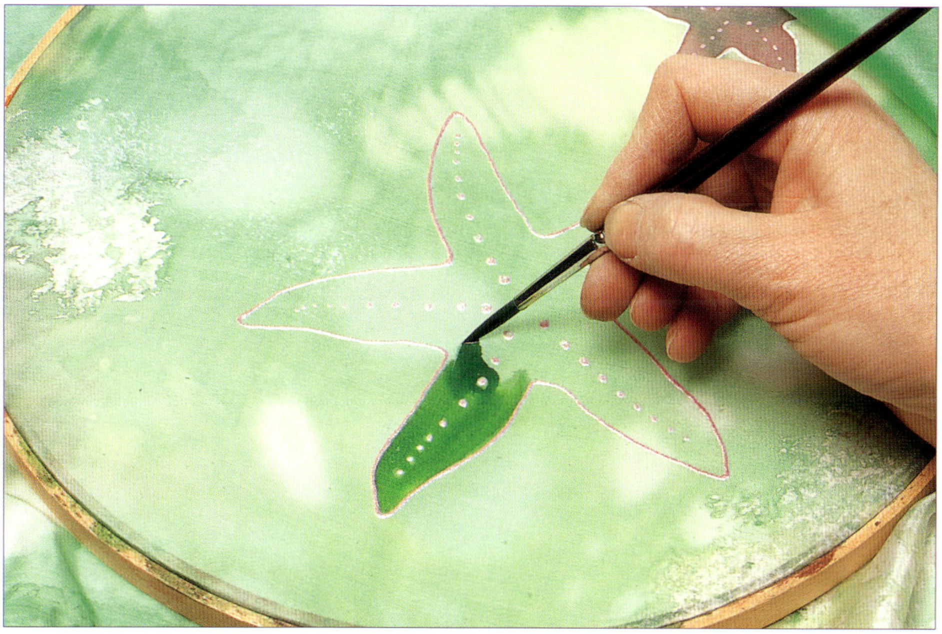

8. Finally, brush a full-strength colour along each edge to colour under the pegs, moving them slightly if necessary. Allow the silk to dry naturally before un-pegging it from the bamboo canes.

9. Pin an area on to the regular frame with silk pins, or stretch an area into an embroidery hoop. Place the pattern motifs under the silk and trace out the patterns in outliner. Once the outliner has dried, paint in the motif using a small brush and full-strength silk paints. Allow this pattern to dry before un-pinning and re-stretching the silk to work another area. Continue until outlined designs have been applied across the whole sarong.

10. Tape the silk on to some plastic sheeting to hold the edge taut. Select a heat-fix outliner, (not clear one as it will wash out) and apply a generous free-hand line along the whole edge. While the outliner is still wet, brush out the line to spread the outliner slightly. Don't worry if it looks a little messy at this stage (see project on page 62).

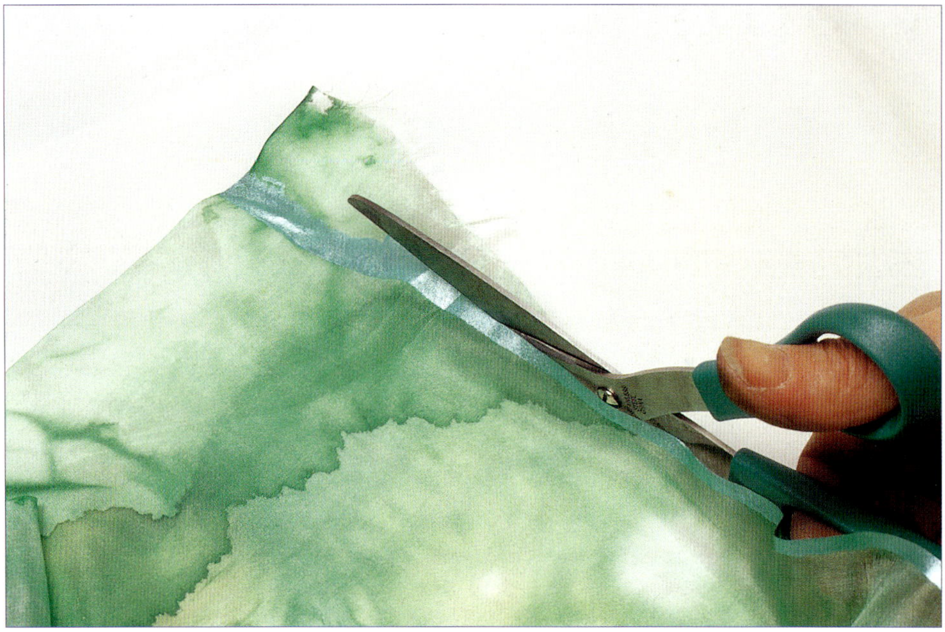

11. Allow the outliner to dry. Then, using a sharp pair of scissors, trim the edge, cutting through the middle of the spread line to form a neat, no sew edge. Repeat at the other end. Use an iron to heat-fix the whole sarong or set the work by dry curing in an oven (see page 15).

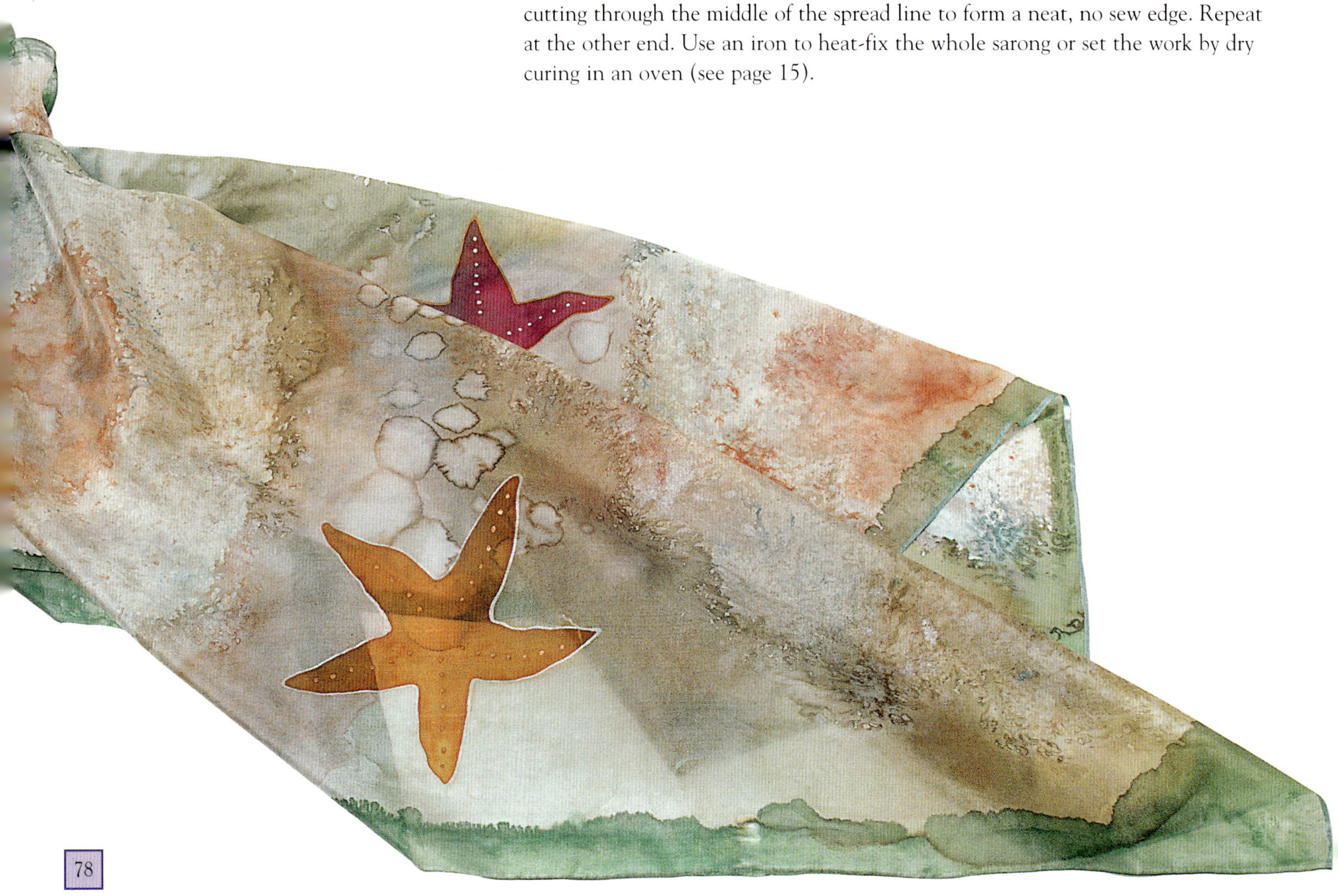

Using clear resist on coloured silk

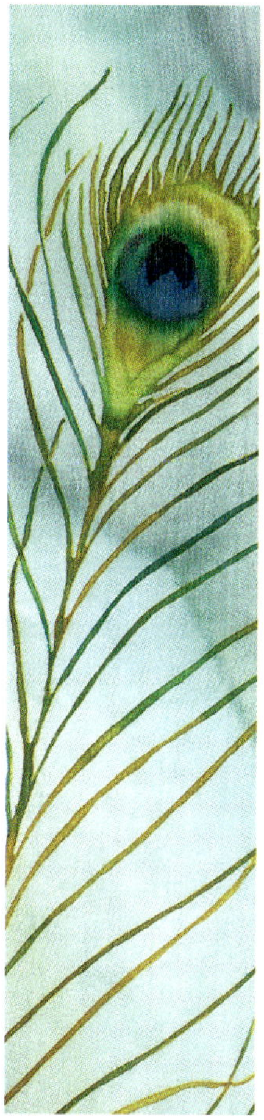

Equipment and materials

- Pongee or habotai silk scarf
- Frame and silk pins
- Steam-fix colours
- Water pot and mixing palette
- Paint brushes and sponge brushes
- Clear outliner
- Hairdryer
- Peacock feathers or patterns
- Steam-fixing equipment
- Template p105

Feathers come in all shapes, sizes and colours and the peacock feathers in this project have been drawn direct from feathers placed underneath the silk. Use the feather patterns at the back of the book if you do not have any real ones. By initially painting the background in a pale colour, and using only clear outliner for the feathers, the resist lines will not show in the completed piece, provided the background is not repainted. Use diluted colours for the background so that the clarity of the colours in the feathers will not be adversely affected.

1. Pin the silk scarf to the frame with silk pins. Prepare the colours for the background by diluting them with water in a large palette well. Apply the background colours across the whole of the scarf, using a sponge brush. Create a smooth or slightly textured pattern with soft watermarks by adding water or more colour while the ground is still wet. Dab all the outer edges with a piece of kitchen paper to remove any excess paints and prevent dye from flowing back from the rolled edges. Allow it to dry naturally.

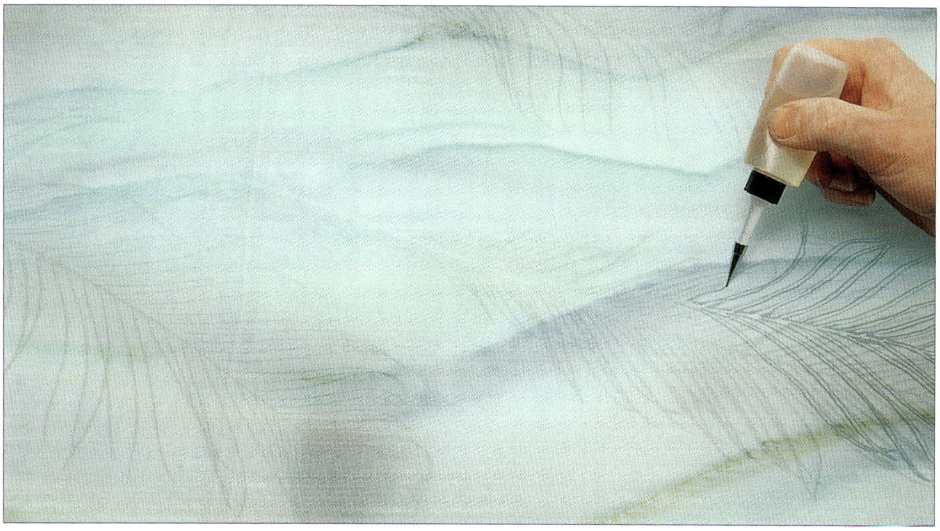

2. Place the peacock feathers or patterns under the painted silk. Look through the silk and trace off the pattern in clear outliner. Remember the outliner will not show in the completed work so do not worry about blobs or heavy outlines.

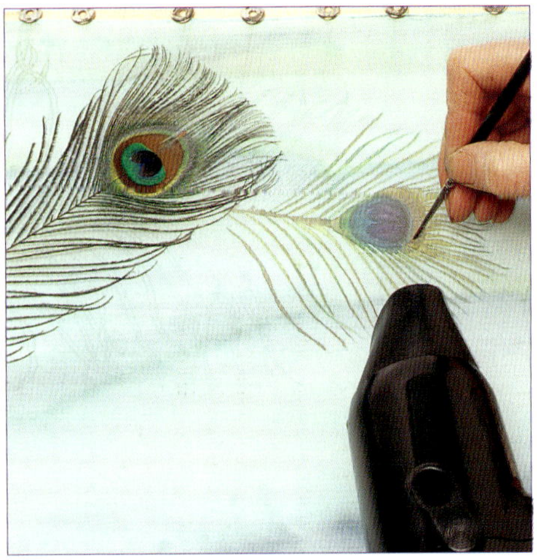

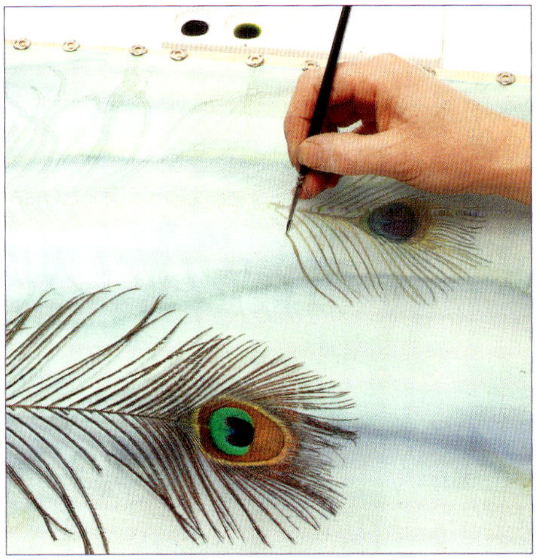

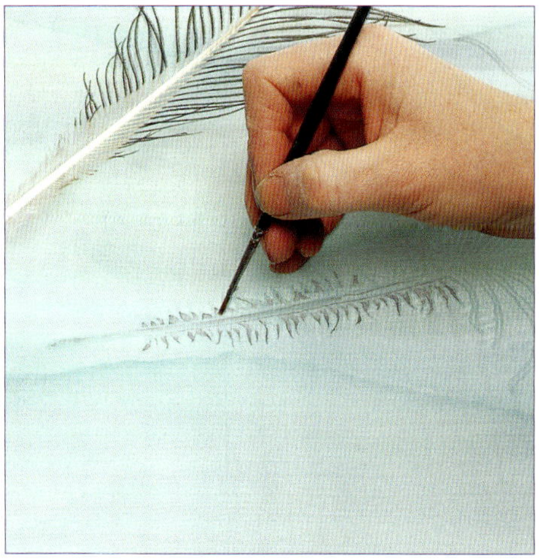

3. Dry the outlines and paint in the eye of the feather using full-strength dyes and a very fine brush to blend the colours. Have a hairdryer ready to help control the patterning for the eye on the feather.

4. Use a fine brush to carefully continue painting in the feather. Use several colours to give shading and depth to the piece.

5. Now paint in and shade the quill of the feather. When all the feathers are painted, steam-fix the work in the usual way, and then wash the silk to remove the outliner. Iron while the silk is still just damp to restore the full sheen and drape of the silk.

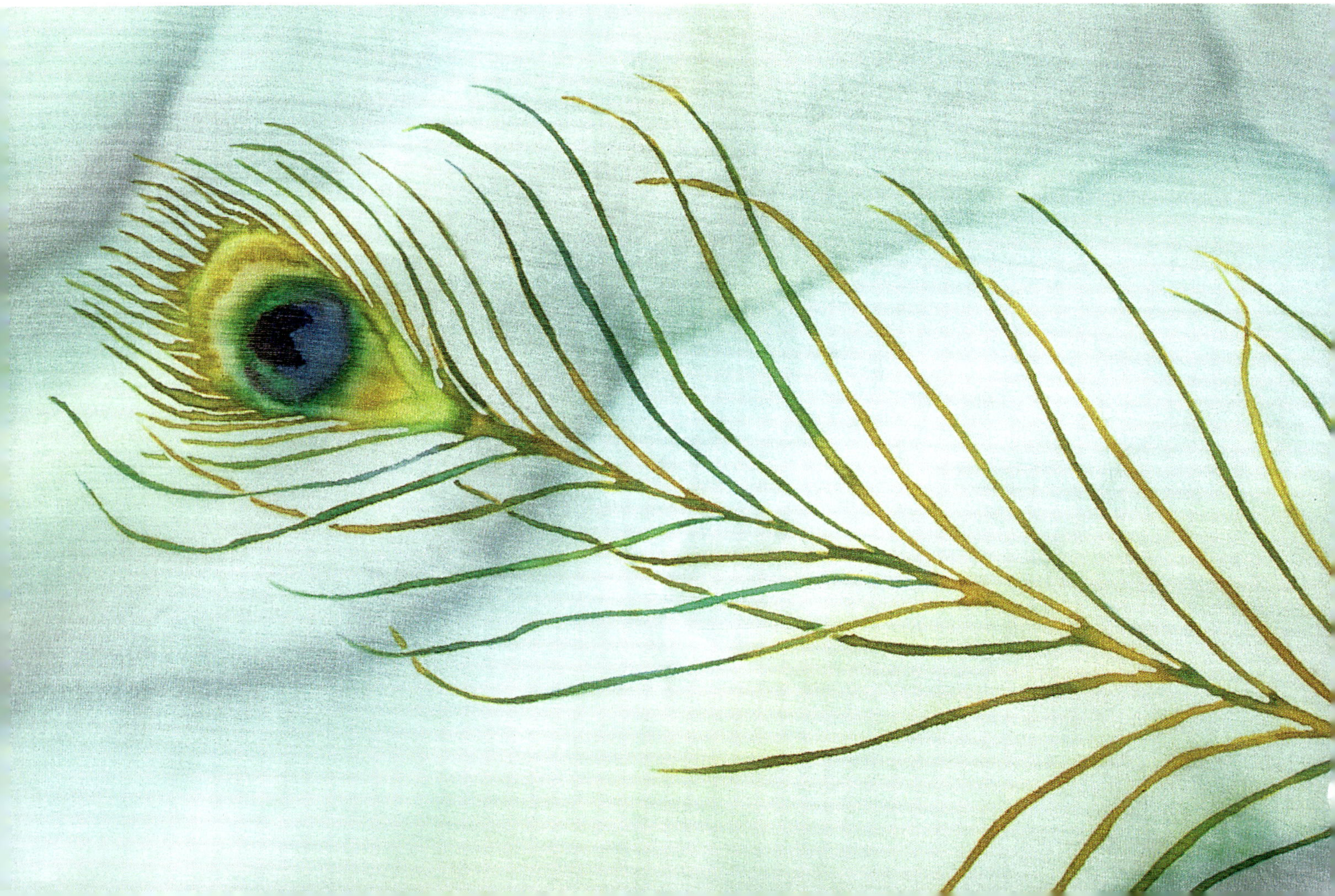

Velvet evening bag

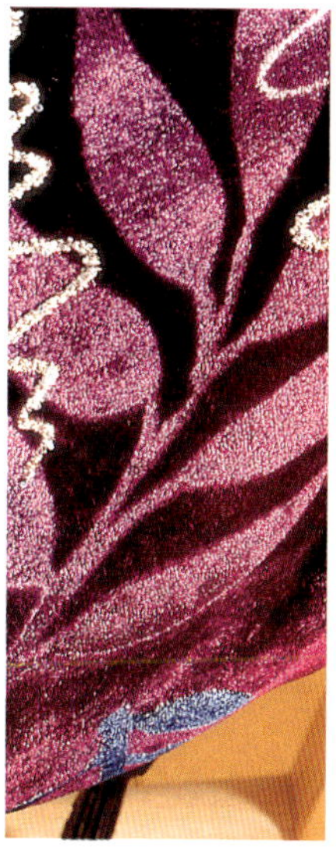

Equipment and materials

A piece of white silk viscose velvet
A selection of steam-fix dyes,
Discharge viscoser, salts and effect colours
Selection of large paint brushes or sponge brushes
Mixing palette and water pot
Kitchen roll
Piece of plastic to protect your work surface
Rubber gloves
Masking tape
Permanent pen and bag pattern
Steaming equipment
Hot stamping blocks and printing blocks
Iron
Spray bottle with water
Plexi-glue and granular beads
Decorative liners
Needle, thread, scissors and other sewing items to make up the finished bag
Template p106

Show off your silk painting skills by working this attractive evening bag that incorporates dyeing, discharging and surface decoration techniques. Use either steam-fix or procion dyes, although steam-fix dyes are probably best as the discharging medium also requires steaming.

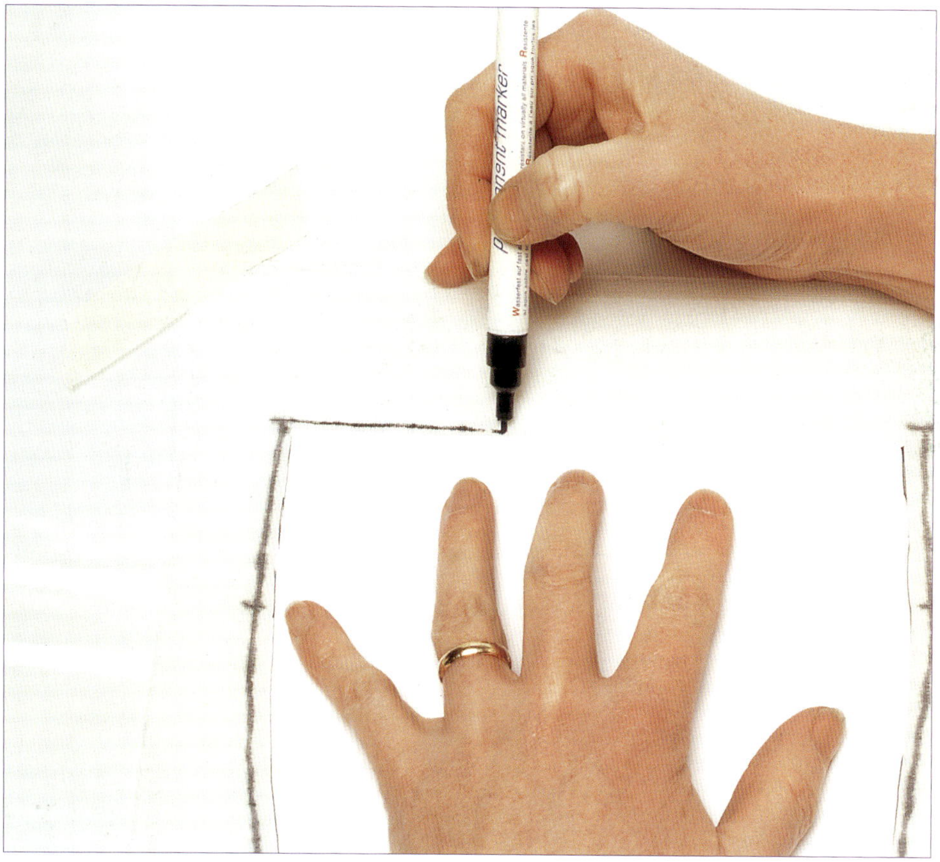

1. Lay the velvet pile-side down on the plastic, and hold in position with masking tape. Draw around the paper pattern in a permanent marker pen to allow you to work patterns to fit the shape of the bag, which is made from three pieces.

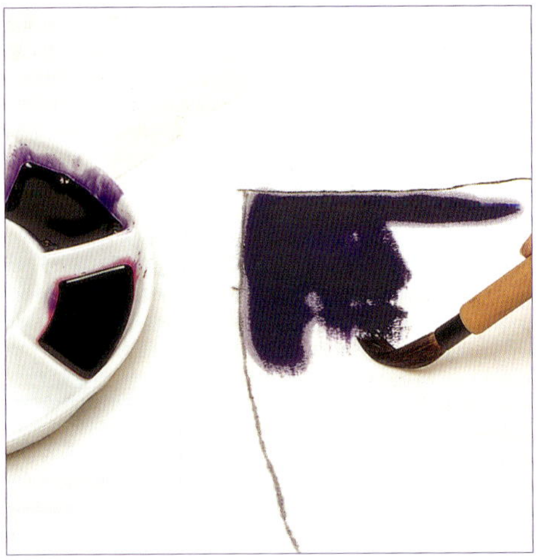

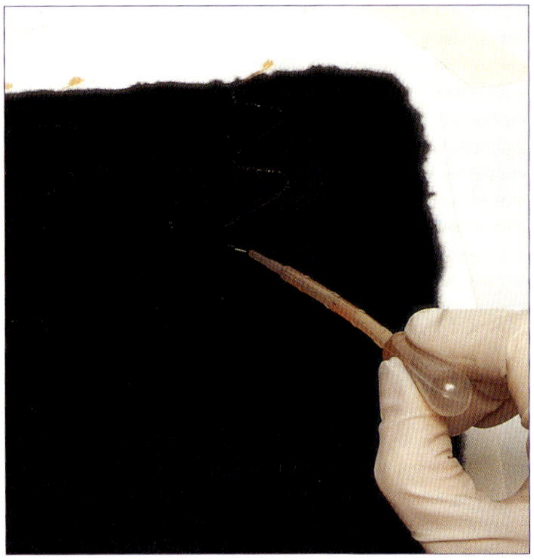

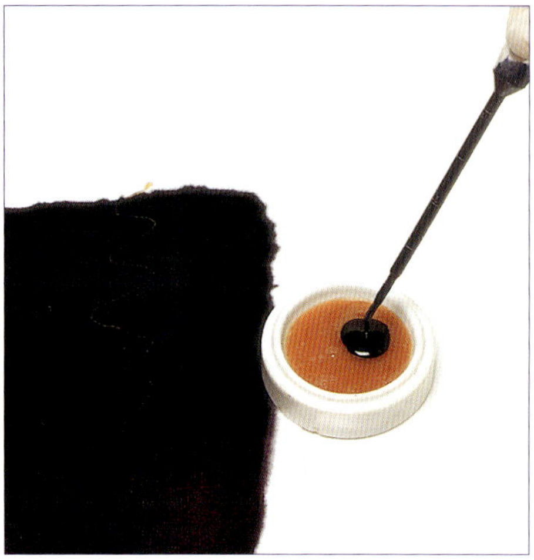

2. Use large brushes to apply and blend the steam-fix dyes to the back of the velvet. Allow to dry.

3. Pour 30 ml (1½ fl oz) discharge viscoser into a dish, add ¾ teaspoon of magic salts, mix thoroughly, and divide this discharge medium into three dishes.

4. Lift up the uncoloured discharge medium from one dish with a pipette and drizzle it on to the pile-side of the velvet and dry with a hairdryer.

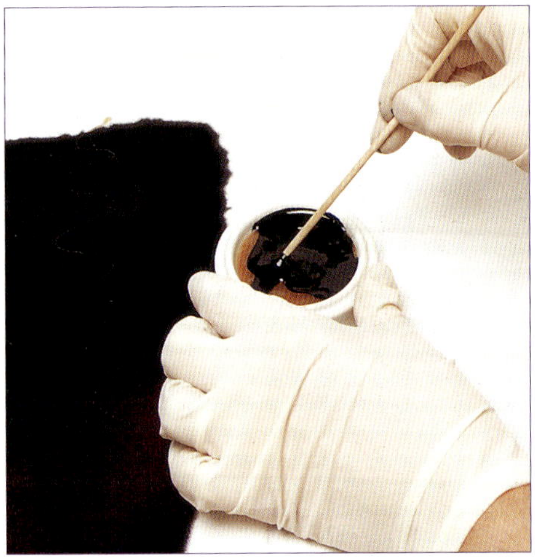

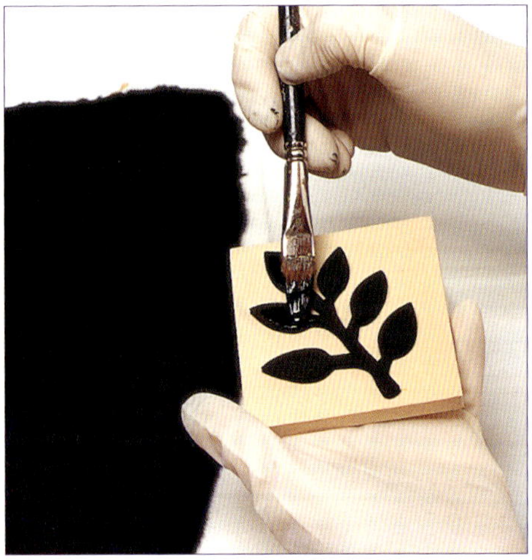

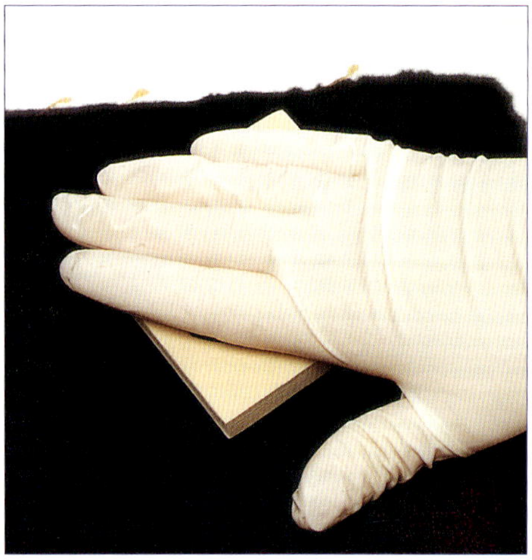

5. Add approx 10 ml (½ fl oz) of effect colour to two of the dishes and mix again to make two different coloured discharge pastes.

6. Apply some coloured discharge medium to a stamping block.

7. Print on to the pile of the velvet inside the pen line. Dry with a hairdryer.

8. Roll up the dry velvet in absorbent paper and steam to set the steam-fix dyes and activate the discharge process. See page 16 for information on steaming. Wash the fixed velvet in warm water to remove the spent discharge medium and any excess dyes. Allow to dry a little. Then iron on the reverse following the lie of the pile.

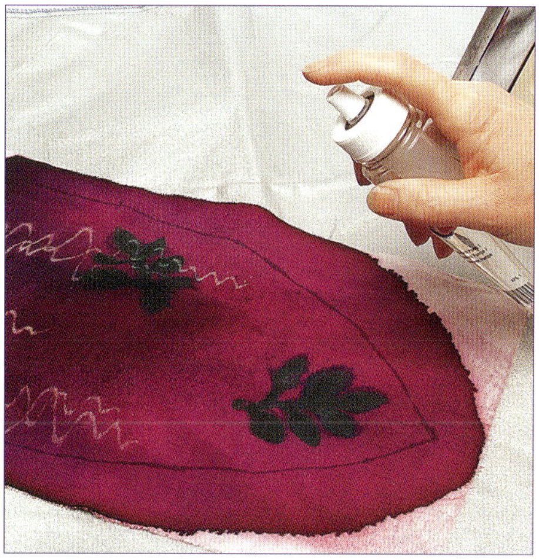

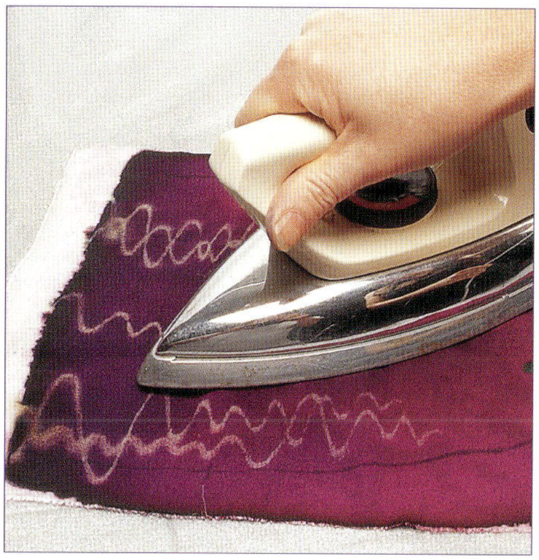

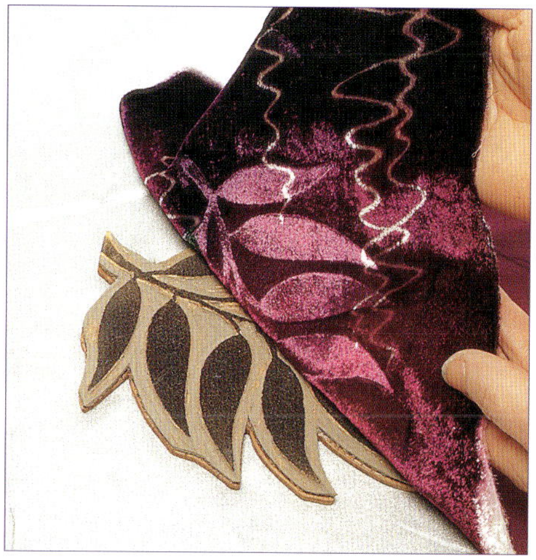

9. Work some hot blocking or stamping with either hot potato, rubber stamps, wooden print blocks or your own lino shapes. Place the block pattern side up, on the ironing board, then place the velvet pile-side down on to the block. Spray a little water on the reverse of the velvet.

10. Place a flat iron on to the fabric and block and hold there for 15–20 seconds.

11. Carefully peel back the velvet to reveal the pattern imprint. Continue this across the velvet.

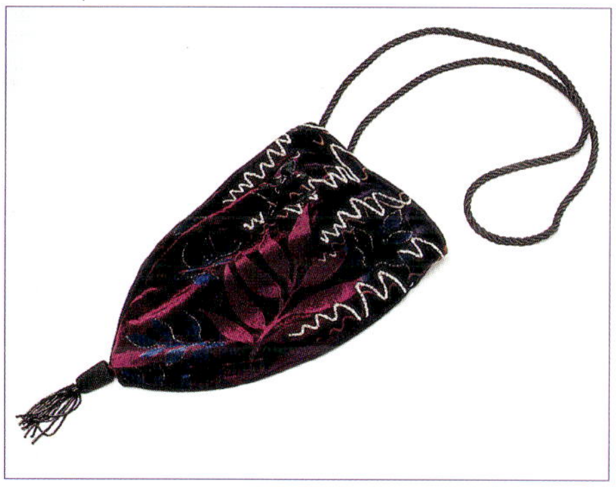

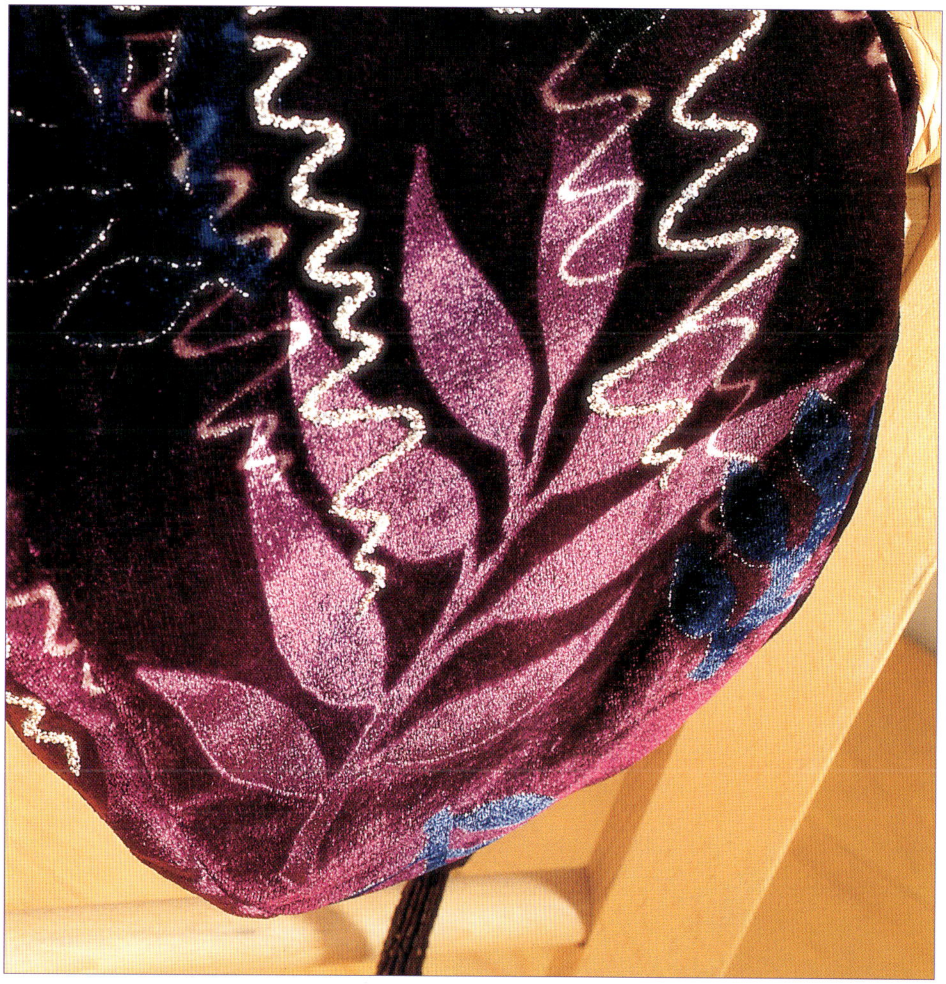

12. Apply a fine line of plexi-glue to highlight some areas, and sprinkle tiny granular beads across the wet glue lines. Allow the glue to completely dry before removing any loose beads. When dry, add fine glitter lines to accent other areas. Allow all pattern mediums to dry completely before making up the bag. Place the right sides together and sew up, leaving the top open to turn and add a lining of painted or dyed habotai silk. Finally, add cording or beaded tassels.

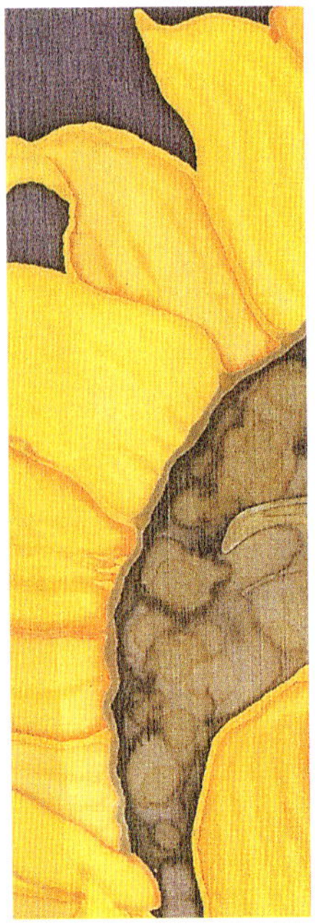

Sunflowers drawn using coloured water-soluble outliners

Creating outliners to blend with the colouring of the flowers or using pre-coloured water-soluble outliners gives a design a softer, less stencilled appearance. The completed work is not stiffened, and the movement of the dyes can be controlled as they are painted on to the silk in the normal way.

Equipment and materials

Ready-edged scarf or piece of silk
Frame and silk pins
Steam-fix dyes
Clear water-soluble outliner
Pre-coloured water-soluble outliners
Pipette applicator bottles and nibs
Mixing palette and water pot
Paint brushes
Pattern
Steam-fixing equipment
Template p107

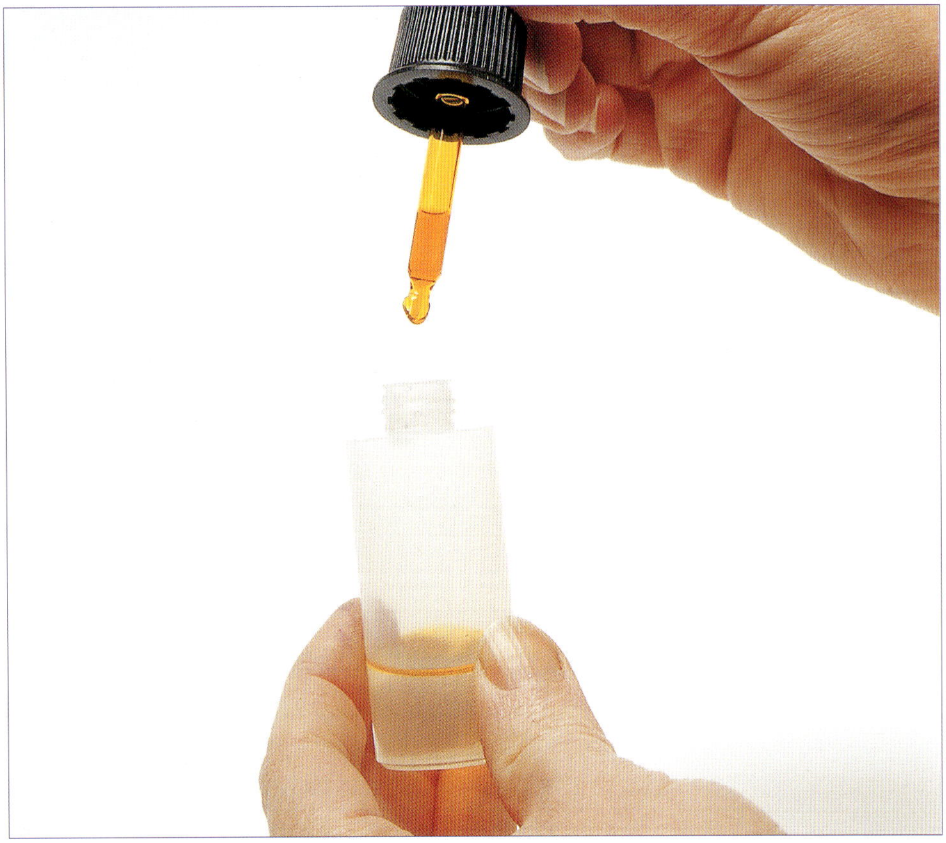

1. Pin the scarf to the frame with silk pins, and arrange the patterns under the silk. Pay attention to the shapes and spaces created. To make your own coloured outliner, pour a little clear outliner into a pipette bottle and add a few drops of dye at a time until you have an acceptable colour and consistency. Too much colour will create a runny outliner medium. Try using dye that has become more concentrated after it has dried a little in the palette. Screw a fine nib on to the tip of the applicator bottle. Alternatively, use pre-coloured water-soluble outliners.

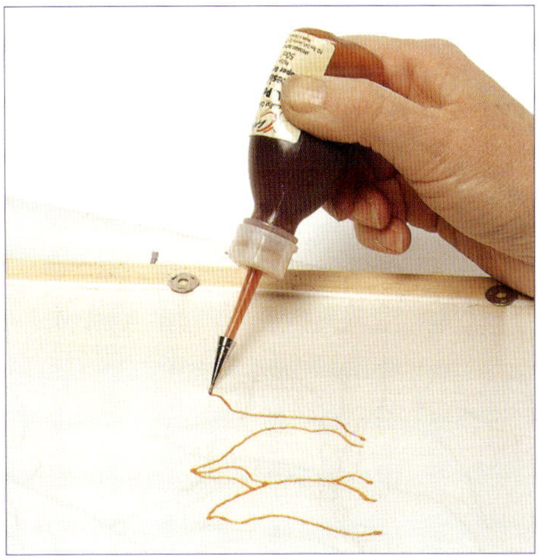

2. Look through the silk to follow the pattern and draw out the design using a selection of outline colours that you feel appropriate. Allow the outlines to dry or use a hairdryer, before painting in any of the shapes.

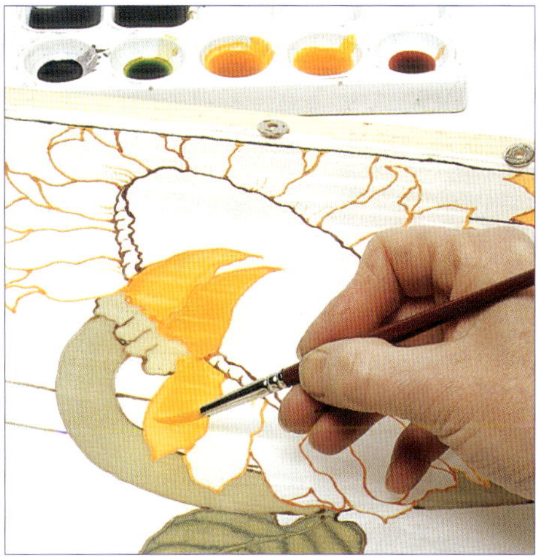

3. Using an appropriately sized brush, carefully paint in the flowers, stems and leaves.

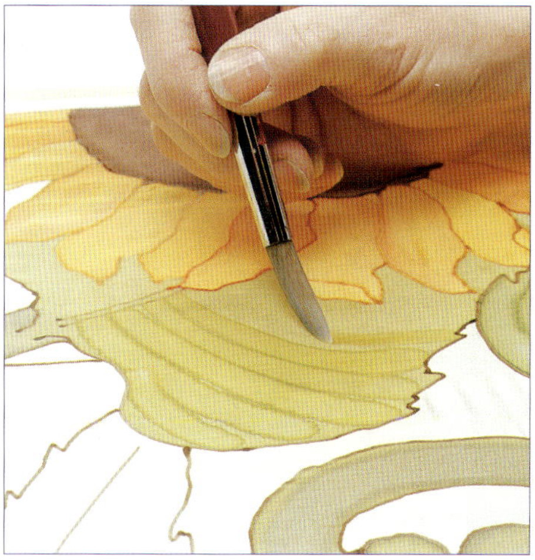

4. Use shading and blending techniques to give depth to the design and make watermarks to create further patterning.

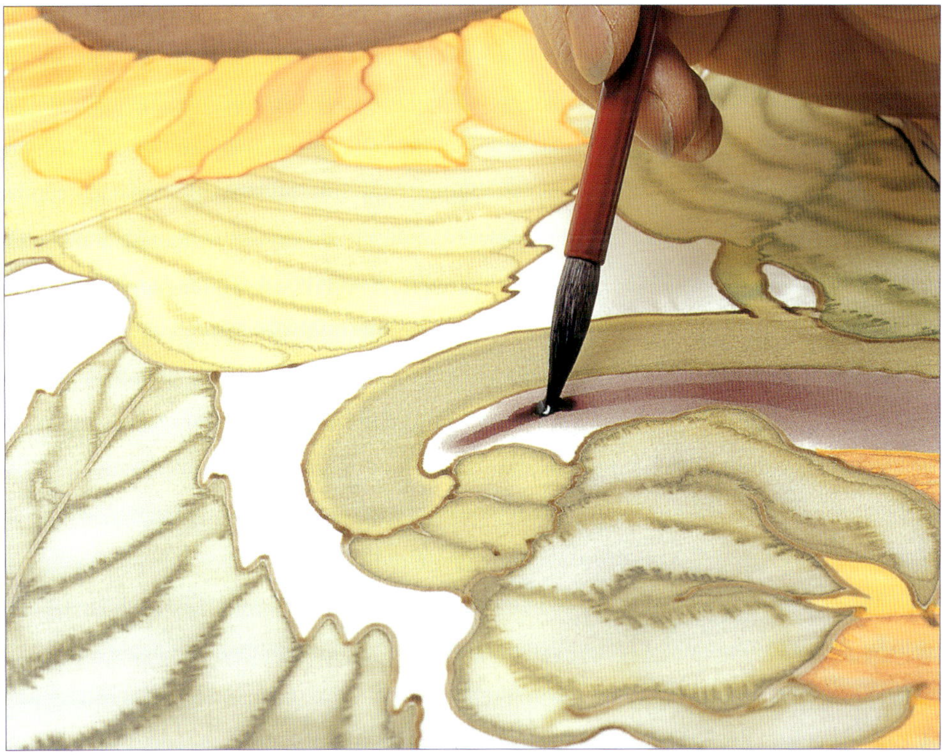

5. Before painting in the background area or borders, consider a variety of different colour options. Then mix up sufficient colour to complete each area. Paint in the background and border areas using a combination of large and small brushes to reach all the nooks and crannies.

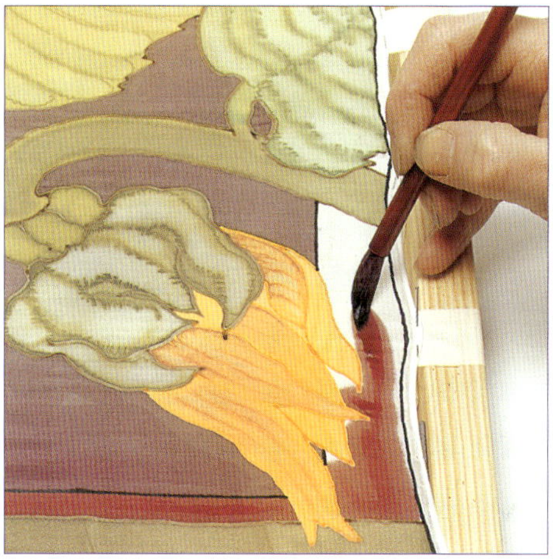

6. Remember to work the border alternatively from one side to another to avoid a join mark.

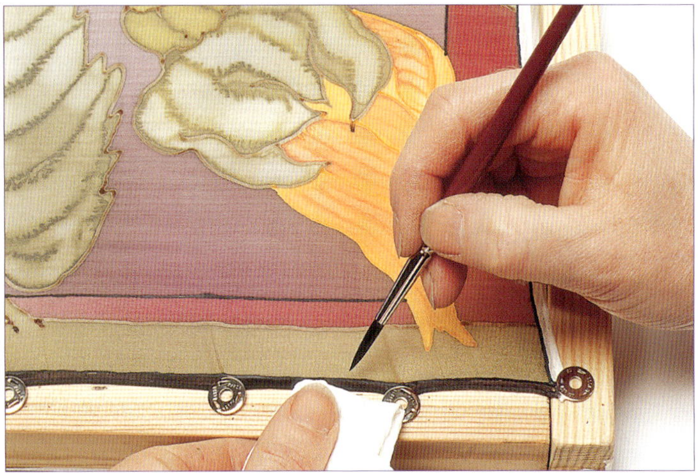

7. Dab the border-rolled edges to prevent flow back. Allow the piece to dry naturally before un-pinning and steam-fixing the scarf.

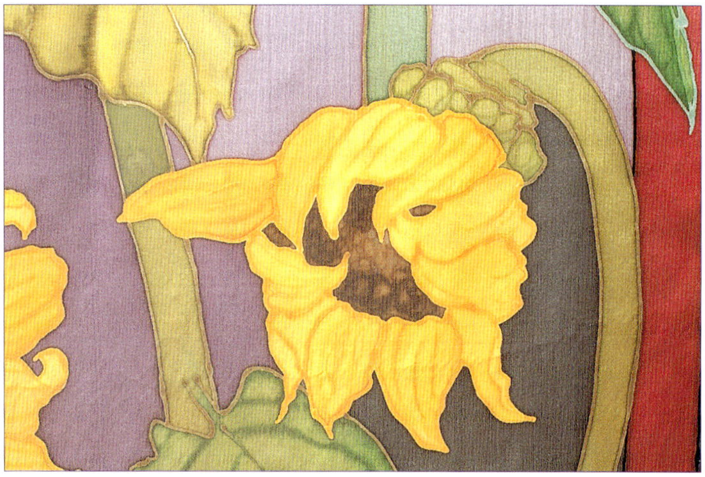

8. Wash the fixed scarf in warm water to remove all traces of outliner. By feeling with your fingers as you wash, you should be able to tell when the glutinous water-soluble outliner medium has gone. Allow the silk to dry a little before ironing.

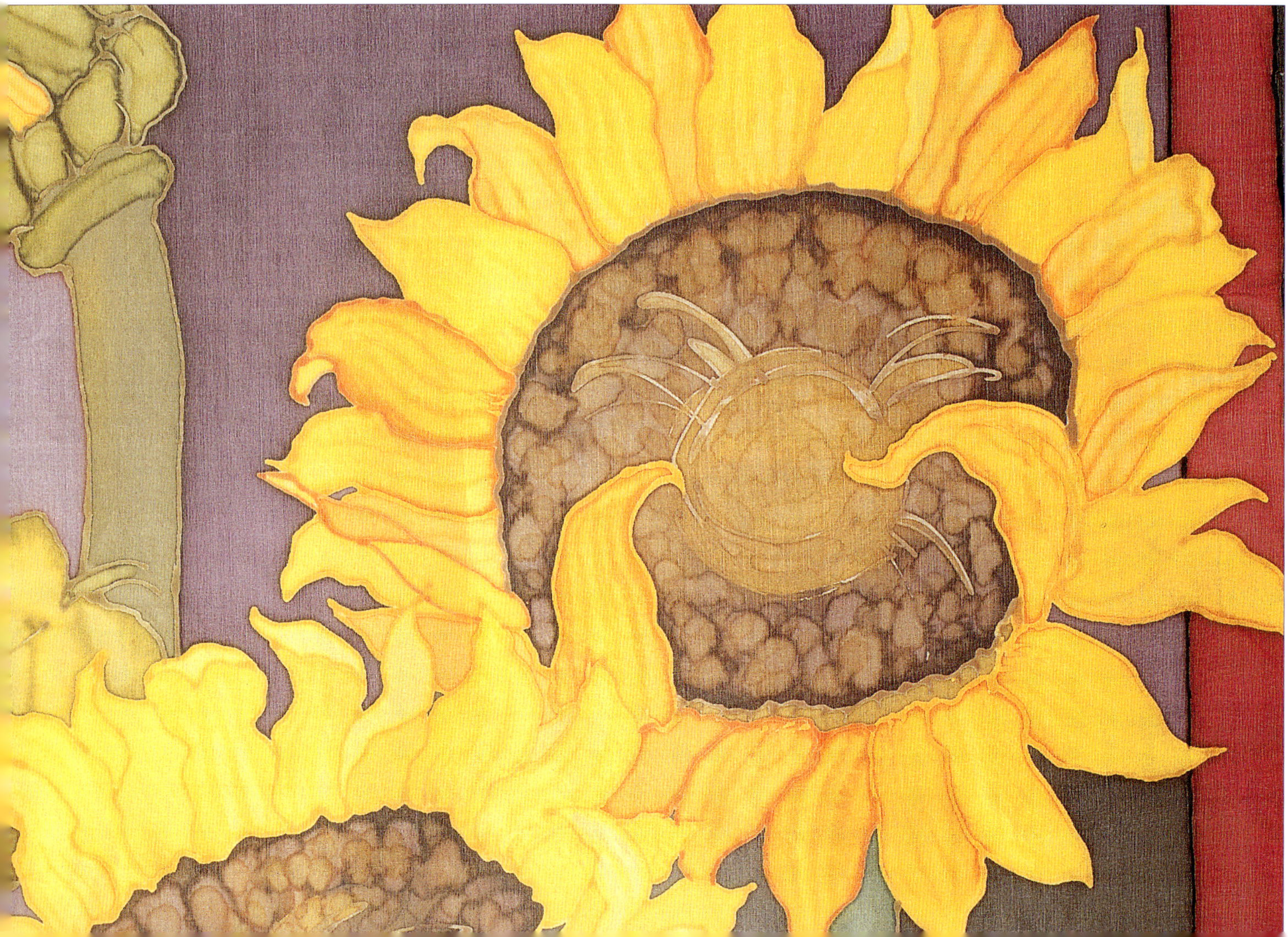

Using silk paint thickener to form a hand-painted design

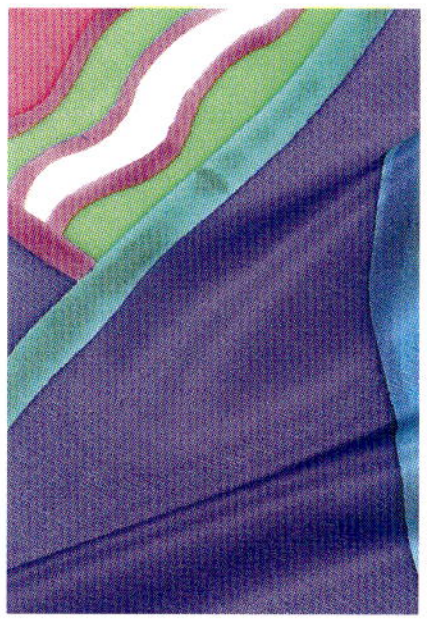

Equipment and materials

A ready-edged scarf

Frame and silk pins

Steam-fix dyes

Steam-fix silk paint thickener

Mixing palette and water pot

Paint brushes

Paper towelling

Hairdryer

Steam-fixing equipment

As you become more proficient with your brush skills you may like to try working free-hand. You don't have to be able to draw pictures to do this, just keep it simple and work an abstract design using straight and curving lines with dots and dashes formed by the brush stroke. Remember, working with the thickener still provides a good element of control when it comes to the painting. It's fun and gives a real sense of achievement and satisfaction if you are not too confident about working free-hand.

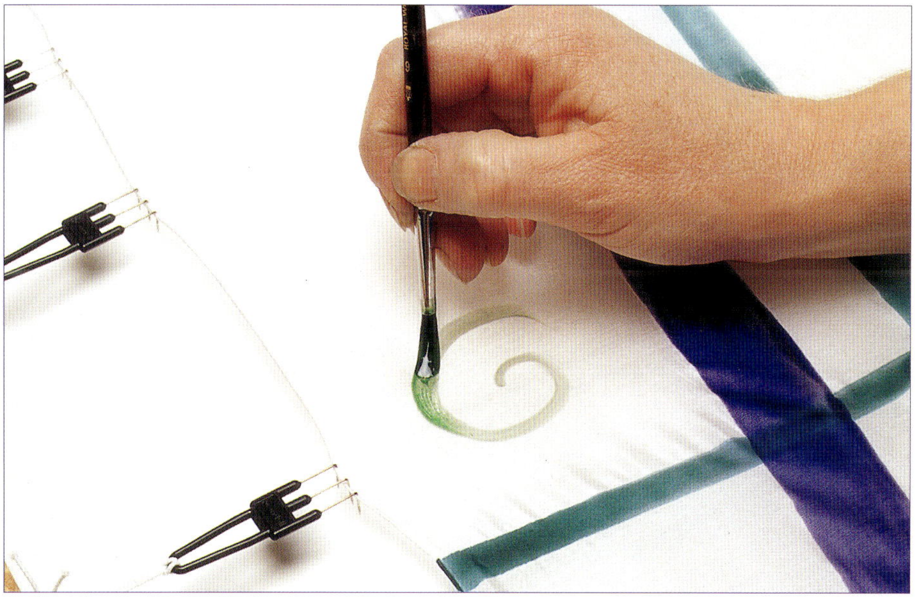

1. Attach the silk to the frame using silk pins. Place some silk paint thickener into the empty palette wells. Add an equal amount of dye to the thickener and thoroughly mix the two together to form a paint medium. Repeat this process for each colour to be applied as a thickened medium. Use a firm brush to apply the colours in simple sweeping shapes across the silk. Allow the shape of the brush to dictate the edge quality of the lines.

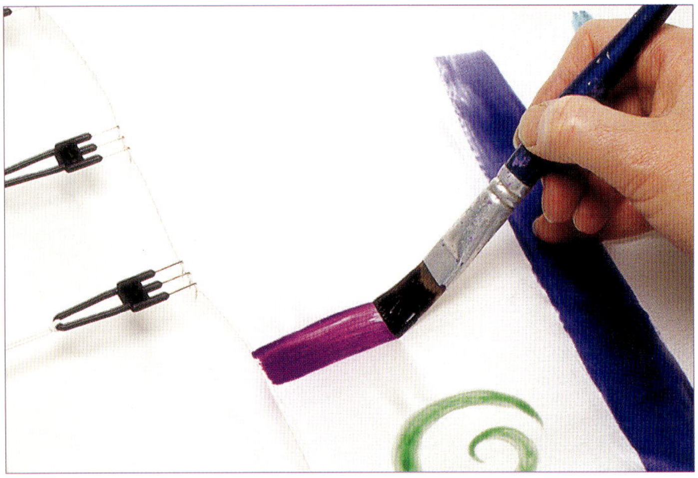

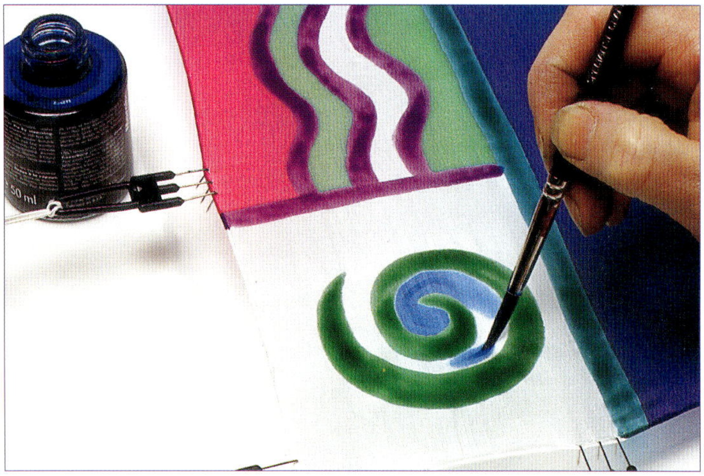

2. Allow the thickener pattern lines to dry. Vary the types of brushes used and try working with a double colour loaded brush for extra variation on the colouring. Leave some areas to paint.

3. Use a paint brush to apply the colour a little distance away from the edges of the brushed pattern lines, allowing the dye to flow to these shapes. Work blocks of colour or shading and patterning as you wish with the liquid dyes

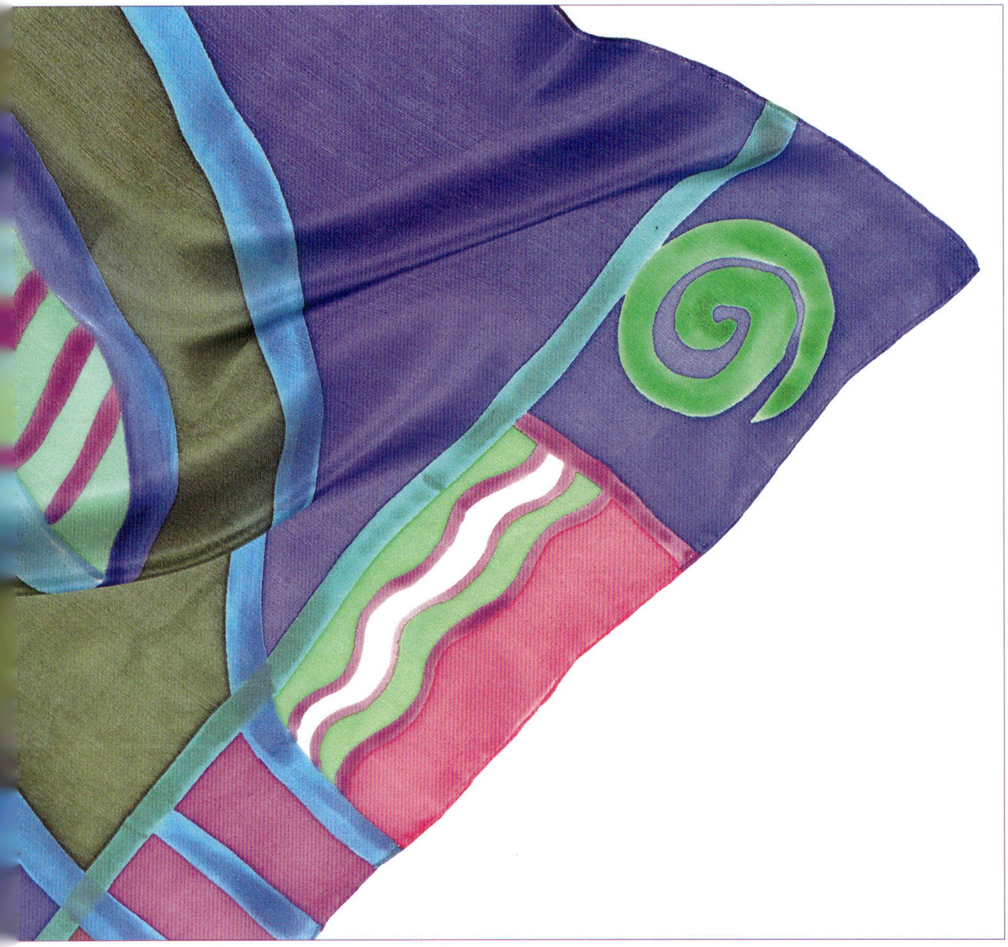

4. When the work is complete, remove from the frame and steam-fix the dyes. Once the design is fixed, wash the silk in warm water to remove the gelatinous thickener and excess dye. As you wash the silk feel with your fingers to tell when all traces of thickener have been removed. Allow the silk to dry a little before ironing to finish.

Cushion worked with a wax resist

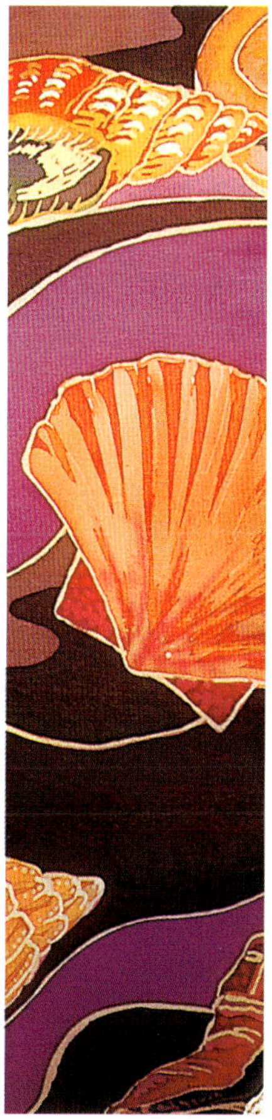

Equipment and materials

- Ready-made open-sided cushion
- Frame and silk pins
- Wax and wax pot, or double saucepan and thermometer
- Selection of cantings (tjantings) and brushes
- Steam-fix dyes
- Brushes for the silk dyes
- Mixing palette and water pot
- Paper towelling
- Patterns
- Iron
- Newspaper to cover table
- Template p108

Working with a wax resist is quite different from working with water-soluble outliners as the wax forms a true resist that permits colour washes to be applied over lines and areas already waxed out. Extra care should be taken when working with hot wax, and ideally you should have a thermostatically controlled wax pot or thermometer to check the temperature. Never leave the pot unattended while it is switched on. Please read the safety advice on page 21 if you have not used wax before.

Tip: If you want to create a crackle effect, brush wax over the whole piece, un-pin and place the waxed silk into a freezer for 10 minutes. This cools the wax and helps to give good crackling. Gently squeeze the silk to form cracks in the wax. Then re-pin the silk on the frame and brush a dark colour across the whole piece. The dark silk dye will run into the cracks and give a batik appearance to the completed work.

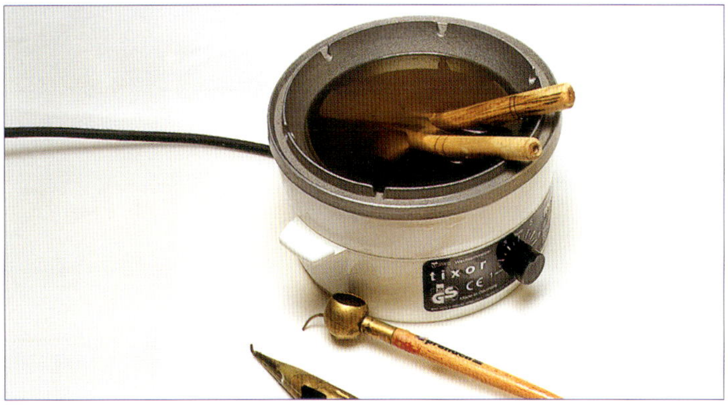

1. Cover the table with newspaper and stretch the silk on the frame using silk pins. Heat the wax to a working temperature of 130° C. Place the patterns under the silk and allow the cantings to warm through in the wax pot before using them.

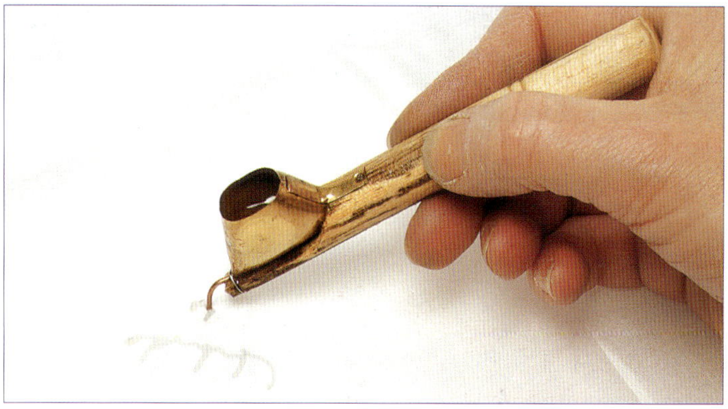

2. Using the pattern as a guide, wax in a few details, which will retain the white colour of the fabric. Hold a piece of paper towelling against the canting spout to stop the flow of wax and prevent drips as you top up with new hot wax. (See page 21 for tips on applying wax.)

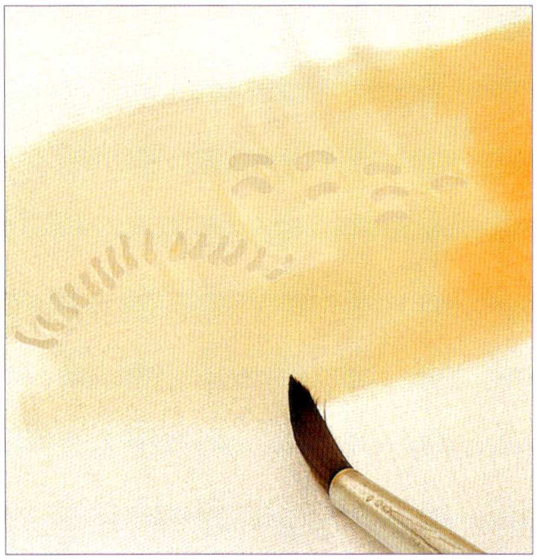

3. Brush the first diluted colours as a pale background wash right over the first layer of dry wax.

4. Use the brush to blend the colours or add any texture patterning. If you use a hairdryer to dry the colours make sure that it is not too hot or it will re-melt the wax and spoil the design.

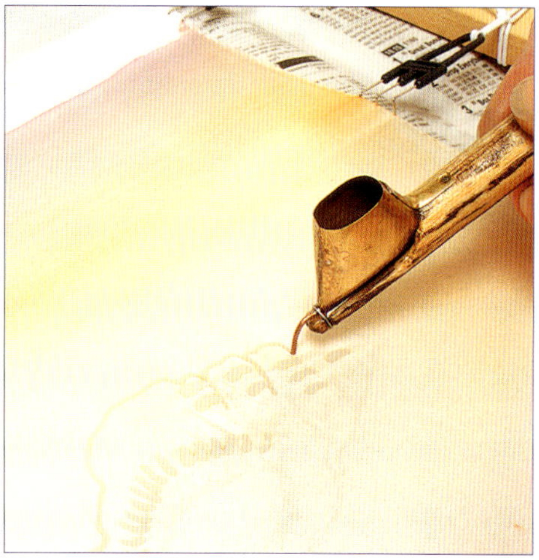

5. Work a second layer of wax, adding more detail to the pattern. This waxing will retain the colours it is applied over.

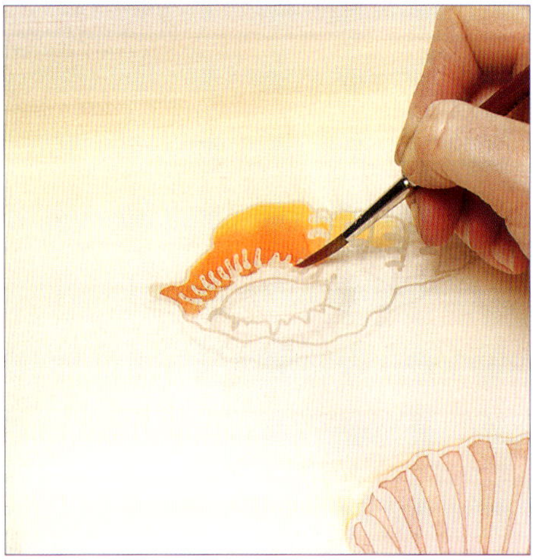

6. When the wax is dry add further colour to the shells.

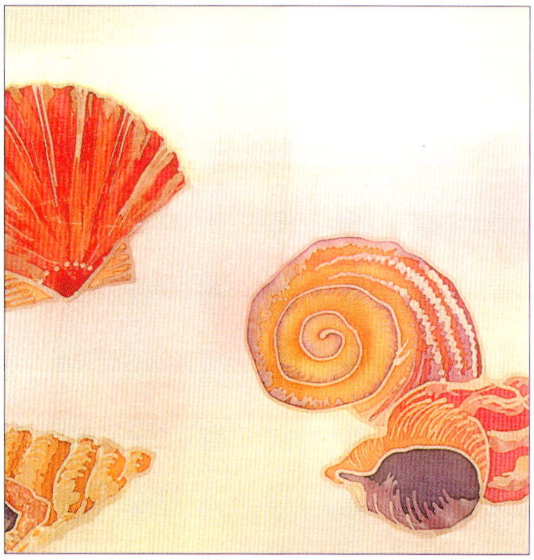

7. Continue waxing in the design and adding colour to create a range of patterning and colouring effects.

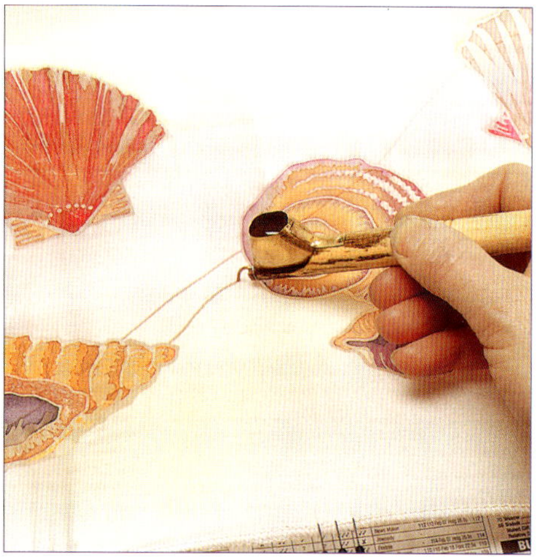

8. Draw wavy lines in wax across the whole piece to create a background pattern.

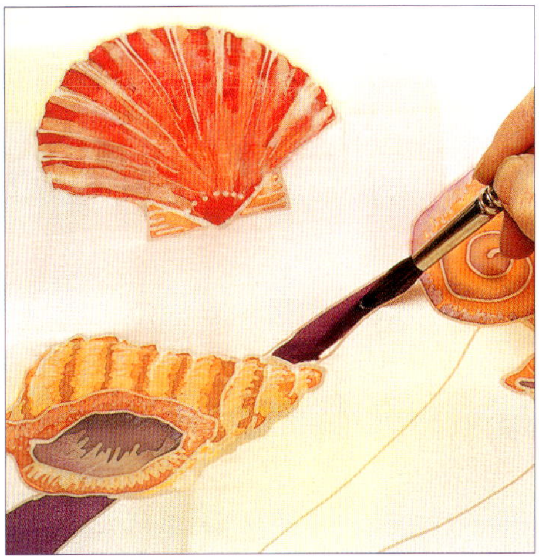

9. Paint in all the stripes to colour the background.

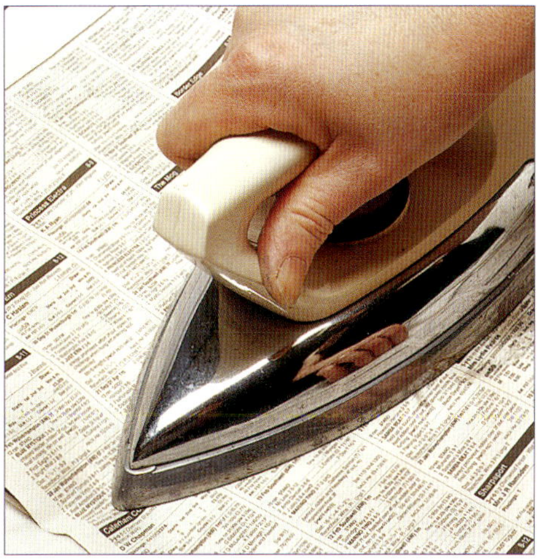

10. Remove the silk from the frame and iron the whole piece between several sheets of absorbent or old newspaper to remove the wax, before steaming the piece in the normal way to set the dyes.

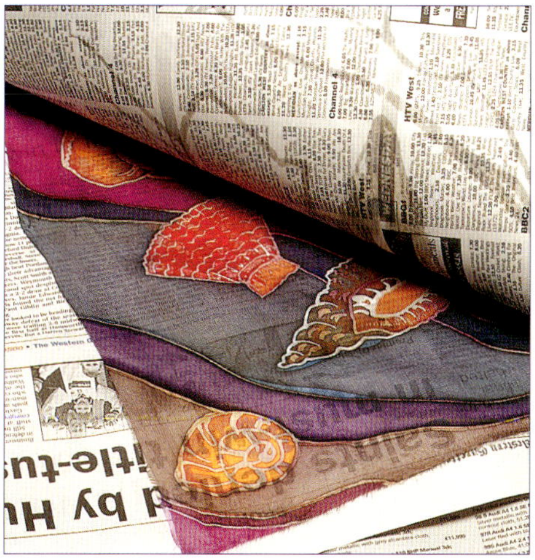

11. Wash the silk in hot soapy water to remove any final traces of wax, and iron once again while just damp to give a good finish. Make the cushion up by sewing along the three open edges, remembering to leave the zip open slightly to allow easy turning through to the right side.

Variations: heat-set paints can be used if you prefer, although they will not flow so readily in the subsequent layers, but ironing to remove the wax will also set the paints.

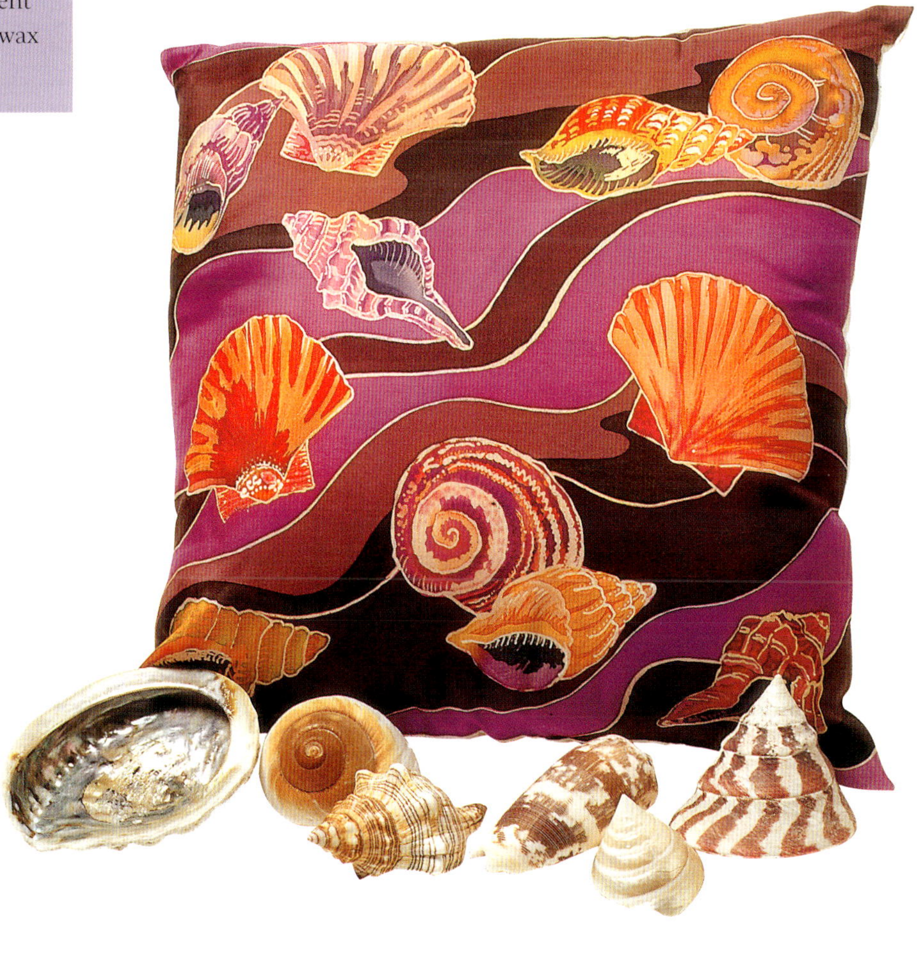

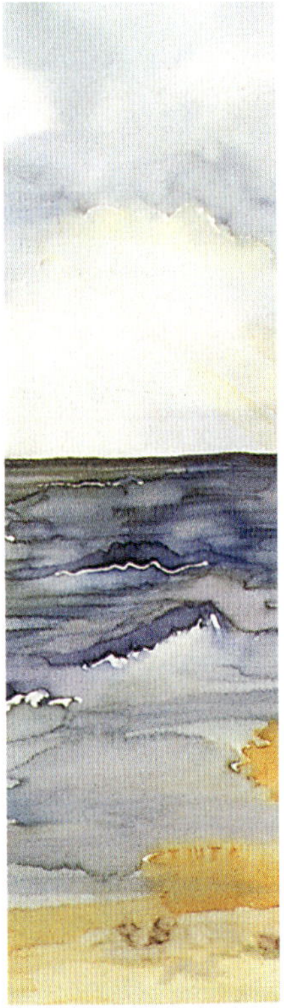

Seascape picture

Painted silk pictures are an excellent way of displaying the variety of effects that can be achieved with silk paints. The vibrant colours and wonderful patterns just seem to glow on the silk fabric. Seascapes or landscapes are great fun to work, using watermarks to imply features. You don't need a pattern, just allow the work to develop as you work. This project uses anti-spread to help control the flow of the dyes without the use of outliner.

Equipment and materials

- Piece of habotai silk
- Frame and silk pins
- Steam-set silk dyes
- Anti-spread
- Paint brushes
- Water pot and mixing palette
- Hairdryer

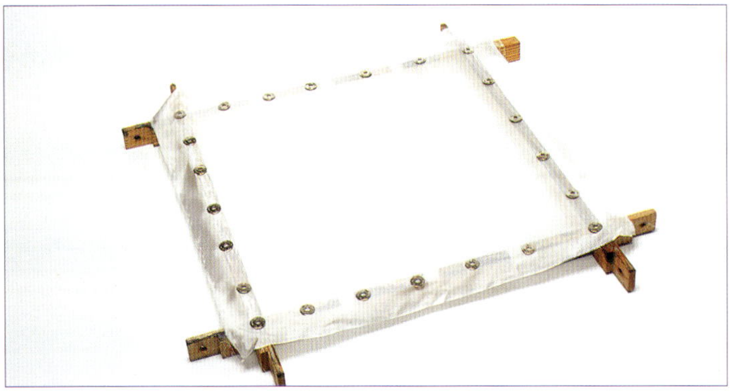

1. Fasten the silk to the frame with silk pins.

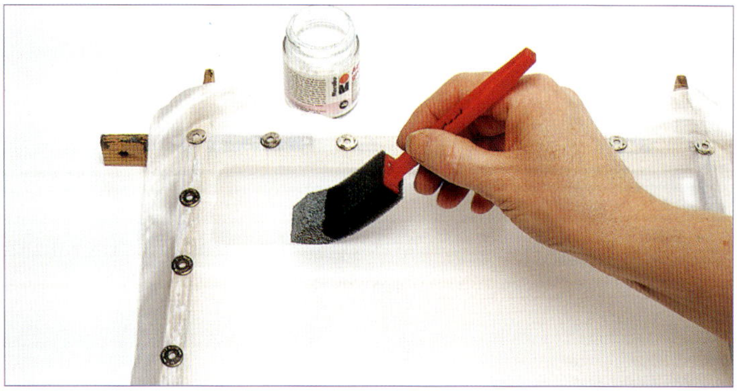

2. Apply a layer of anti-spread to the silk with a large brush and allow it to dry while you prepare the colours, diluting some with water for paler tints and washes.

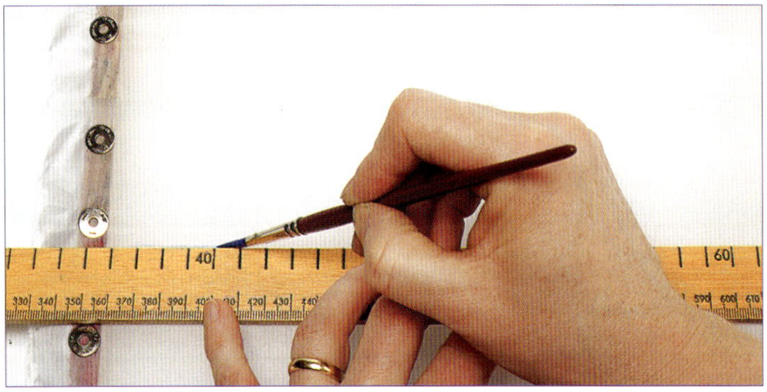

3. Draw in the horizon with a rule and a fine brush to hold just a little dye. The wet colour will not run on the treated silk.

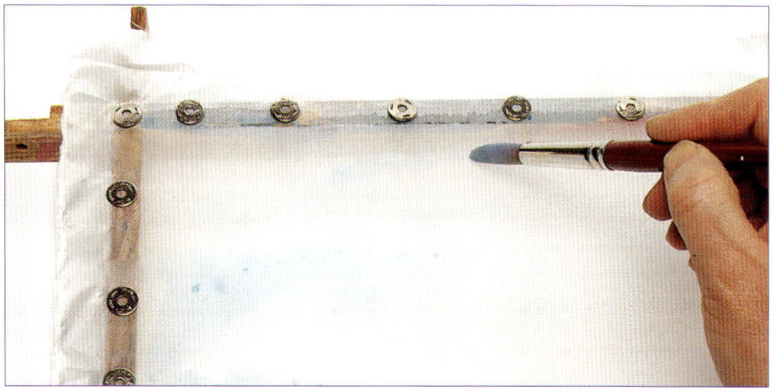

4. Start with the sky, applying a light wash of sky colours over the area. Use water to retain any cloud area as white.

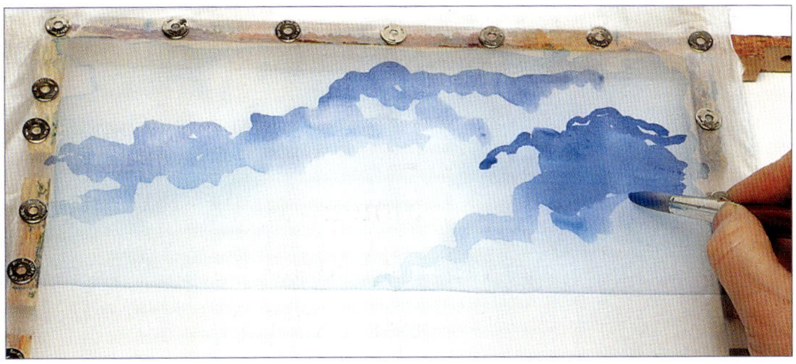

5. Allow this to dry, then repeat with slightly darker colours, to add depth. Create a layered effect by re-painting a few areas, or re-wet the whole area to blend in the darker tones. The dyes will not run on dry areas of silk.

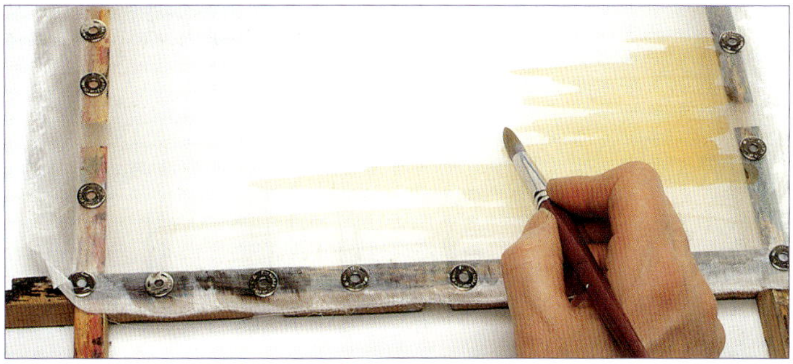

6. Repeat this process with the sea, using slightly darker colours, again working in layers, allowing each layer to dry before adding another to create the impression of waves. Any colours applied wet-on-wet will still blend if you want a more shaded effect, or use a hairdryer to dry areas quickly.

8. Continue building up the design working wet-on-wet for blended colours and wet-on-dry to form layers.

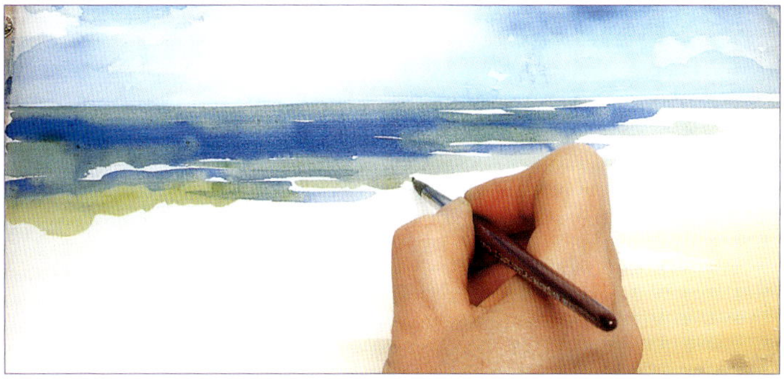

7. Use water to dilute the colours and help blend the beach area with the edge of the waves, working wet into wet.

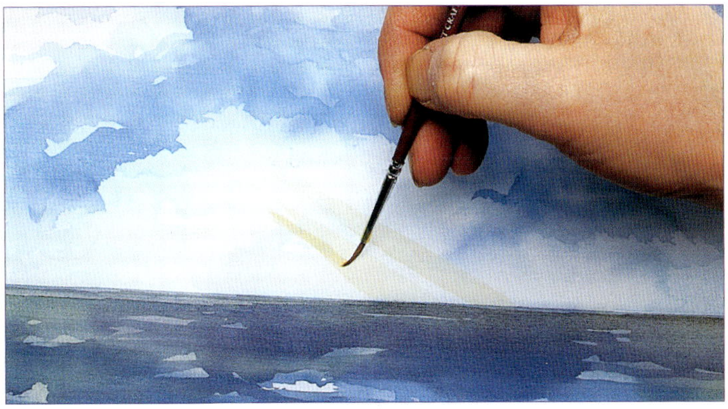

9. Working wet-on-dry, add small pebbles and seaweed to the beach, and some rays from the sun to create a depth to the picture.

10. When the design is complete remove the silk from the frame and steam to set the colours. Mount the work in a frame to enhance the completed picture.

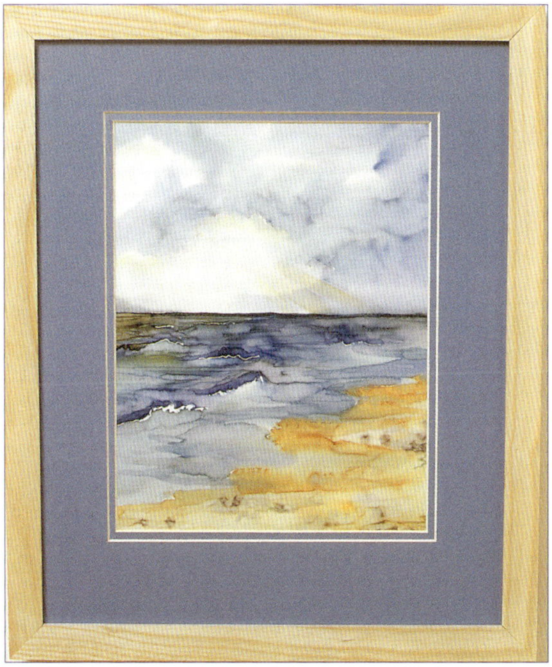

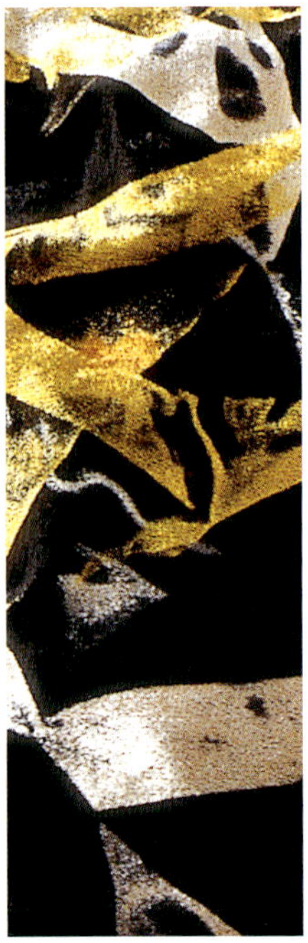

Velvet cushion using discharge paste and illuminants

This project uses a simple screen printing technique worked on black velvet, using a discharge paste to bleach out the black. Illuminants provide colour to create a beautiful animal print effect.

Equipment and materials

- Black silk viscose velvet
- Frame and silk pins
- Discharge paste
- Illuminant colours
- Screen printing frame stretched with screen mesh
- Squeegee
- Masking tape
- Plastic sheeting
- Plastic gloves
- Steaming equipment

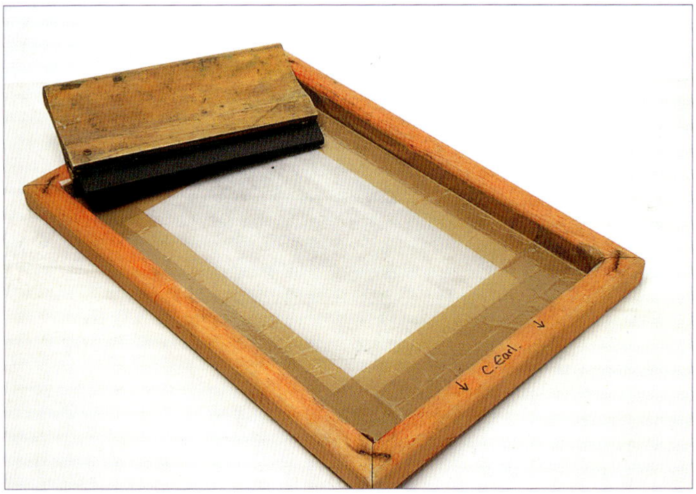

1. Cover the table in plastic and lay the black velvet pile-side up on to the table. Arrange the velvet into a series of loose folds or pleats. Put on the plastic gloves.

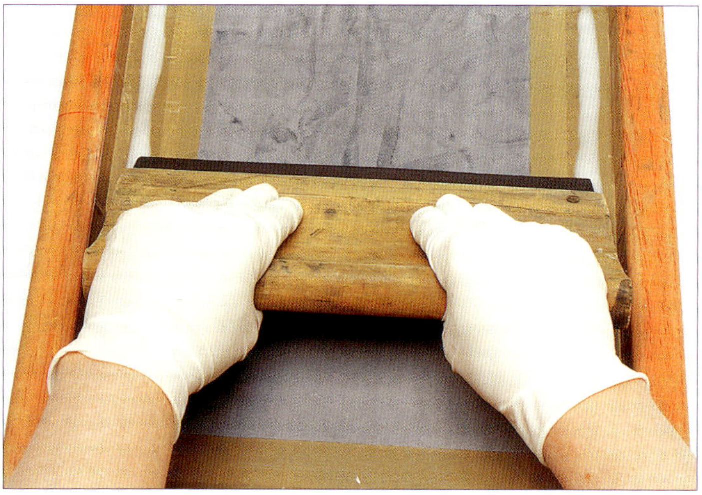

2. Place the screen printing frame on top of the velvet and pour a good quantity of discharge paste, without any added colour, into the top trough edge of the frame. Use a squeegee to pull the discharge paste down and through the screen mesh. It may be easier if someone holds the frame while you do this. Take the squeegee back across the frame several times until all the discharge paste has been worked through the mesh.

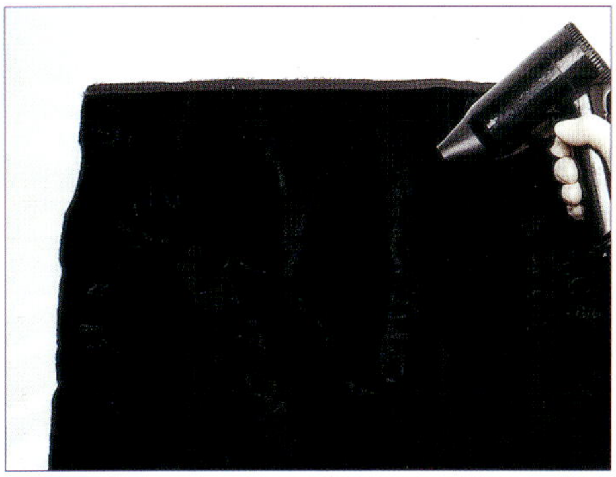

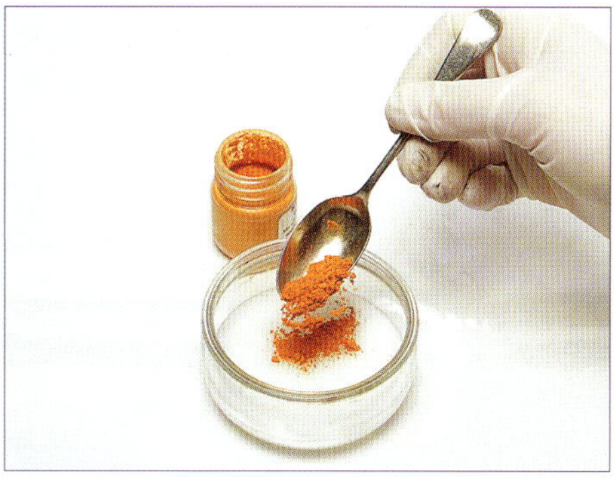

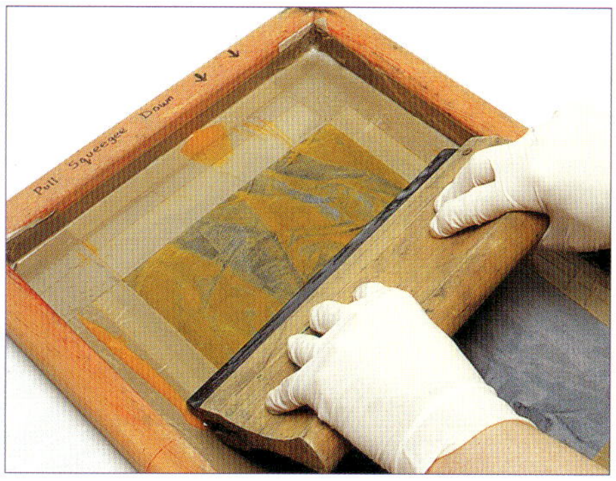

3. Remove the frame, open up the velvet and dry with a hairdryer.

4. Pour a further quantity of discharge paste into a dish and add $\frac{1}{4}$ to $\frac{1}{2}$ teaspoon of yellow illuminant powder, then mix thoroughly.

5. Re-arrange the black velvet, pile-side up, into a series of new folds, trying to get different areas to work on. Place the screen back on top of the velvet, and pour the coloured discharge paste into the top trough of the screen. Use a squeegee to pull this across and through the screen mesh. Open up the velvet and dry with a hairdryer.

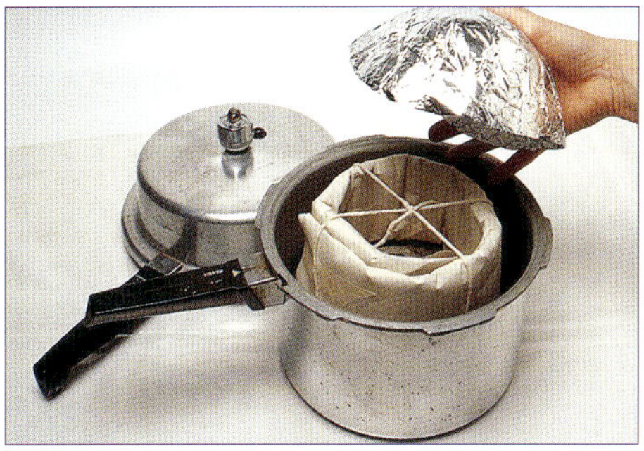

6. Roll up the work and steam (see page 16) to activate the discharge process. Areas where discharge paste has been applied will turn to pale brown, while the areas treated with illuminants will take on new colour.

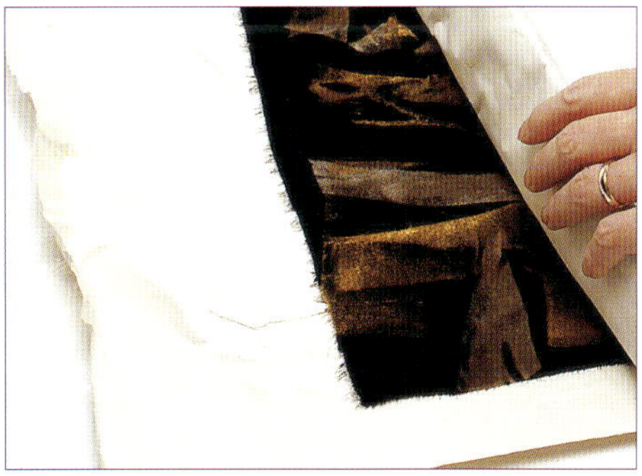

7. Wash the work in cool water to remove the spent discharge paste, and allow to dry a little before ironing on the reverse side of the velvet following the lie of the pile. Make up into a cushion, adding braiding, tassels or surface decoration if you wish.

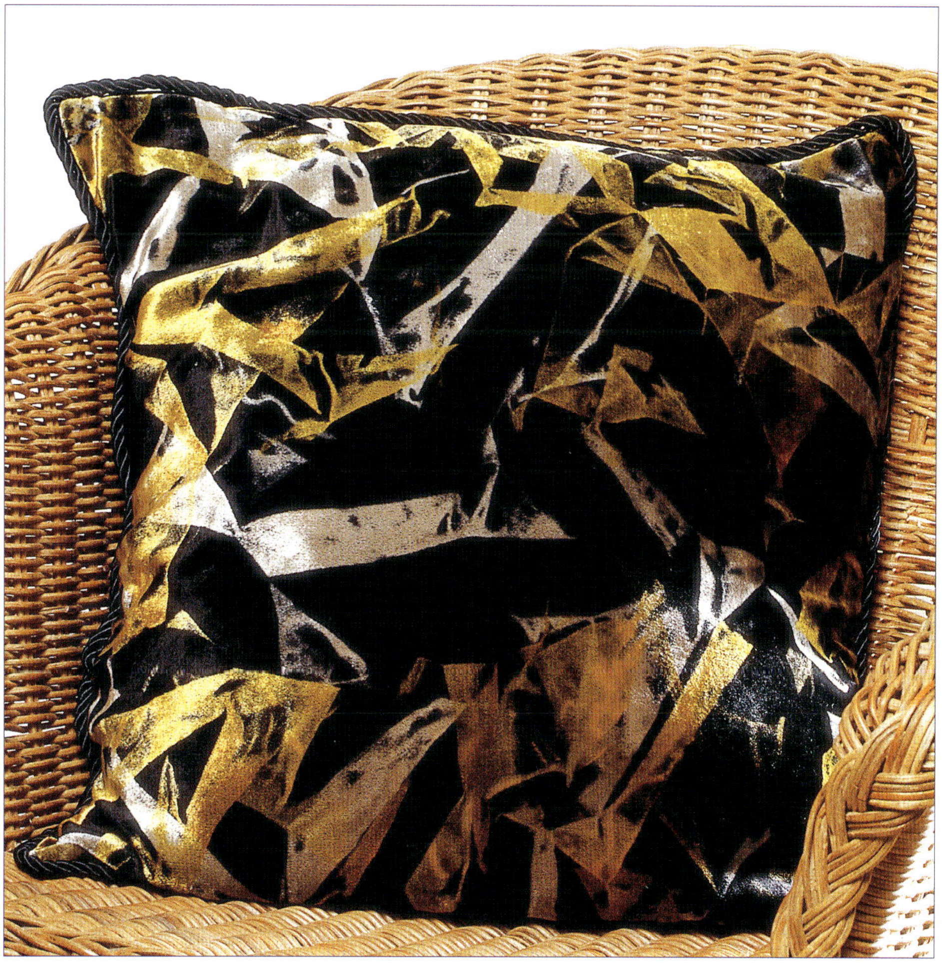

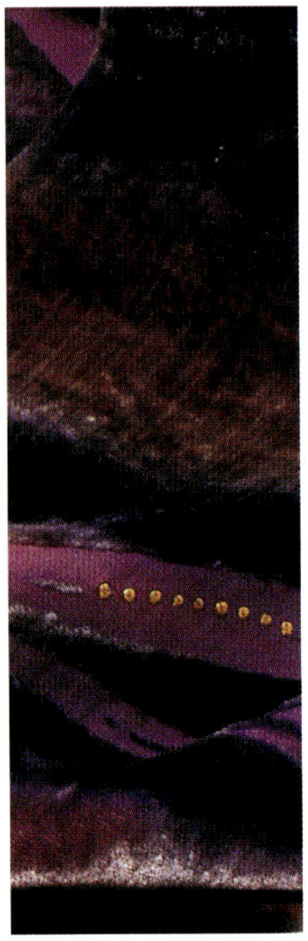

Devorée velvet scarf with an abstract design and decorative foils

This simple pattern is a good project to practise the devorée process and can be worked using steam-fix or procion dyes. The simple lines can be highlighted further with decorative foils. The design is formed from brush strokes, so a pattern is not required.

Equipment and materials

- A long length of silk viscose velvet
- A selection of either steam-fix dyes or procion dyes and soda ash
- Mixing palette and water pot
- Large paint brushes or sponge brushes
- Masking tape
- Fibre etch fluid
- Paper towelling
- Plastic sheeting
- Plastic gloves
- Hairdryer
- Iron
- Decorative foils and plexi-glue

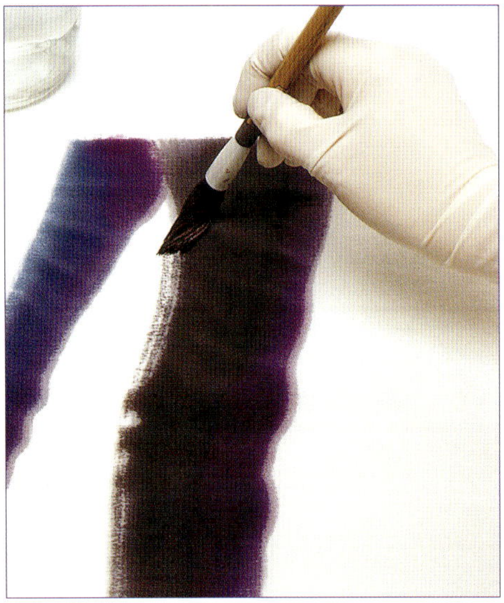

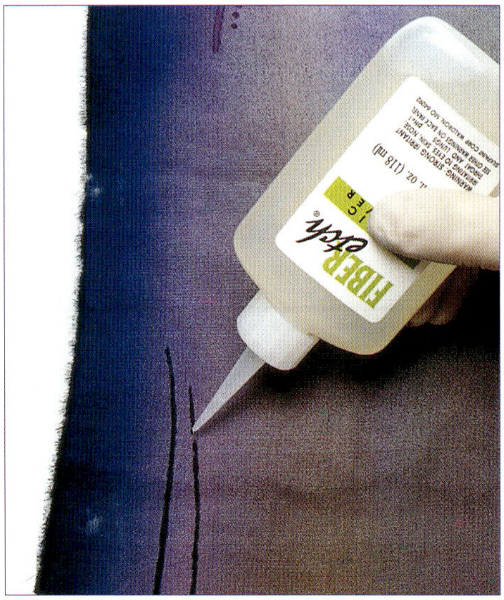

1. Cover the table with plastic and hold the velvet taut with masking tape, pile-side down. Select a range of colours in your chosen dye, and remember to add the soda ash to the dye if using procion dyes (see page 38). Use large paint brushes to apply the dyes in broad strokes across the backing of the velvet. Build up the colour, blending and overlapping as you go until the whole length is coloured. Do not worry about watermarks showing on the backing, as they will not show on the pile side.

2. Allow the colours to dry, and steam if using steam-fix dyes, or allow the work to cure if using procion dyes. Wash and dry the fixed velvet, re-stretch and tape back into position on the table, pile-side down. Apply the fibre etch solution as evenly as you can, direct from the nozzle on the bottle (see page 39 for information on the devorée process), picking out areas that you wish to highlight with a devorée effect.

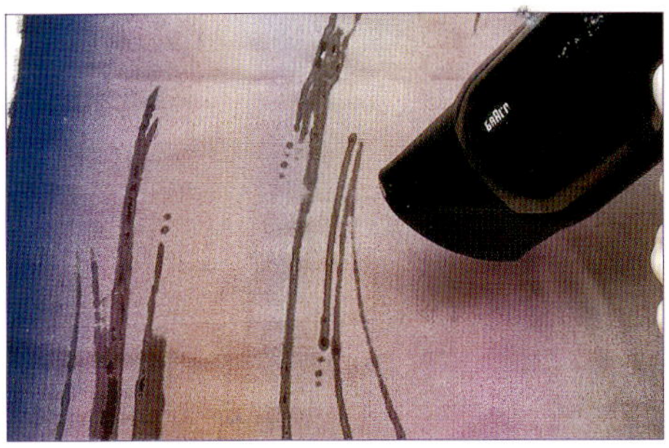

3. Dry the fibre etch with a hairdryer.

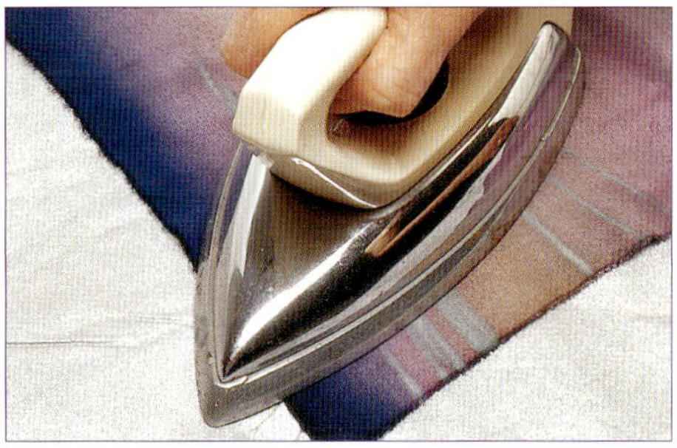

4. Then carefully iron all areas treated with fibre etch, with the iron set at silk/wool until the fibre etch has turned pale brown.

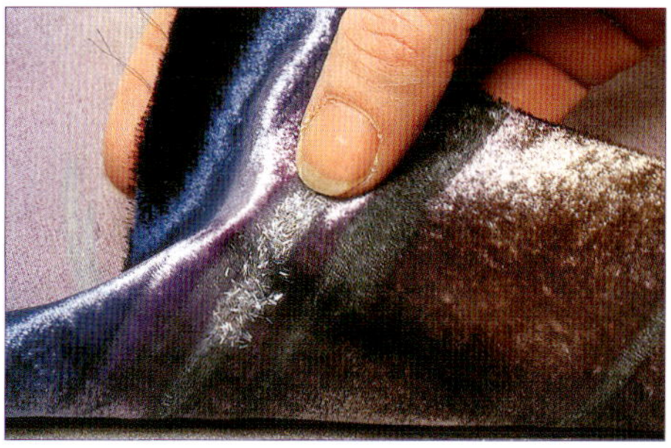

5. Check that the pile will release by gently rubbing ironed areas with a finger, then wash the velvet in warm water to release all the pile and reveal the devorée pattern. Dry the velvet and iron on the reverse while still just damp.

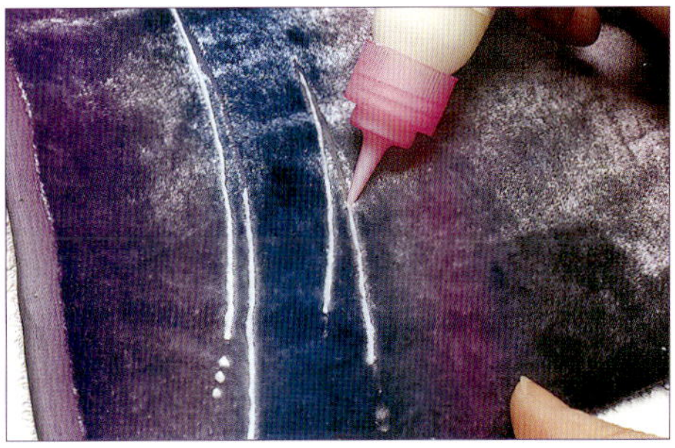

6. Lay the dry velvet out, pile-side up and apply plexi-glue to any areas that you wish to highlight with decorative foils. Allow the glue to dry. It will then become transparent.

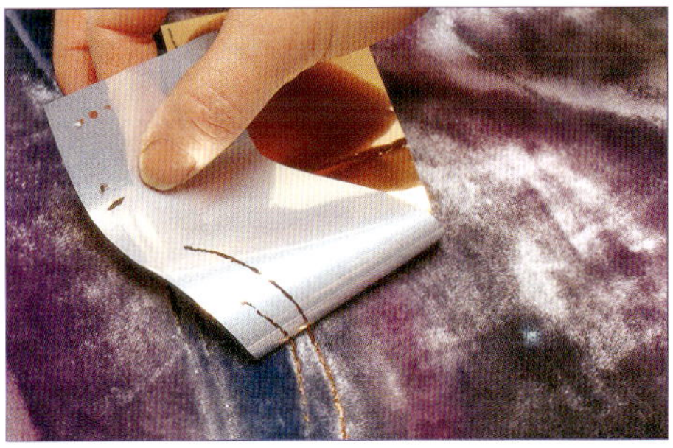

7. Lay a piece of decorative foil, colour side up, on to the transparent glue line, and gently press the foil to transfer the colour. Continue until all glue lines have been foiled.

8. Make up the scarf by placing right sides together and tacking along the edges before sewing, leaving a small opening to allow for turning through. Close the opening with a few stitches once the scarf has been turned right side out.

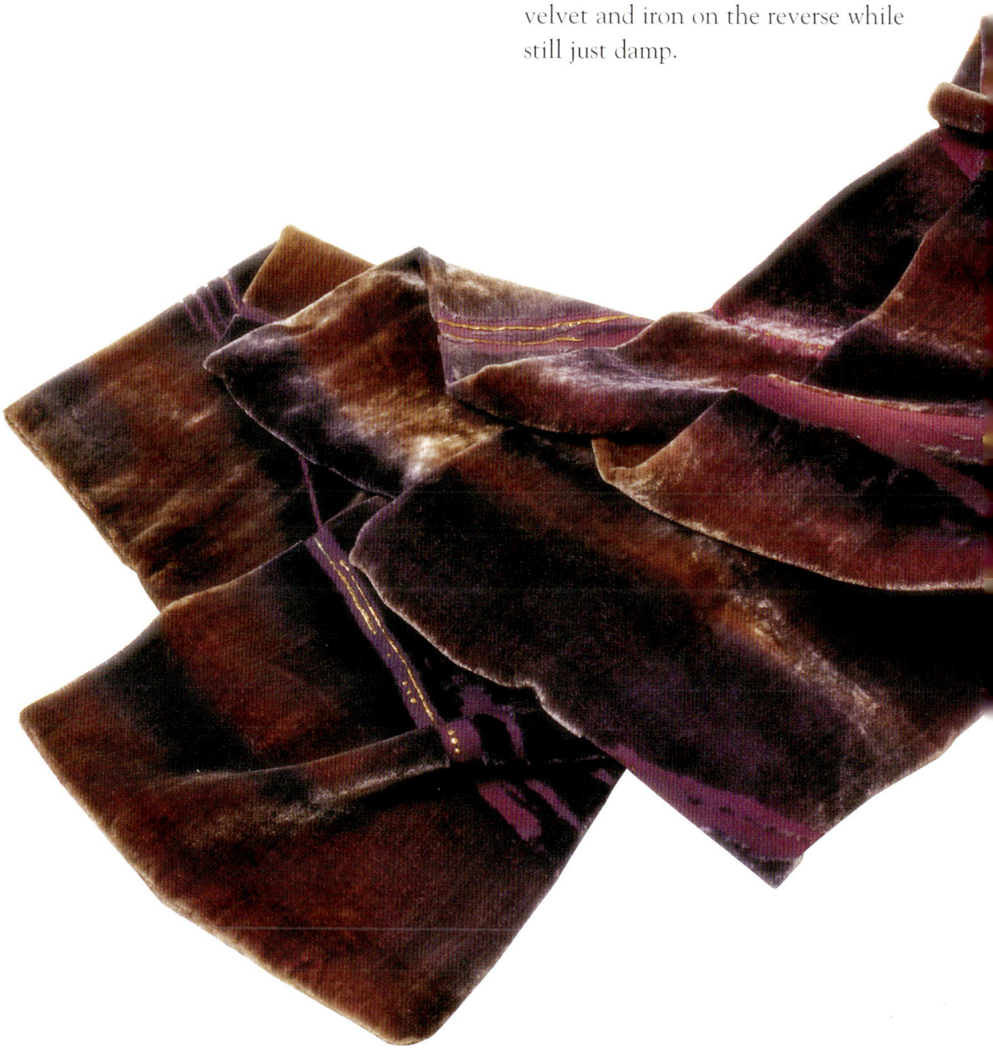

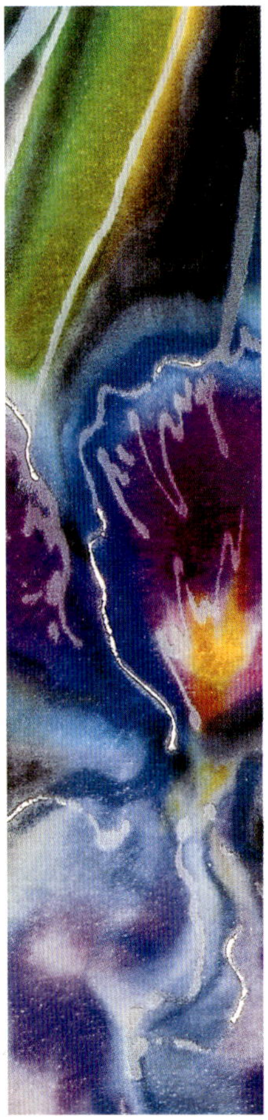

Painted devorée velvet scarf with foil highlights

This scarf is worked in a similar way to the previous project, but the floral pattern is painted, working the design free-hand or from guidelines drawn in with a vanishing water-soluble pen.

Equipment and materials

Length of silk viscose velvet
A selection of either steam-fix dyes or procion dyes and soda ash
Mixing palette and water pot
Large paint brushes or sponge brushes
Masking tape
Fibre etch fluid
Kitchen paper
Plastic sheeting
Plastic gloves
Vanishing pen and pattern (optional)
Hairdryer
Iron
Decorative foils and plexi-glue

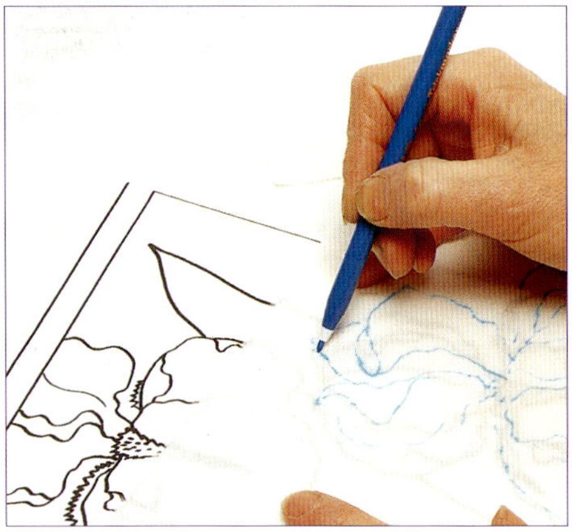

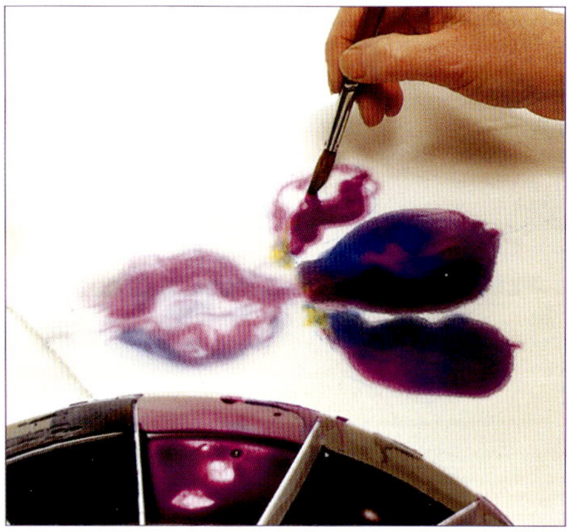

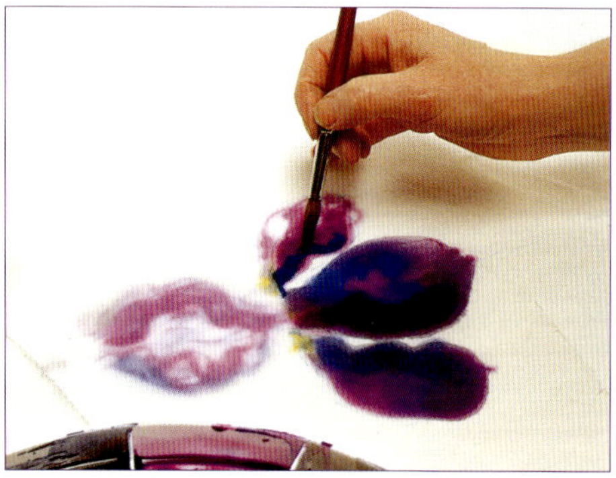

1. Cover the table with plastic and hold the velvet taut with masking tape, pile-side down, with the pattern sheet under the velvet if you want to trace the lines out with a vanishing pen. You can also use the pen to give a few guidelines when working free-hand. All pen lines will disappear once the dyes are applied.

2. Use large paint brushes to apply the dyes (remember to add soda ash if using procion dyes). Use overlapping strokes to mix and blend the colours as you work, and use a hairdryer to help control the flow of the dyes.

3. Use water to keep any areas white or pale and start painting in the flower heads first. Just use the tip of the brush to help achieve fine control of the pattern where necessary.

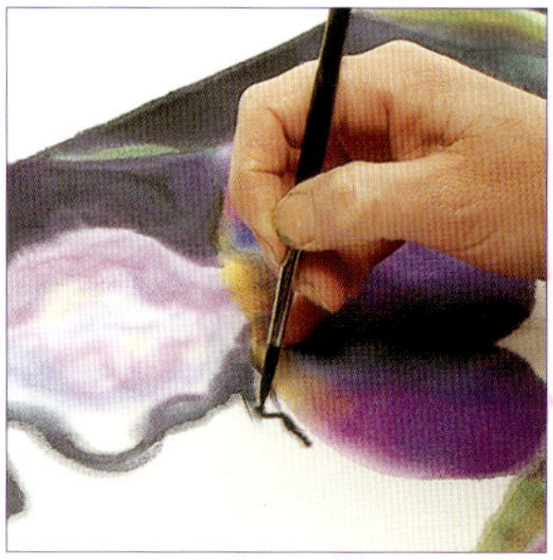

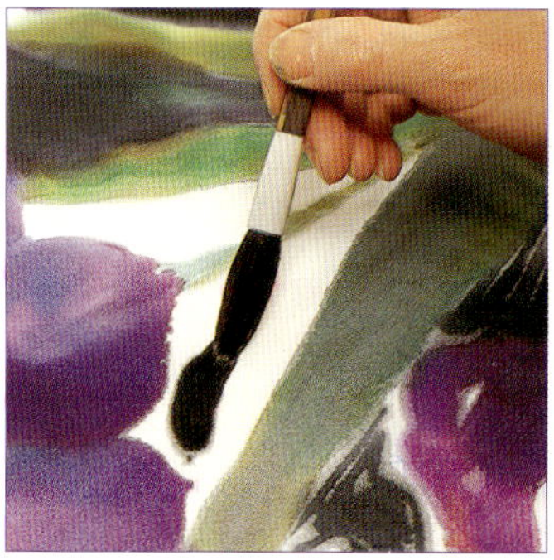

4. When the flower heads are painted, brush in the leaves and stems. If the flowers are still wet, it will help to prevent the flow of dye into these areas, otherwise control the spread of the dye using a smaller brush and less brush contact with the velvet.

5. Paint in the background. Leave a good spreading distance, otherwise the background colour will swamp the pattern.

6. Add a little of the violet and green from the flower colours to give the dark background more depth.

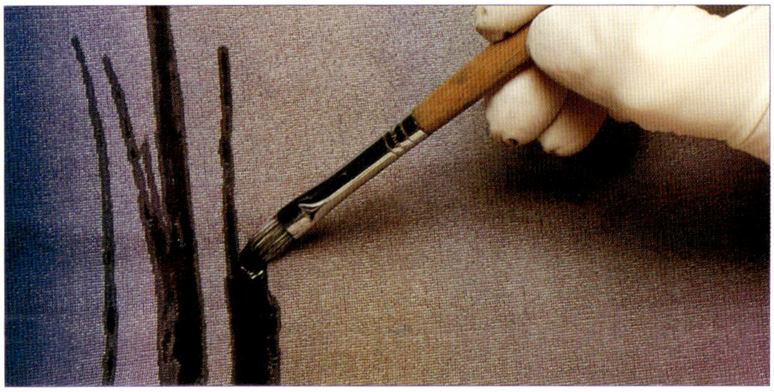

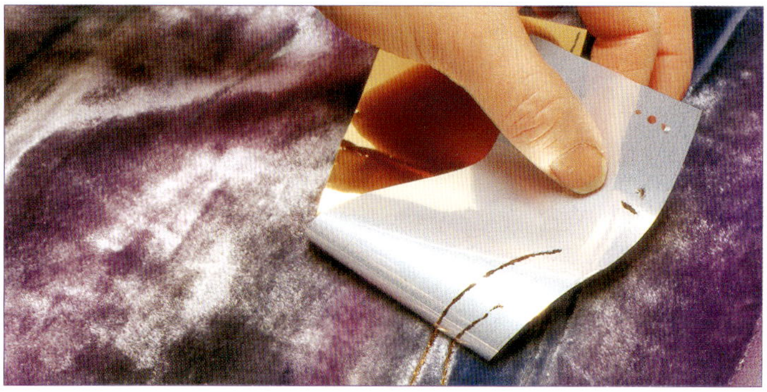

7. Allow the colours to dry and steam if using steam-fix dyes, or allow the work to cure if using procion dyes. Wash and dry the fixed velvet, then re-stretch and tape back into position on the table, pile-side down. Apply the fibre etch solution as before (see page 96), using the devorée process to highlight parts of the flowers and leaves.

8. Add decorative foil highlights with plexi glue as described on page 97 or see page 49.

9. Make up the scarf by placing right sides together and tacking along the edges before sewing, leaving a small opening to allow for turning through. Close the opening with a few stitches once the scarf has been turned right side out.

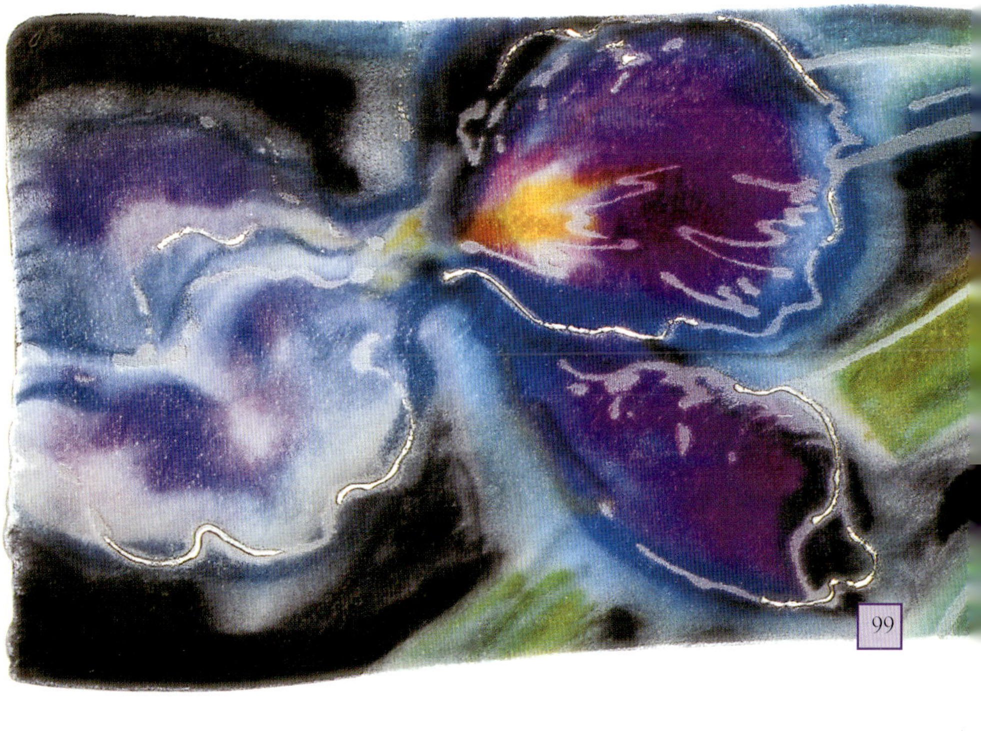

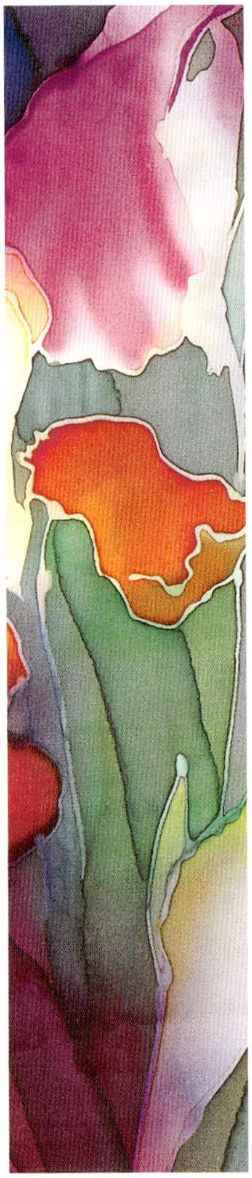

Working with washes, watermarks and minimal resist

This project requires much more skill in handling and applying the dyes, as the control element comes from the way the colours are allowed to spread, rather than controlling the spread of the dye with resist mediums. The pattern is built up in a series of layers. Because minimal resist is used, the pattern continually develops and watermarks form as further colour is applied on to already painted areas. The finished result is worth the effort as it gives a beautiful watercolour appearance to the work.

Equipment and materials

Ready-edged silk scarf
Silk painting frame and pins
Steam-fix dyes
Clear water-soluble outliner
Mixing palette and water pot
Paint brushes
Paper towelling
Hairdryer
Steam-fixing equipment
Template p109

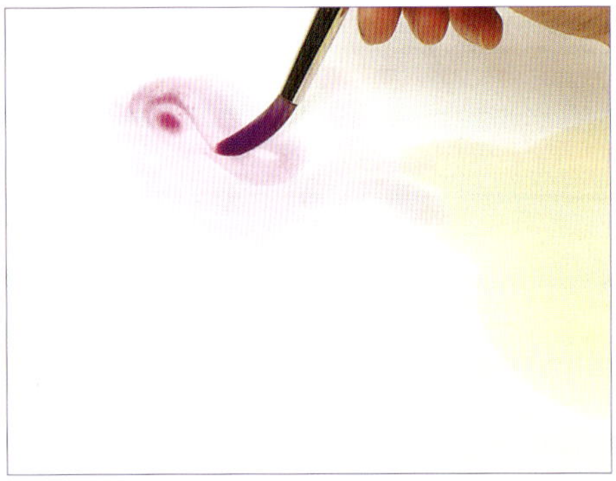

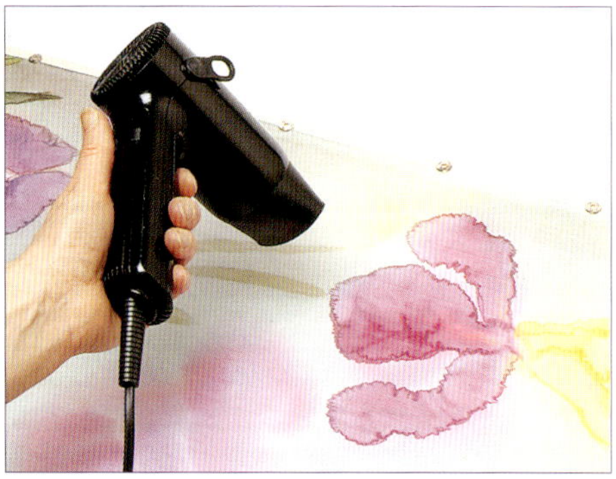

1. Pin out the silk using silk pins, and place the selected colours into the mixing palette, diluting them with some water. If you feel unsure about working free-hand, place a paper pattern of a flower head under the silk as a guide, rather than a pattern to be rigidly followed. This will allow the design to evolve as you work.

2. Using the diluted colours, roughly paint in the flower heads positioning them at varying heights and spacing them so that they are at the top, bottom and edges of the scarf, then add soft background colours across the whole piece, allowing these colours to blend wet into wet.

3. Allow the work to dry then start adding more detail to it, re-painting the flowers with deeper colours and adding some leaves and stems, using careful brushwork and a hairdryer to help control the spread of the dyes. Continue layering up the design, re-working areas and creating watermarks as the new layers displace earlier dry layers of dye.

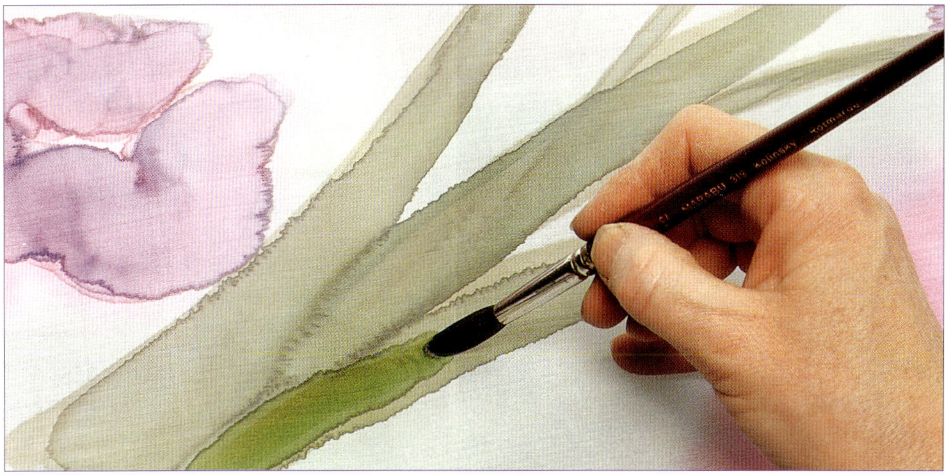

4. To work more detail into the design, create deliberate watermarks to form leaves and stems, but remember that the leaves first painted in will be in the background, and once dry, further leaves painted on top of those already painted will appear to be in the foreground. Before re-working areas check what impact it will have on the whole piece, as you may form watermarks in the wrong places.

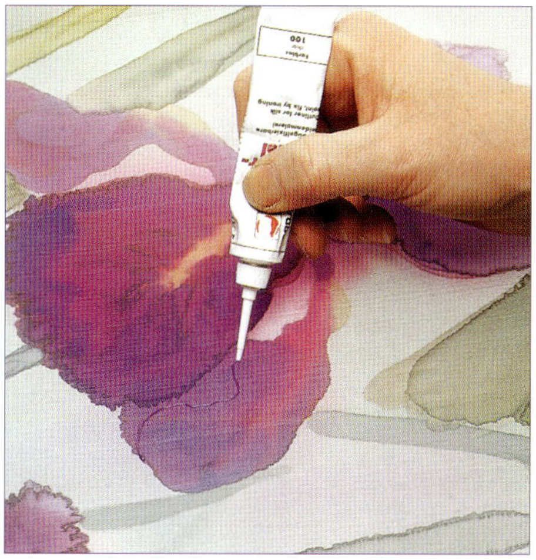

5. Use a little clear outliner to add sharper definition or give tighter control on the movement of the dyes in areas that you do not want to disturb.

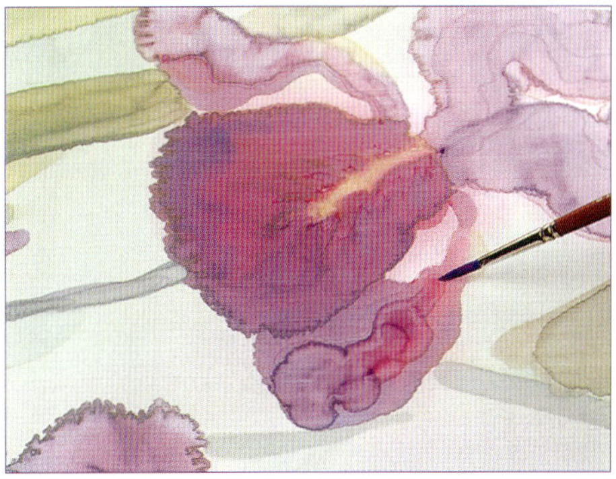

6. Continue building up the design until you are happy with the result.

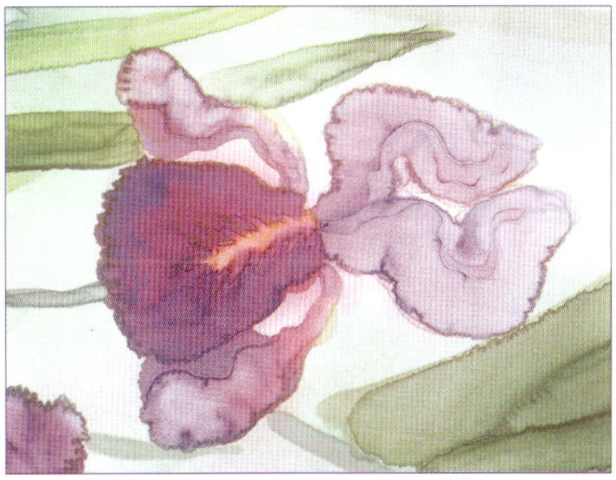

7. Dry, then steam the completed piece, and wash and iron in the usual way to finish.

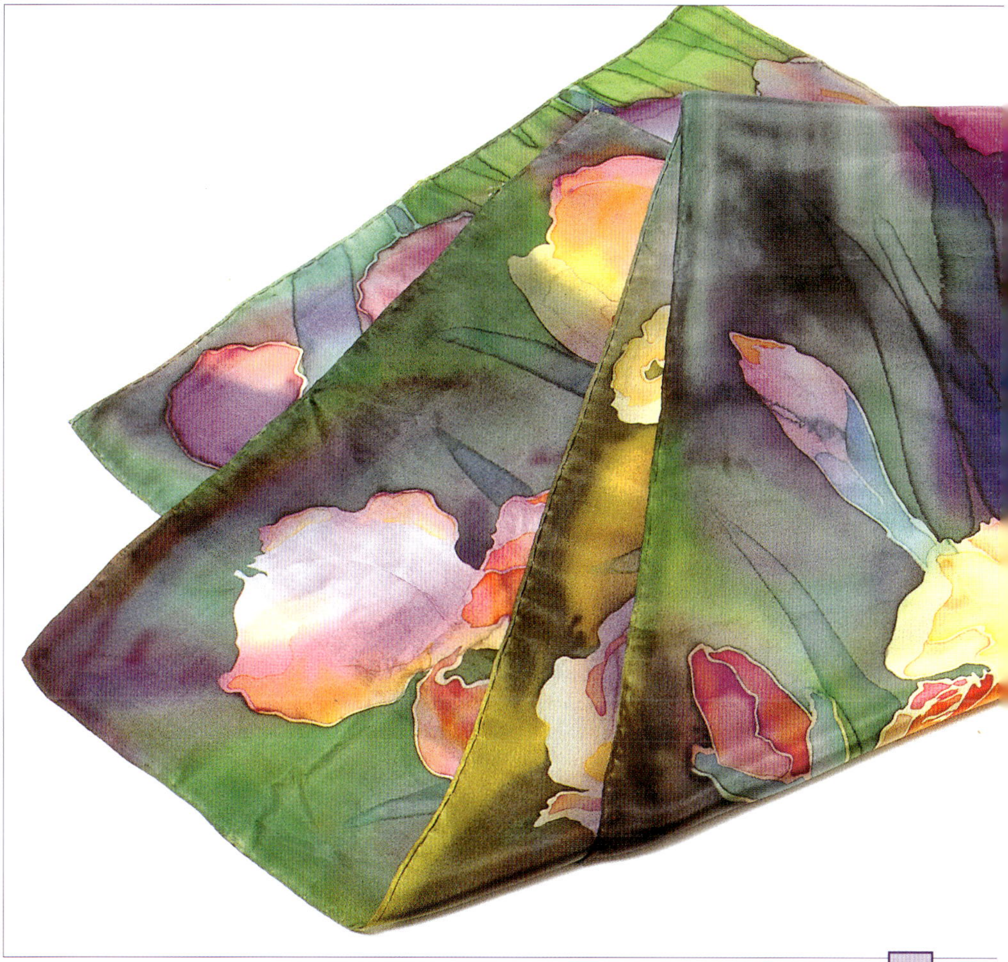

Templates

Freesia scarf
Increase by 200%

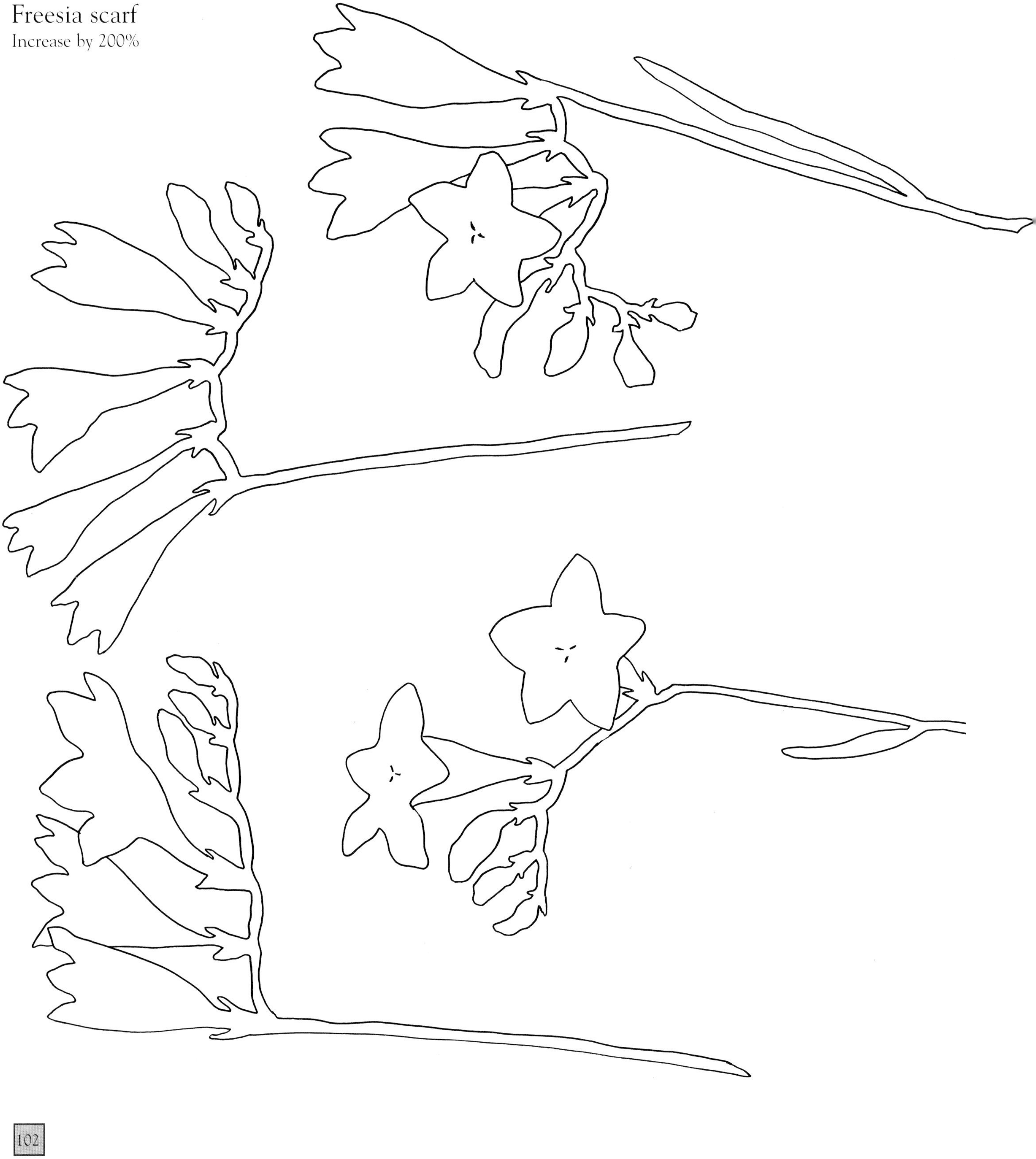

Silk painted cards

Increase by 200%

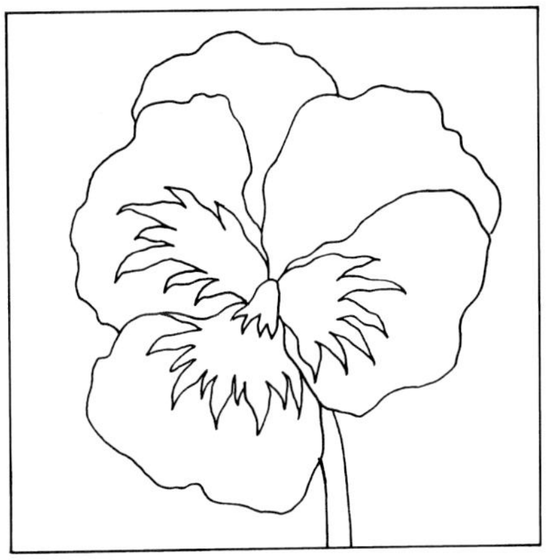
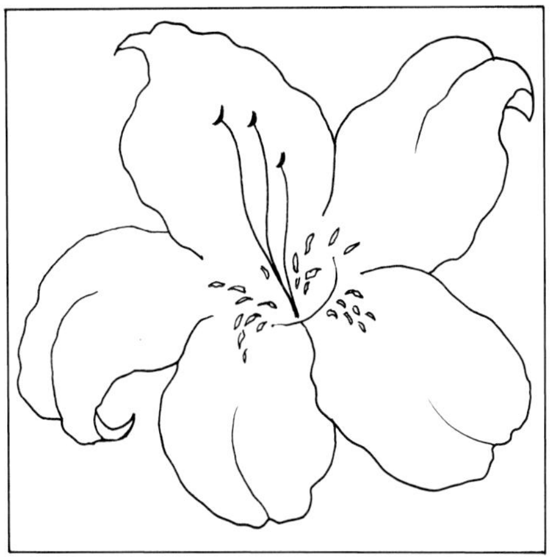
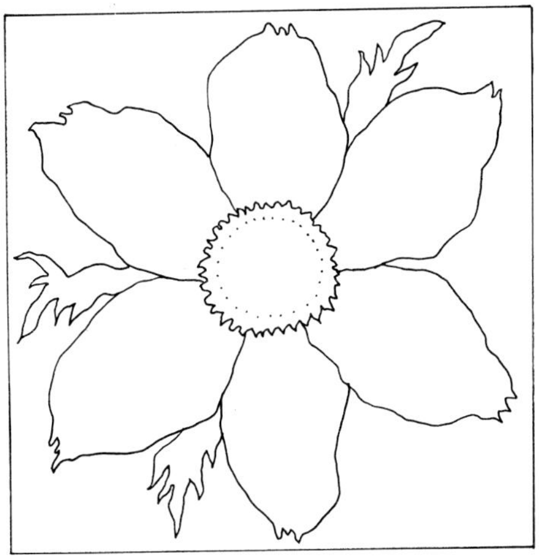
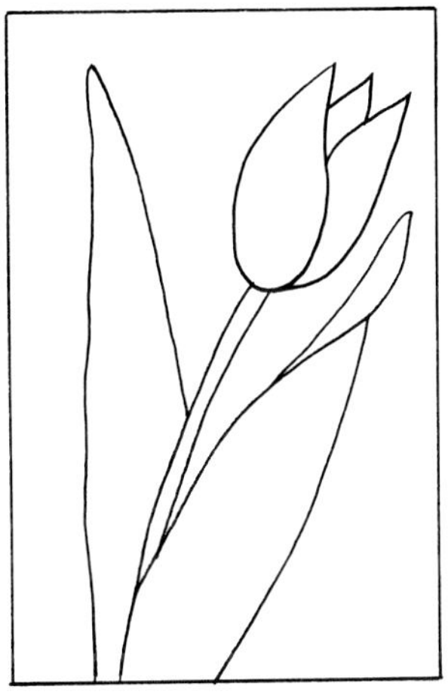
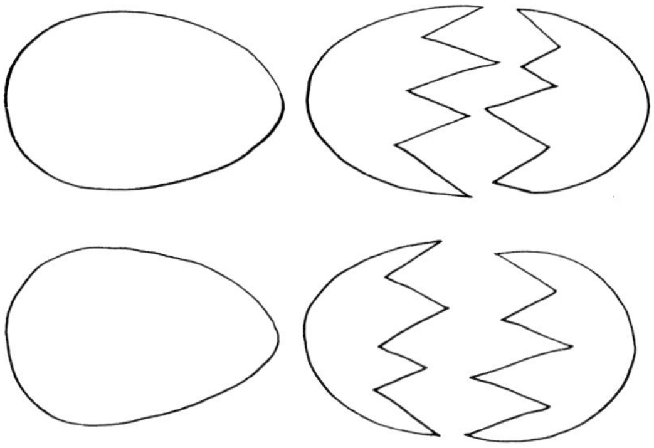

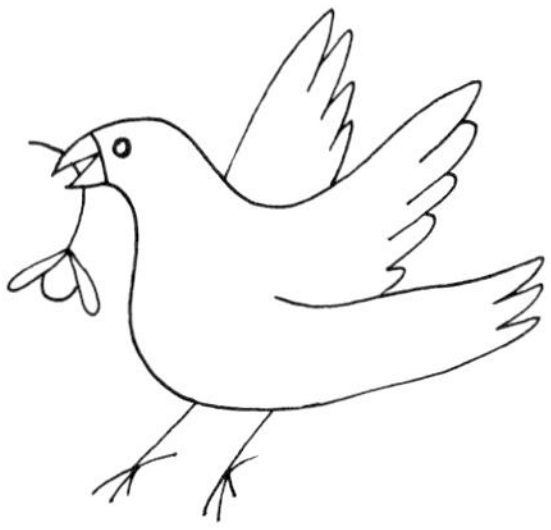
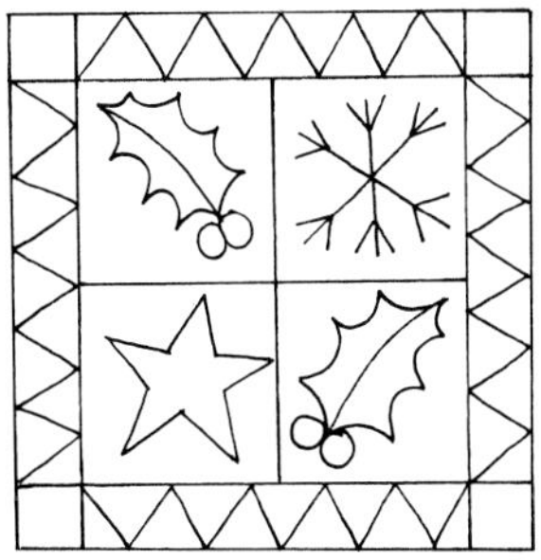

Silk sarong

Use at this size

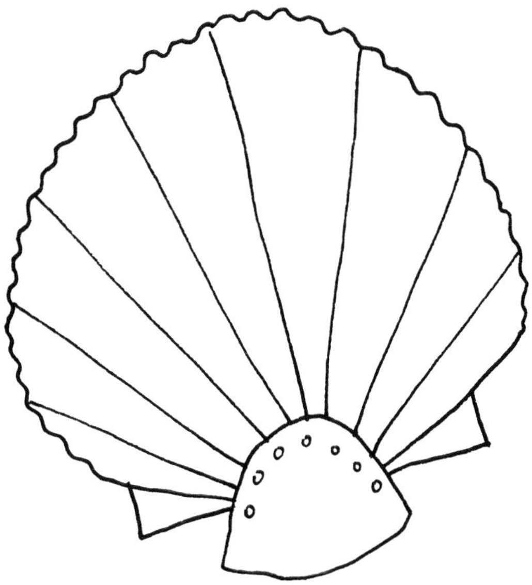

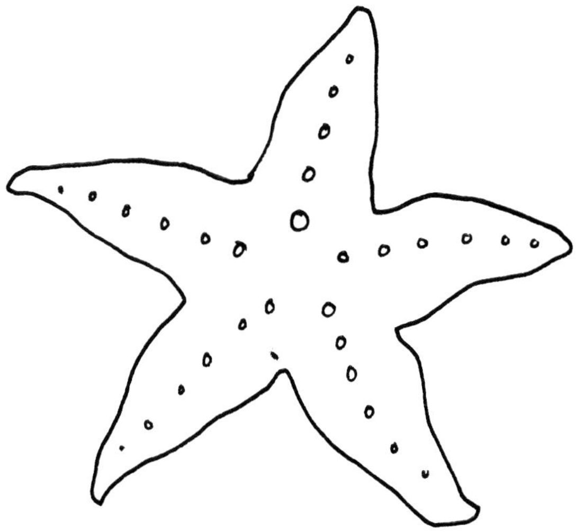

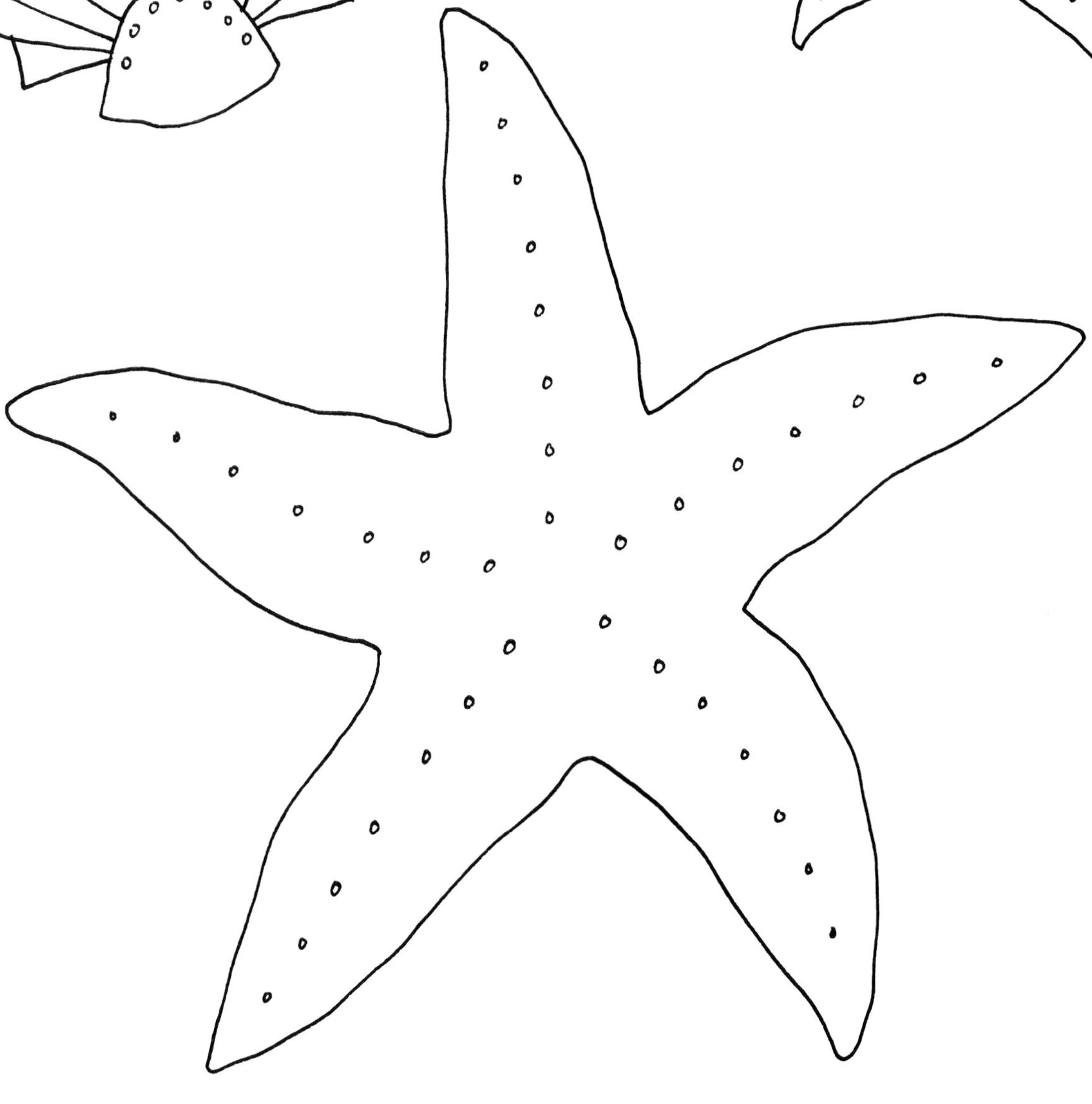

Using clear resist on coloured silk

Increase by 200%

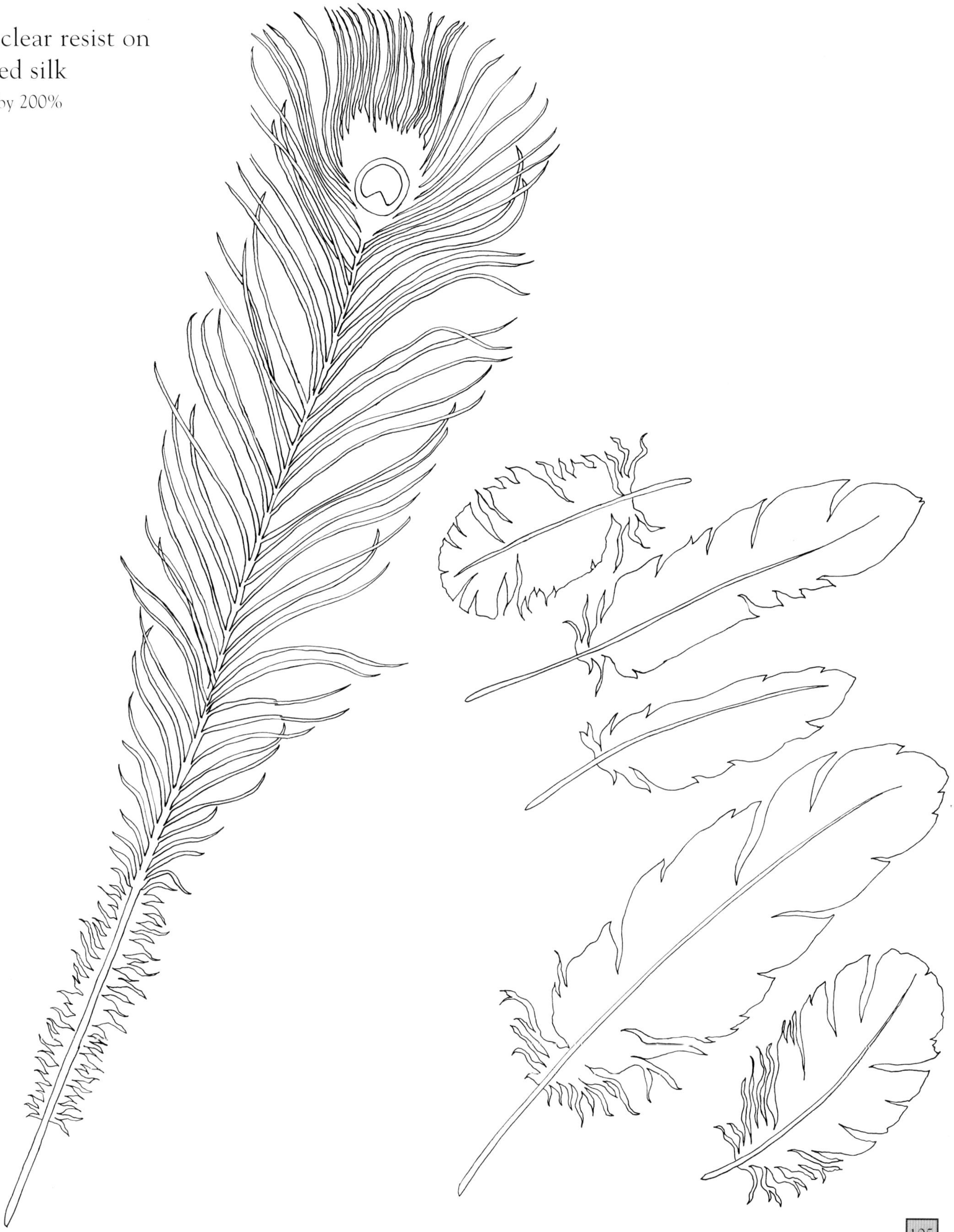

Velvet evening bag

Increase by 133%

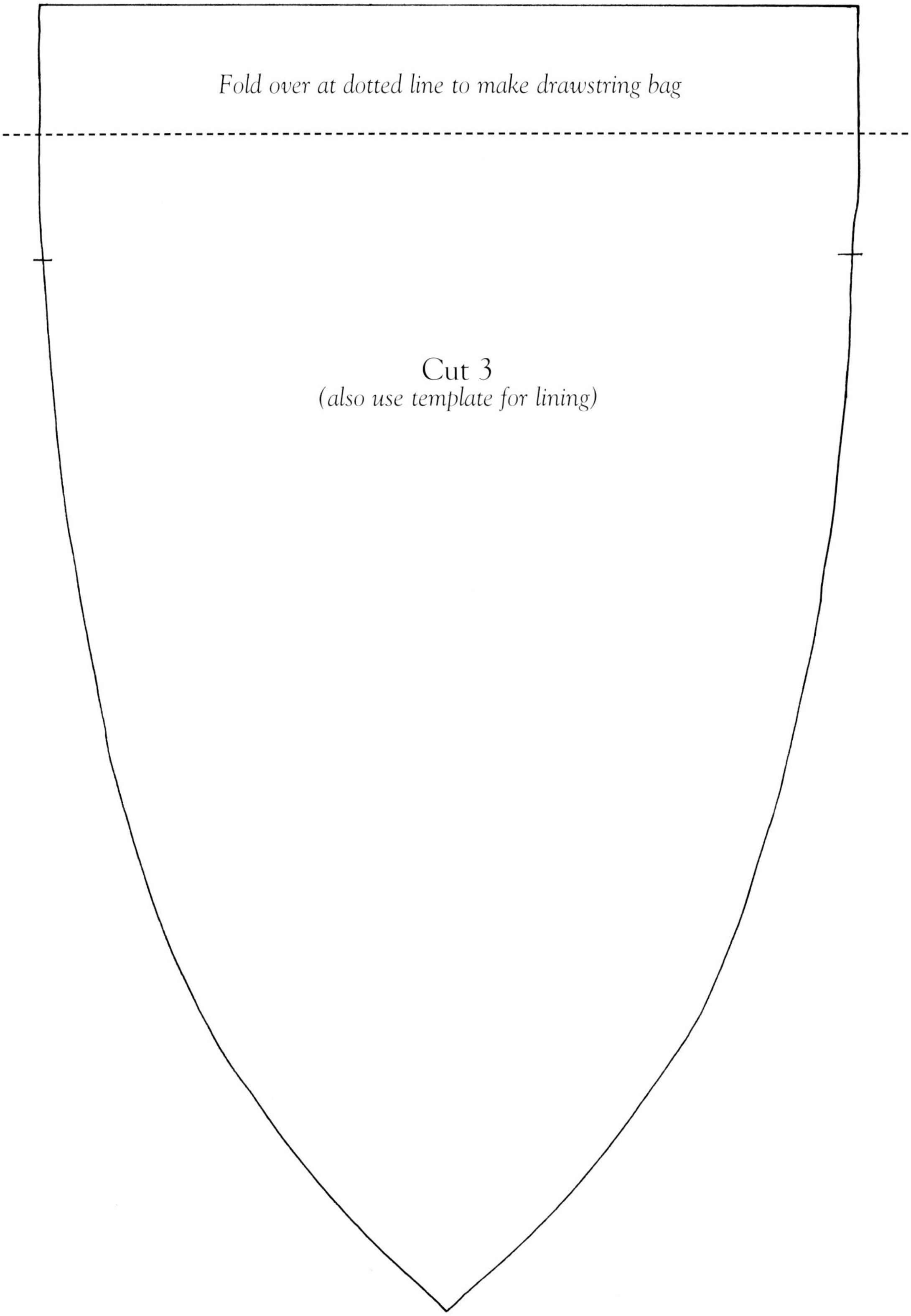

Sunflowers drawn using coloured water-soluble outliners

Increase by 300%

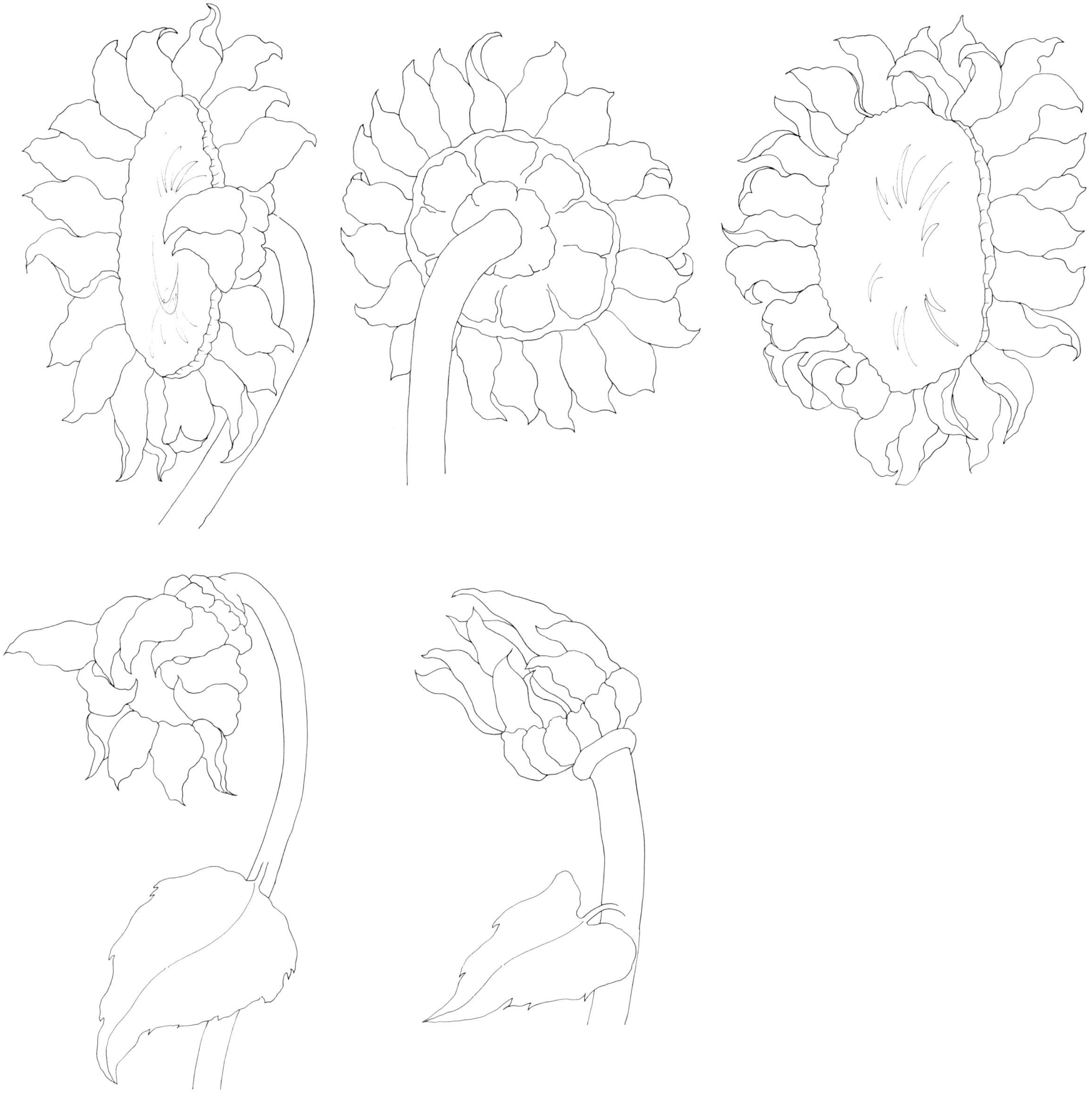

Cushion worked with a wax resist

Increase by 133%

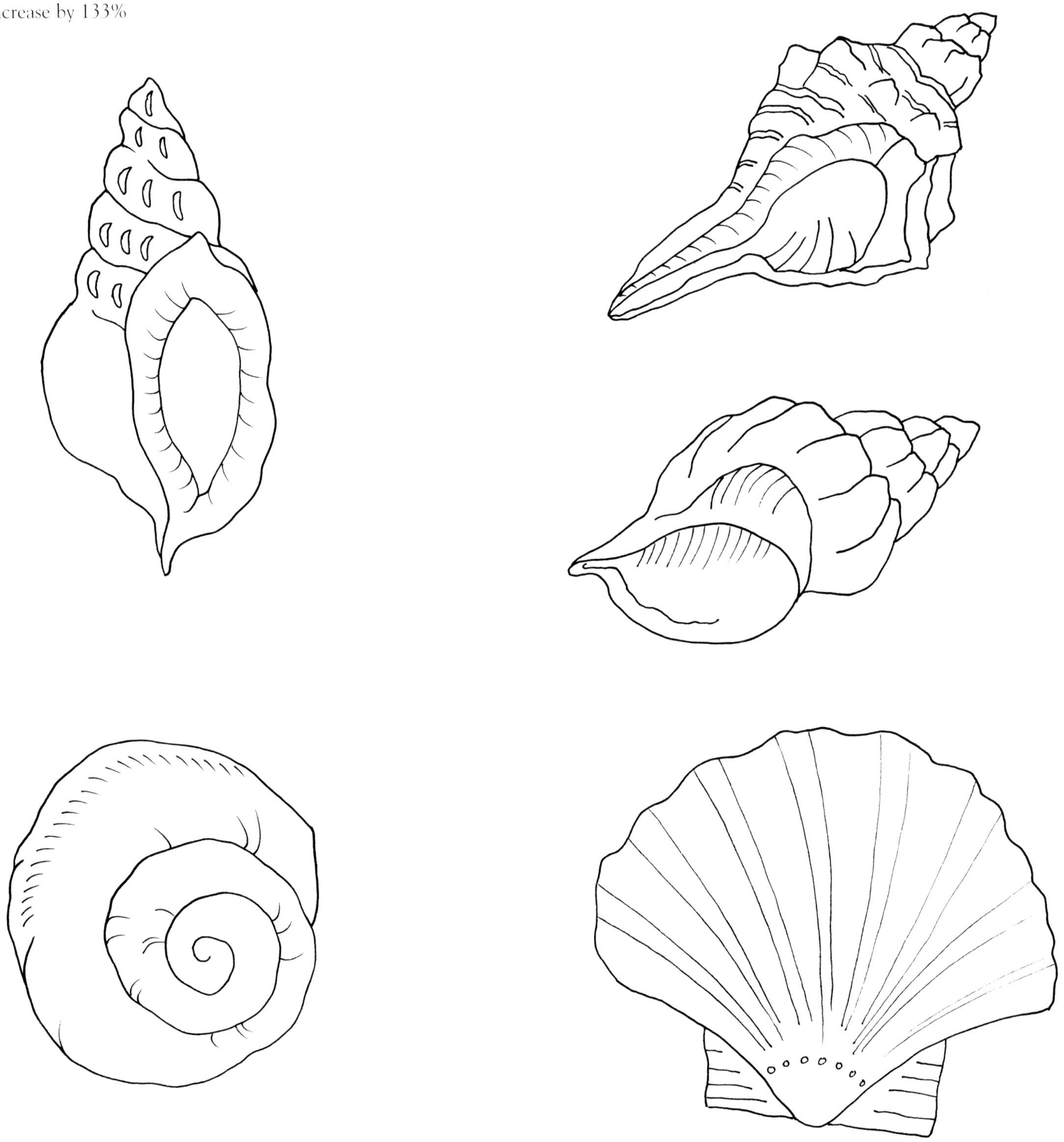

Painted devorée velvet scarf
Working with washes, watermarks and minimal resist

Increase by 300%

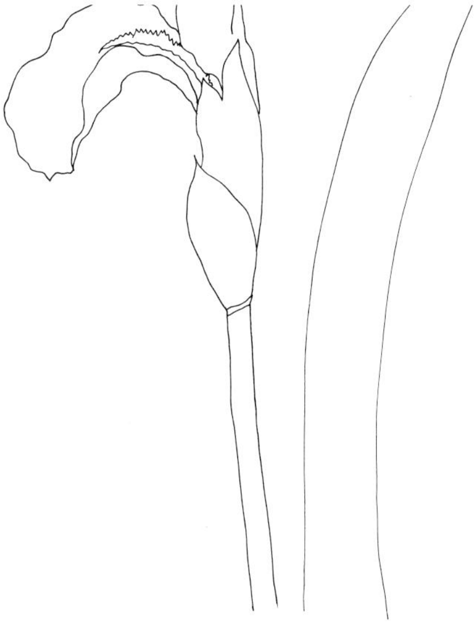

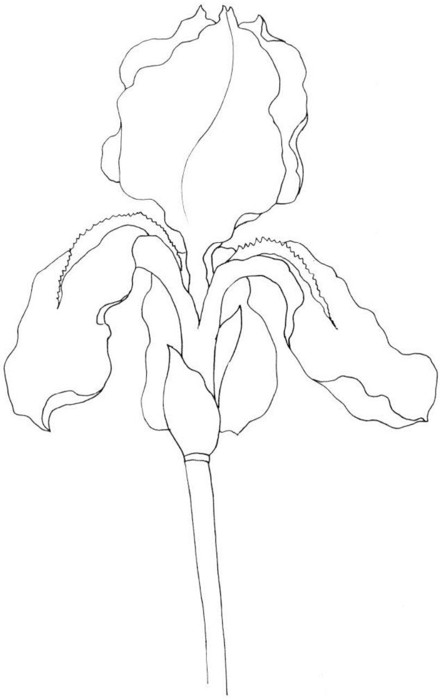

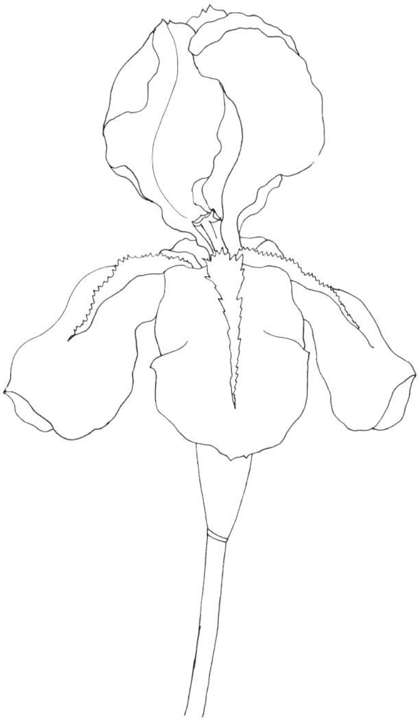

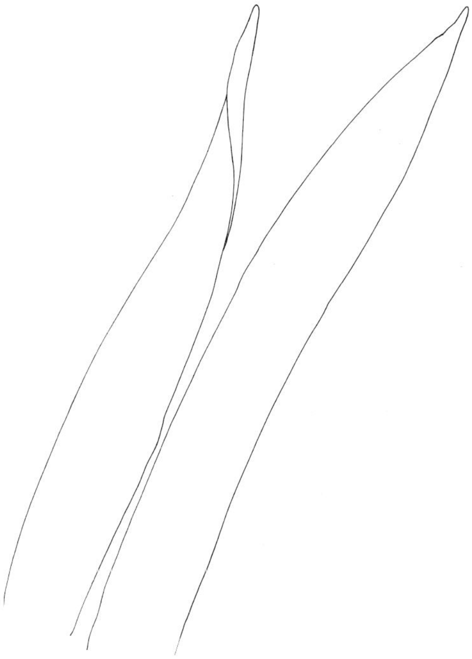

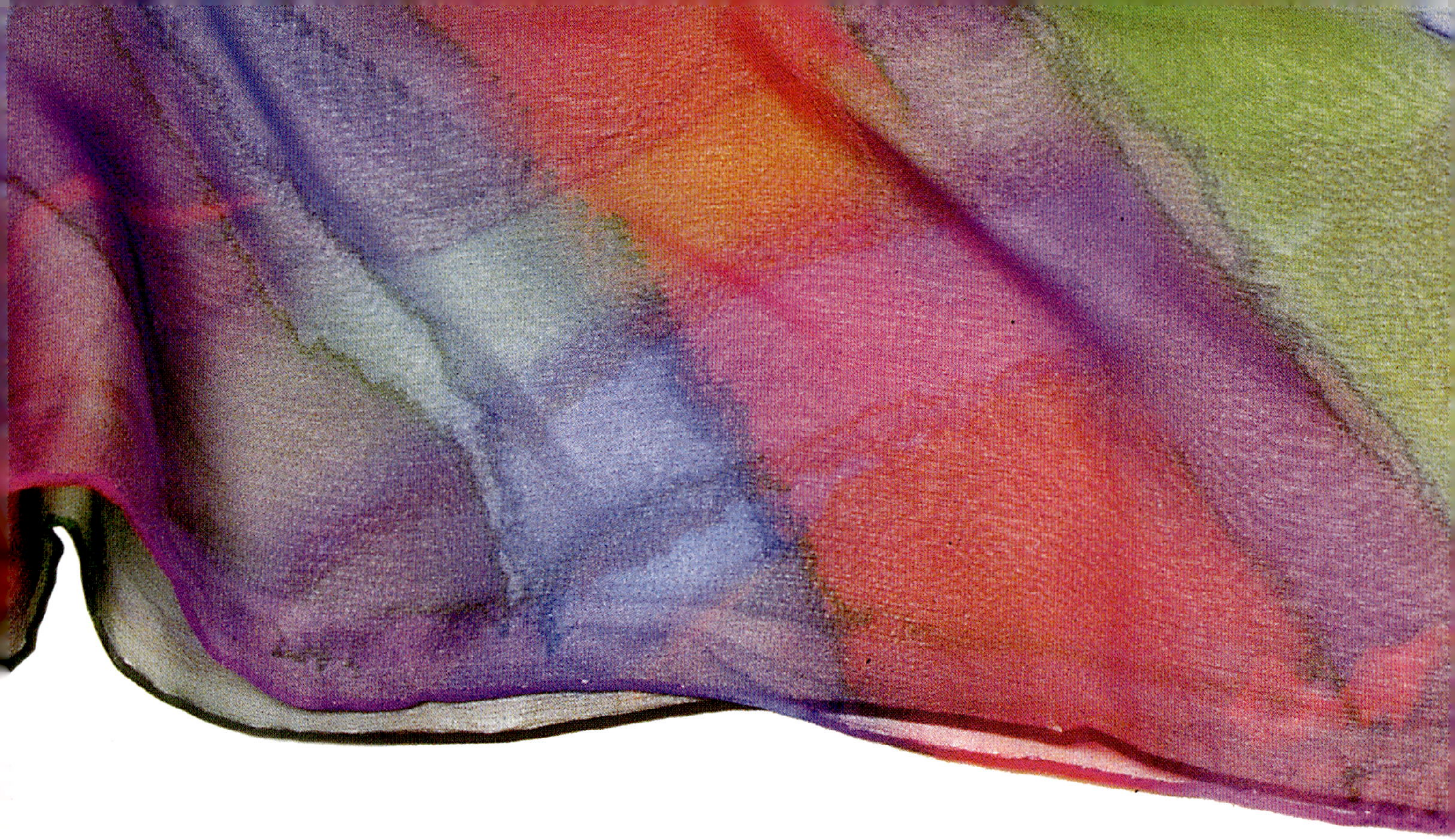

Index

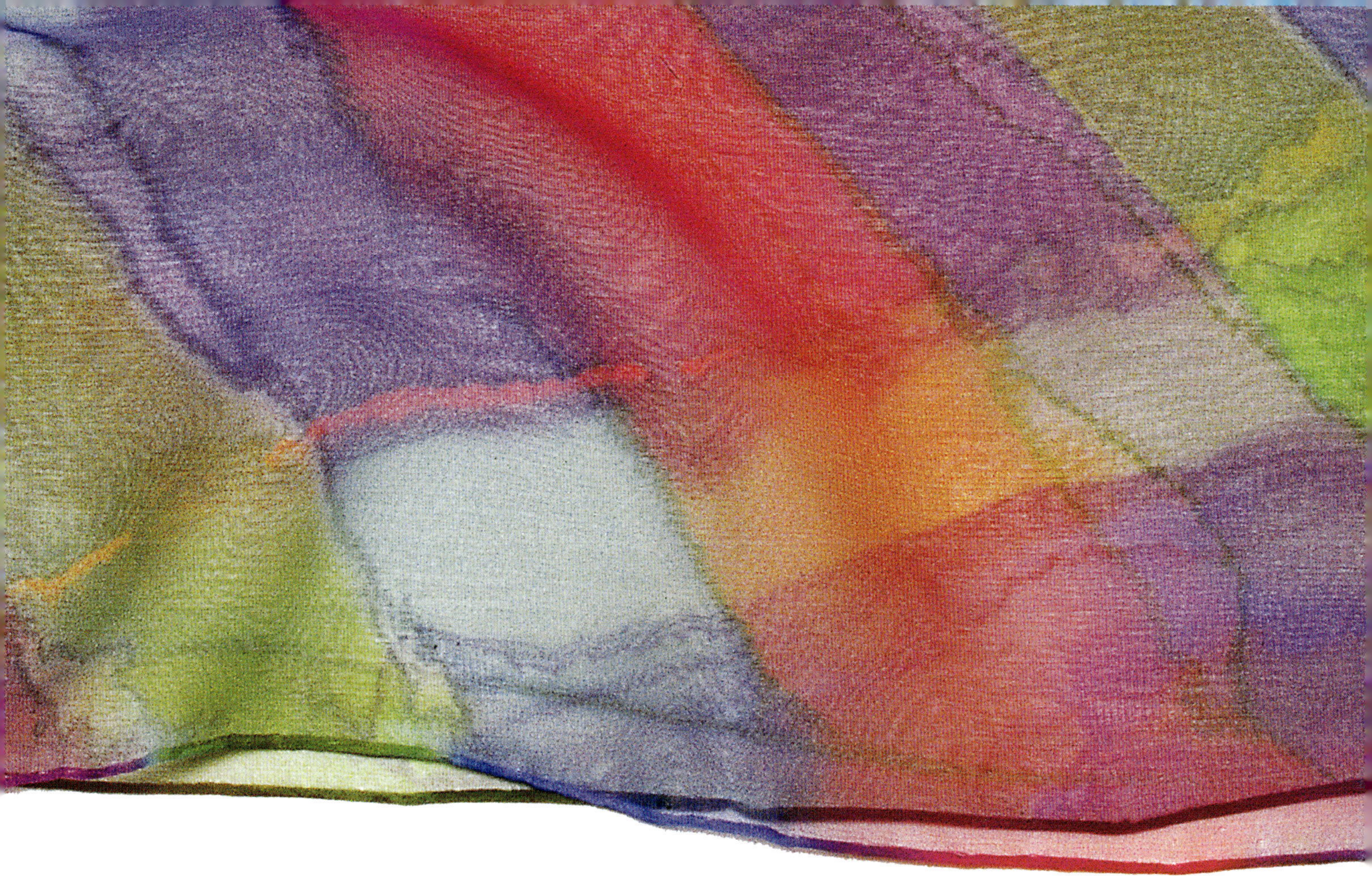

Credits and acknowledgements

I would like to thank my family for being so supportive to me whilst I was writing this book, and the following suppliers who generously gave materials and equipment for use and illustration in the production of this book.

Edding (UK) Ltd, Merlin Centre, Acrewood Way, St Albans, Herts, AL4 0JY.
Rainbow Silks, 7 Wheelers Yard, High Street, Great Missenden, Bucks, HP16 0AL.
Specialist Crafts Ltd, P.O. Box 247, Leicester, LE1 9QS

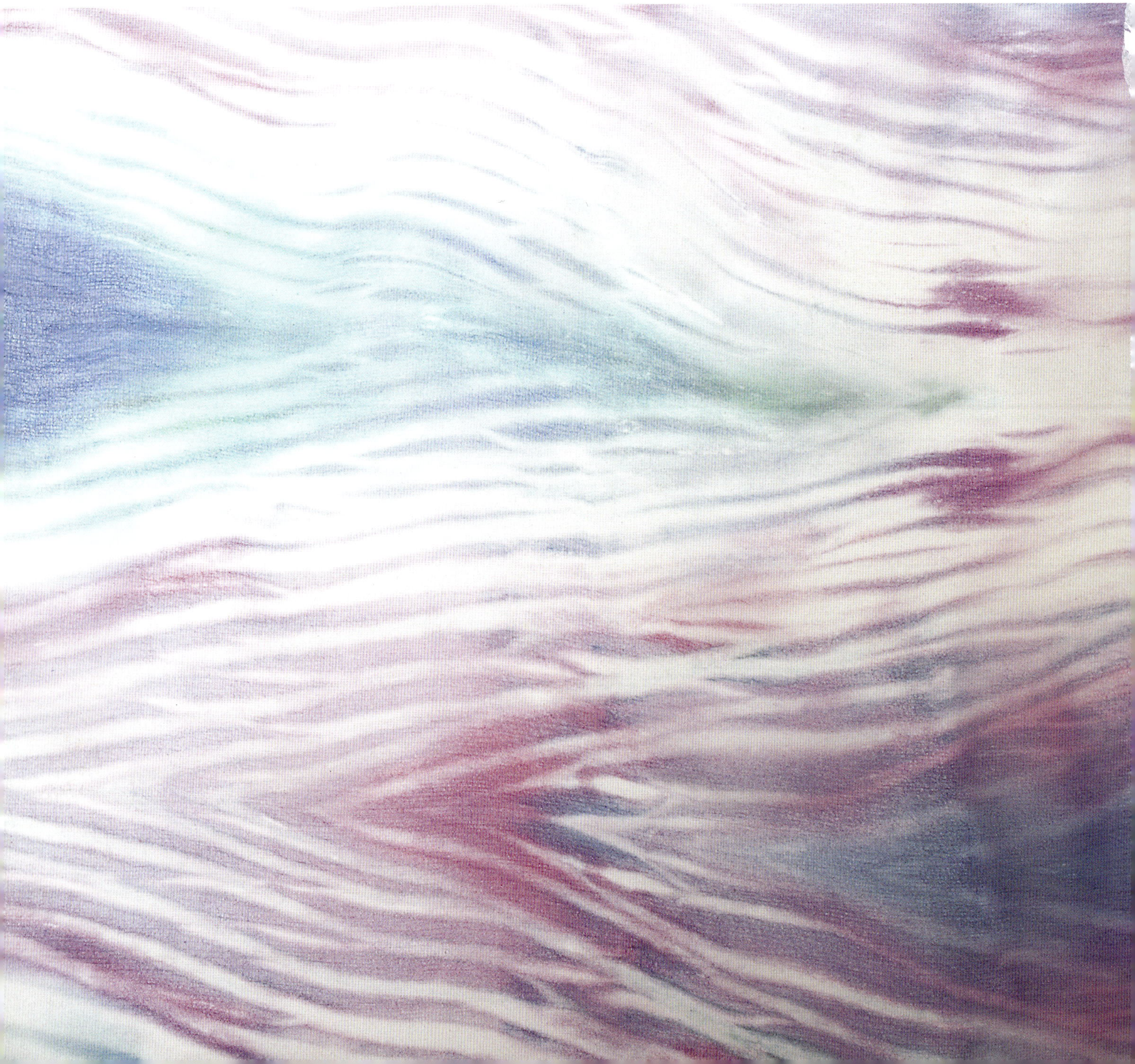